From Your Friends at **The MAILBOX®**

The **BIG BOOK** of

MONTHLY IDEAS

Preschool–Kindergarten

Kelly White
4451 Deerwood Drive
Fredericksburg, VA 22401

Project Manager:
Karen A. Brudnak

Editor:
Leanne Stratton

Art Coordinator:
Teresa R. Davidson

Cover Artists:
Nick Greenwood
Clevell Harris
Kimberly Richard

D1605266

www.themailbox.com

©2001 by THE EDUCATION CENTER, INC.
All rights reserved.
ISBN #1-56234-432-3

Manufactured in the United States

10 9 8 7 6 5 4 3 2 1

ABOUT THIS BOOK

Get a year's worth of seasonal and holiday ideas in this handy resource! We've compiled outstanding curriculum-related activities, ready-to-go reproducibles, and timely themes from our best-selling Monthly Idea Books for preschool–kindergarten. You'll find

- Super starters for the first days of school
- High-flying activities for Thanksgiving
- Dozens of December holiday delights
- Outstanding ideas for commemorating the birthday of Martin Luther King Jr.
- A fresh bouquet of activities to celebrate spring themes
- Thoughtful thank-yous for Mother's Day and Father's Day
- Sunny suggestions for summertime fun
- And much more!

TABLE OF CONTENTS

In Praise Of Pets

A pet and a child make a perfect pair! Teach your little ones about kindness and responsibility with this unit in praise of pets.

ideas by Linda Blassingame, Jayne Gammons, and Lori Kent

What Is A Pet?

Begin your pet ponderings by providing youngsters with a collection of magazines containing pictures of both wild and domestic animals. Ask the children to find and cut out animal pictures. When each child has cut out several pictures, gather the children together for a group time. Ask students to answer the question, "What is a pet?" Record their answers on a bulletin-board-paper house shape. Then explain that a pet is an animal kept for pleasure, usually in a home or in a yard. Further explain that pets must be fed, groomed, regularly taken to a veterinarian, and loved. Then, as a group, look at the pictures and decide which animals would make the best pets. Glue the pictures that the group selects around the comments on the house shape. Keep the remaining pictures for use in "Our Class Pet."

Dogs are pets.

My pet cat gets lots of hugs!

Pets live in your house with you.

Did we get a lion?

No! A lion has big teeth.

Did we get a guinea pig?

Yes! We can keep him in a cage. We can hold him.

Our Class Pet

If you don't already have one, now's the perfect time to purchase a classroom critter! Make a list of the types of pets your children own, adding any other animals that are common pets. As a group discuss the care and type of surroundings that each animal requires. Then decide which animal would make the best pet for your class. When the group has reached a consensus, ask for parents' support in buying the animal and setting up its new home. Take a picture of the pet; then use the picture and the wild-animal pictures collected in "What Is A Pet?" to create a class book.

Title a large construction-paper cover "Our Class Pet." Program the first page to read "Our class wanted a pet." Glue each of the wild-animal pictures onto a separate sheet of paper. Program each page as shown, substituting youngsters' thoughts as to why each different animal would be an unacceptable pet. Glue the picture of your class pet to the final page, programming the page with reasons why the pet was chosen for adoption. Bind the pages together to complete a class book that's sure to be "pet-ticularly" popular!

Pet Preferences

There's a perfect pet for every personality. Find out your students' pet preferences; then use the results for some math fun. Informally poll individual children to find out which pet from the selections on pages 11 and 12 they would choose to own. Based on students' choices, duplicate onto construction paper the appropriate number of each pattern. Direct each child to color and cut out his pattern; then staple it onto a personalized sentence-strip headband. During one or more group times, ask each child to wear his headband. Then choose from the following activities:

Sights And Sounds
Ask the group to sort themselves by the pet preferences displayed on their headbands. For added fun have each child move and make the sounds associated with his animal to help in finding the members of his group.

"Purr-fect" Patterning
Line up a number of students so that the pets displayed on their headbands create a pattern. Once the pattern has been identified by the remainder of the class, have each child from left to right in the line make her animal's sound or movement.

"Grrr-eat" Graphing
On a length of bulletin-board paper, create a floor graph with two columns. Assign a pet label to each column. To graph students' pet choices, direct students wearing the corresponding headbands to stand on the graph. Record the results of each graph you create.

meow meow

ruff ruff

squeak squeak

susan hodnett

PuPPy Love

BuRied TreasuRe

Burying and digging up treats is a favorite pastime of man's best friend. Prepare this center so your little ones can bone up on counting and number sets. Duplicate ten dog patterns (page 11) onto construction paper. Label each dog with a different numeral from one to ten. Cut out each dog pattern; then tape it to a resealable plastic bag. Hide 55 Milkbone® dog bones in your sensory table's sand. To use the center, a child digs in the sand to retrieve the bones. He then fills each bag with the corresponding number of bones. Now that's doggone fun!

Good Dog!

Teach youngsters some new tricks with this canine role-playing activity. Program individual index cards with dog commands—such as *fetch, sit, lie down, roll over, bark, beg,* and *come*—and corresponding picture cues. Give one child in a pair the set of cards. Encourage him to show his partner a card and read the command. His partner pretends to be the dog and performs the trick. When all of the commands have been read and performed, the partners switch roles. Ready for a treat?

Paws"For Reading

Any Kind Of Dog
Written by Lynn Reiser
Published by Greenwillow Books

I'll Always Love You
Written by Hans Wilhelm
Published by Crown Books For Young Readers

fetch

roll over

sit

8

The Cat's Meow

Cool Collars

Youngsters will feel like fancy felines when wearing these captivating cat collars. To make a collar, direct a child to cut through a paper plate's rim to its center, then cut out the center of the plate. Next have him paint the resulting collar. When the paint is dry, personalize the collar with the cat name the child would like to be called. Then invite him to decorate his collar with a variety of craft materials such as sequins, fake jewels, beads, pom-poms, and jingle bells. Here, kitty, kitty!

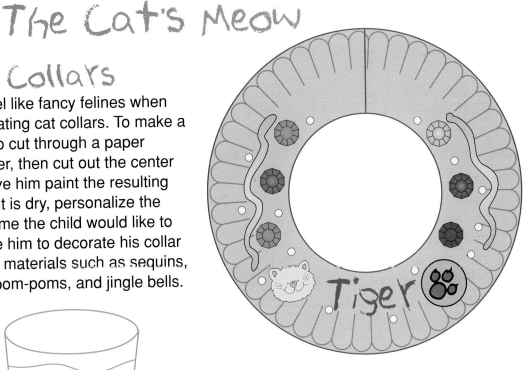

Kitty-Cat "Crunchies"

Entice your litter with this cat snack. For each child personalize a paper bowl with her chosen cat name (see "Cool Collars"). Have each student decorate her bowl with a variety of cat-related stickers; then invite her to prepare a snack of Kitty-Cat "Crunchies" by combining equal portions of fish crackers, triangular crackers, and pretzel sticks in her bowl. Serve the snacks with cups of milk. These treats are sure to leave your little kittens meowing for more!

Catnap

Prepare your students for catnaps and a cat tale with some of these soothing cat movements. Have students stretch like cats by arching their backs and dropping their hands down to their feet. Next have students lie on the floor and roll their bodies into balls, then stretch their bodies out long and lean. Finally have students curl up in a group area while you read a book aloud. "Purr-fect!"

Cat Tales

Have You Seen My Cat?
Written by Eric Carle
Published by Scholastic Inc.

My New Kitten
Written by Joanna Cole
Published by Morrow Junior Books

The Tenth Good Thing About Barney
Written by Judith Viorst
Published by Atheneum Books For Young Readers

The Age Of Aquariums

Your little ones are just the right age to enjoy this fishy water-center idea. Gather the listed items and place them near your filled water table. Encourage youngsters who visit the center to arrange the gravel and aquatic items in the water to "set up" the aquarium. Invite youngsters to use the net to catch fish put in the water. If desired explain that when a pet fish is brought to a new aquarium, it needs time to adjust to the temperature of that aquarium's water. To demonstrate how to care for a new fish, put a plastic fish in a clear bag filled with water. Tie the top of the bag; then let the bag float in the water table until the pet fish "adjusts" to its new home. Also demonstrate how to use the thermometer to check the water temperature. During cleanup time, have a child fill the sieve with the gravel and replace the gravel in the bucket. Provide towels for drying the remaining aquatic items.

aquarium gravel in a bucket
sieve
shells
plastic plants
landscaping pieces
plastic fish
small net
water thermometer
towels

Pennies For Pets

Conclude your unit with a project that you can count on to foster kindness for our animal friends. Explain that many animals that do not have homes live in animal shelters. Further explain that workers at shelters care for home-less pets while seeking good homes for the animals. Suggest that the class donate pennies to help a local organization care for animals until they are adopted as pets. Send home duplicated copies of the parent note (page 12) explaining the project. Use construction paper to decorate an empty facial-tissue box to resemble a dog or cat. As students bring in donations, have them drop the pennies into the decorated box. After a desired amount of time, have children help to roll the pennies. Then plan a class trip to the chosen organization to deliver the donation. If a trip is not possible, deliver the donation to the shelter and take several pictures of the site to help the chil-dren understand how their pennies will help pets.

Pet Patterns
Use with "Pet Preferences" on
page 7. Use the dog pattern
also with "Buried Treasure"
on page 8.

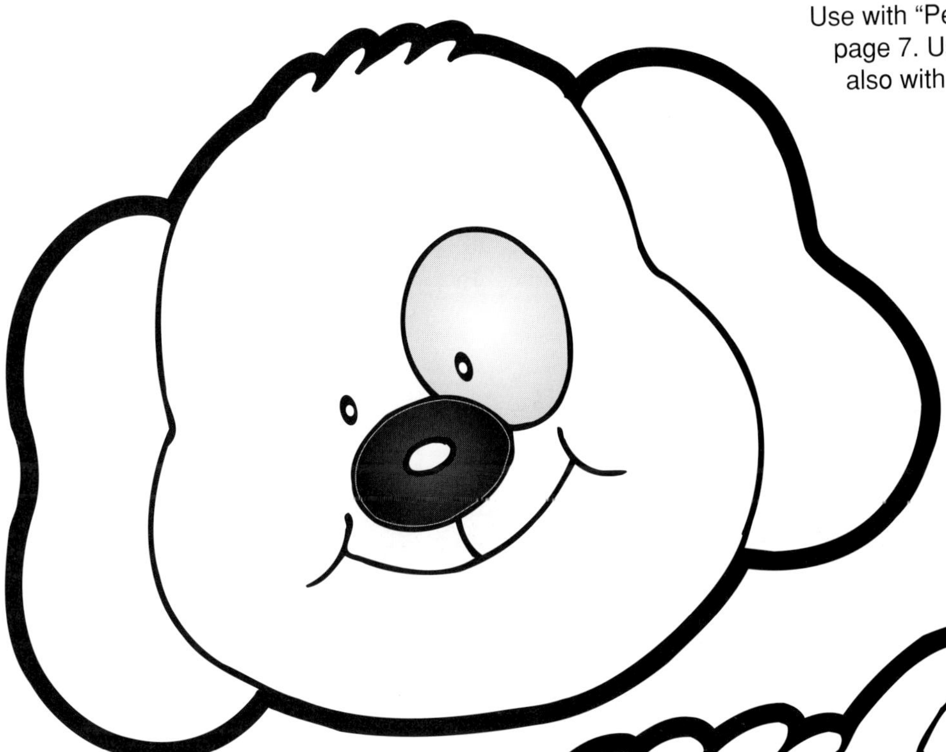

Pet Patterns
Use with "Pet Preferences" on page 7.

Parent Note
Use with "Pennies For Pets" on page 10.

Dear Families,

Please help us with a new project—Pennies For Pets. During our pet unit, we have learned that animals need food, shelter, and love. We will collect pennies until _____
(date)
to help _____ care
(organization)
for and find homes for pets.

Woof, woof! Meow!
(Thank you!)

_____'s class
(teacher)

At The Grocery Store

Attention, shoppers! You'll find a cartload of fun, cross-curricular ideas waiting for you when you stroll the aisles of this grocery-store unit.

ideas contributed by Barbara F. Backer

Where Do You Shop?

"Where does your family shop for food?" Begin your grocery-store unit by asking students this very simple question during circle time. Write students' responses on a sheet of chart paper. Then, after everyone has had an opportunity to reply, provide each child with a newspaper containing grocery-store advertisements. Instruct each student to cut out an advertisement that has the name or logo of the store where his family shops. Have each student glue the logo onto the chart next to his name. Tally the results to see which store is the most popular.

What Do We Know?

Get your little ones revved up and ready for a trip to a grocery store with this activity. Invite students to tell you some things they know about the grocery store; then write each child's response on a sheet of chart paper. On another sheet of chart paper, write students' responses to the question, "What do you want to know about the grocery store?"

Create a display for your little ones' grocery-store knowledge by mounting each chart to a bulletin board as shown, leaving enough room for a fourth chart. When you return from your field trip, display a fourth chart titled "What We Learned" (see "To Market, To Market" on page 14). Surround the charts with a border of photos taken during your trip; then top it all off with the heading "To Market, To Market."

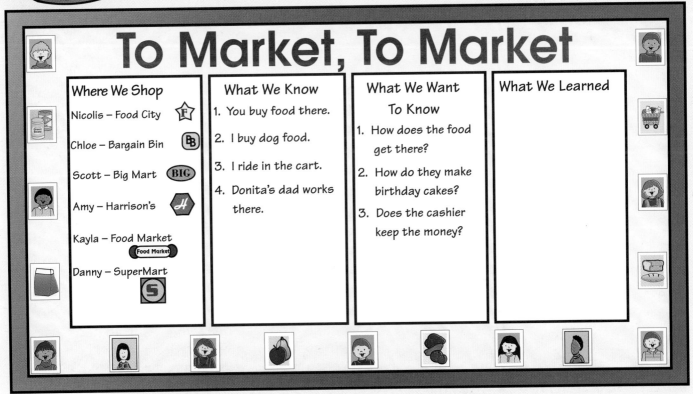

To Market, To Market

Where We Shop	What We Know	What We Want To Know	What We Learned
Nicolis – Food City	1. You buy food there.	1. How does the food get there?	
Chloe – Bargain Bin	2. I buy dog food.	2. How do they make birthday cakes?	
Scott – Big Mart	3. I ride in the cart.	3. Does the cashier keep the money?	
Amy – Harrison's	4. Donita's dad works there.		
Kayla – Food Market			
Danny – SuperMart			

To Market, To Market

The grocery store can be a busy, fascinating place for youngsters! Arrange a field trip to a local grocery store to give students a behind-the-scenes look at the action. In advance contact the store manager to request that your students be given a tour of the store—including such areas as the loading dock and stockrooms. Also advise him of the things students would like to know about the market (refer to the chart made in "What Do We Know?" on page 13).

Before your trip duplicate onto tagboard a nametag (on page 16) for each child. Instruct each child to color, then cut out his nametag. Write his name in the space provided using a black marker. Laminate the nametags; then hot-glue a bar pin (available at craft stores) to the back of each tag.

During your field trip, point out the numbered overhead signs. Explain to students that each sign tells shoppers which items can be found in that aisle. Conduct a scavenger hunt by asking a student to name a food; then guide a group to find the aisle in which the named food is located.

When you return to the classroom, make a chart of the things your students learned at the grocery store. Hang this chart on the bulletin board created in "What Do We Know?" on page 13.

Bag Of Thanks

Have students express their gratitude to their grocery-store guide with this thank-you note. Duplicate onto construction paper a class supply of the grocery-bag pattern on page 16. Instruct each child to color the food items and cut out her note. Write each child's dictation for her thank-you message on the front of the bag; then have her sign her note. Bind all the pages together between construction-paper covers; then place the resulting book inside a brown paper bag. Deliver the bagged book to the grocery store. Now that's a bagful of heartfelt thanks!

14

Sing A Song Of Grocery Stores

Follow up your trip to the grocery store with this little ditty that encourages students to recall some things they saw while at the store. After each verse select a different child to name something she saw at the grocery store; then substitute her name and item in the corresponding phrases.

(sung to the tune of "Mary Had A Little Lamb")

(chorus)
We went to the grocery store,
Grocery store, grocery store.
We went to the grocery store,
And this is what we saw.

(verse)
[Shevonne] saw [some ice cream],
[Some ice cream], [some ice cream].
[Shevonne] saw [some ice cream],
When we went to the store.

A Cart With A View

Your little ones will love taking home these books to share about their visit to the grocery store. Duplicate the verses on page 17 for each child. To make a book, have a child cut out a set of verses on the bold lines, then glue each verse to the bottom of a sheet of paper. On each page instruct the child to draw a picture of something he saw at the grocery store. Then write the student's completion to the verse on the line provided. (For the purposes of this activity, it won't matter if the food the child names was actually in the aisle specified on each page.) Continue in the same manner until all the pages are complete. Sequence and bind the pages between construction-paper covers. Urge students to take their books home to share with their families.

Sitting in the grocery cart,
I had a lot of fun.
I saw _a birthday cake_
In aisle number **1**.

Nametag

Use with "To Market, To Market" on page 14.

Thank-You Card

Use with "Bag Of Thanks" on page 14.

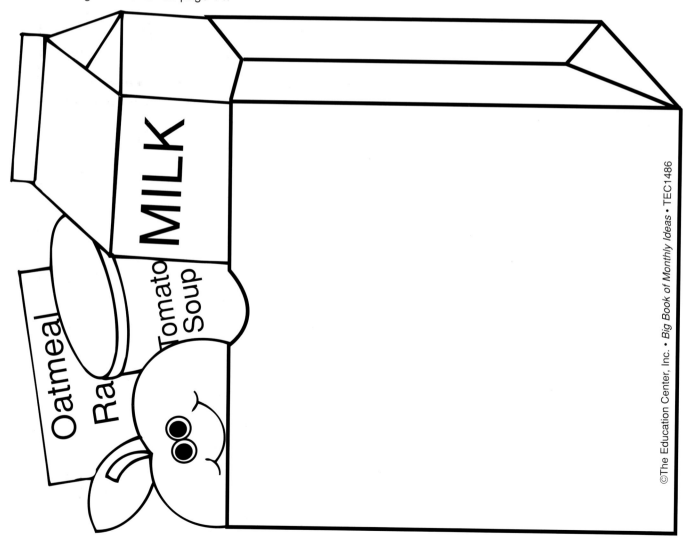

2.

Sitting in the
grocery cart,
You know it's true;

I saw _____

In aisle number **2.**

©The Education Center, Inc. • Big Book of Monthly Ideas • TEC1486

4.

Sitting in the
grocery cart,
Near the front door,

I saw _____

In aisle number **4.**

©The Education Center, Inc. • Big Book of Monthly Ideas • TEC1486

1.

Sitting in the
grocery cart,
I had a lot of fun.

I saw _____

In aisle number **1.**

©The Education Center, Inc. • Big Book of Monthly Ideas • TEC1486

3.

Sitting in the
grocery cart,
Happy as could be,

I saw _____

In aisle number **3.**

©The Education Center, Inc. • Big Book of Monthly Ideas • TEC1486

Cookies, Crackers, Math, & Me

Get ready to crunch and munch your way into math skills with those incredible edibles—cookies and crackers! Help little ones develop skills with shapes, patterning, counting, measurement, graphing, and numeral recognition with these activities that are good enough to eat.

ideas contributed by Ada Goren and Suzanne Moore

Cracker Matchers

Crackers come in so many shapes and sizes, they're the perfect tool for reinforcing matching skills. To prepare for this activity (and for "Shape Up With Crackers"), purchase—or ask parents to donate—several types of crackers in different shapes and sizes. For each child, prepare a zippered plastic bag containing five matching pairs of crackers, ten in all. Distribute a bag of crackers and a paper towel to each child. Ask each youngster to empty her bag and match the pairs of crackers atop her paper towel. When all the matches have been made, ask a volunteer to tell how she found each match. Lead children to understand that they used their sense of sight to determine the likenesses of their crackers in shape and size. Then make the matching a bit more challenging.

Give each child a second paper towel. Ask her to remove one cracker from each pair and replace it in the plastic bag, leaving the bag lying flat on the tabletop. Then have her cover the bag with the second paper towel. Have her identify one of the crackers still showing, then reach into the covered bag and attempt to find the matching cracker using only her sense of touch. Of course, little ones will want to munch their matches when they're all through! Wouldn't you?

Shape Up With Crackers

Move from matching to identifying shapes with this delicious rhyme. For each child, place a few differently shaped crackers into a zippered plastic bag. You'll also need a set of attribute blocks (or poster-board cutouts) in corresponding shapes. Place these in their own plastic bag. To begin, give each child a bag of crackers. Then pull one attribute block or poster-board shape from the bag, and have students identify its shape. Then have youngsters recite the following rhyme as each child looks for that shape of cracker in his bag. If he has a cracker of that shape, he may crunch into it before the next shape is pulled.

Mmmmm!
Crackers, crackers, what a treat!
[Shape] crackers are good to eat!
Mmmmm!

Pam Crane

Snack-Mix Measurement

Serve up a class-size portion of introductory measurement skills with this activity. In advance, purchase—or ask parents to donate—the ingredients listed in the snack-mix recipe. Bring in a measuring cup and ask little ones to help you measure and mix this tasty treat. First model proper measurement techniques, pointing out the lines on your measuring cup and showing students how to fill a cup to its exact volume. Then encourage student volunteers to try their hands at measuring the recipe ingredients into a big bowl. Give every child a turn to stir the mixture with a large wooden spoon. Then, working with one small group at a time, have each child carefully measure a half-cup serving onto a paper plate. Before having them munch the mix, have students sort and graph the ingredients (see "Egg-Carton Graphs").

Egg-Carton Graphs

These lightweight, compartmentalized containers are perfect for making real graphs with small items—including small cookies and crackers. To make one, cut the lids from two egg cartons. Connect the bases with brads. You now have a four-column graph! Need more columns? Just add another egg-carton base or two!

To sort and graph the ingredients from "Snack-Mix Measurement," supply each child in a small group with an egg-carton graph. Have her sort the four ingredients into the four columns on her graph, then compare her results. Use this opportunity to introduce the mathematical terms *most, fewest,* and *equal.*

Crunchy-Munchy Mix

(makes 16 half-cup servings)

2 cups Ritz® Bits® minicrackers
2 cups Goldfish® crackers
2 cups miniature pretzels
2 cups cinnamon-graham stars

To Twist Or Not To Twist?

Mmmm...sandwich cookies! Some folks just take a big bite, while others twist off one cookie layer and eat the filling first. To find out which way each of your students prefers to eat a sandwich cookie, prepare a two-column graph on a large piece of bulletin-board paper. At the top of one column, glue a construction-paper cookie with a "bite" taken out of it. At the top of the other column, show two construction-paper circles—one with cotton glued onto it to resemble cookie filling.

Ask each child to write his name on a sticky note and place the note in the column illustrating his preferred cookie-eating method. Then pass out sandwich cookies and have little ones demonstrate their preferences firsthand! After the treat, discuss the results of the graph. Extend this activity on another day by graphing whether little ones prefer to dunk their cookies in milk before eating them.

"Chocolate Chip, Peanut Butter, Chocolate Chip, Peanut Butter..."

Cookies make for some palatable patterning practice! In advance, ask parents to send in an assortment of cookies. Working with one small group at a time, have students wash their hands before beginning this activity. Spread a supply of cookies on a table; then demonstrate a simple pattern involving two types of cookies, such as *chocolate chip, peanut butter, chocolate chip, peanut butter.* Ask a volunteer to extend your pattern, using the cookies on the table. Repeat this exercise a few times, using different types of cookies. Then ask students to work together in pairs. Encourage one child to create a simple two-cookie pattern; then ask his partner to extend it.

More advanced youngsters may be ready for more difficult patterns, involving varying repetitions or a greater number of cookies. However far your patterning practice takes you, end the activity by asking each child in the group to select one cookie from those remaining in the packages. Then challenge the children to arrange themselves in a pattern before inviting them to eat their cookies.

To Twist Or Not To Twist?

⬤ ⬤ ⃝	◗
Juan	Todd
Katie	Kyle
Dallas	Allie
Cara	

Cookie Questions

Conduct a survey—and a little counting practice—to find out the favorite cookies of your youngsters' families and friends. First duplicate the cookie survey sheet on page 22 for each child. Tell little ones to take the sheet home and ask each family member (or any friends they'd like to have participate) to indicate her favorite type of cookie by drawing a happy face in a square beside it. Instruct students to have their parents assist them in counting the number of happy faces beside each type of cookie and in writing the corresponding numeral in the column marked "Total." Have your young pollsters return the survey sheets on the designated day. If desired, count the total number of people in your extended classroom family who prefer each type of cookie and determine an overall favorite.

"Nummy" Number Cookies

There's no more delicious way to reinforce numeral recognition than to make number cookies. To prepare for this activity, check your local craft or discount store to find a set of numeral-shaped cookie cutters. Then purchase a few rolls of refrigerated sugar-cookie dough or prepare your favorite recipe in quantity.

Divide your class into small groups and have each group work with an adult. Have everyone wash her hands before beginning. Invite youngsters to help roll out the sugar-cookie dough on a floured surface. Then have each child press a numeral-shaped cutter into the dough. Ask her to place the unbaked cookie on a baking sheet and identify the numeral. To add practice with creating sets, provide M&M's®, raisins, or chocolate chips. Have each child count out the corresponding number of cookie decorations to press onto her unbaked cookie. Invite children to continue taking turns making cookies until your dough is depleted. Then bake the cookies according to package or recipe directions.

Invite a neighboring class to help you nibble your number cookies, or send each school helper a small plastic bag containing a few cookies and a note that reads, "We *number* you among our best friends!"

Cookie Questionnaire

Draw a happy face beside the type of cookie you like best.

Name							Total
chocolate chip							
peanut butter							
sugar							
oatmeal							

Name _____

Please return this survey sheet to school on _____.

(date)

©The Education Center, Inc. • *Big Book of Monthly Ideas* • TEC1486

Note To The Teacher: Use with "Cookie Questions" on page 21.

SEPTEMBER

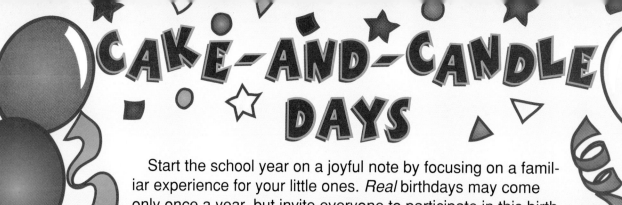

CAKE-AND-CANDLE DAYS

Start the school year on a joyful note by focusing on a familiar experience for your little ones. *Real* birthdays may come only once a year, but invite everyone to participate in this birthday theme full of ideas to span the curriculum. "Happy learning to you; Happy learning to you;…"

by Ada Hamrick

Who's Having A Birthday?

Your students are sure to ask who's having a birthday when they see a decked-out classroom on the first day of your birthday unit. Put students in a birthday mood by hanging party streamers from the classroom ceiling and adding a few well-placed balloons*, a "Happy Birthday" banner, some brightly wrapped packages, and a copy of the birthday-party announcement (on page 28) at each child's seat or cubby. Your excited students will be happy to learn that they're all invited to join in the birthday celebration!

Begin by sharing the story *Happy Birthday, Dear Duck* by Eve Bunting (Clarion Books). Then give each child an opportunity to relate a story about a special birthday. Ask children to compare Duck's birthday party with their own experiences.

(*Please note: Uninflated balloons create a choking hazard for small children. Keep them out of the reach of youngsters.)

You've Come A Long Way, Baby!

Once you've introduced your birthday unit, you'll have the perfect opportunity for noting each person's growth and how he has changed from year to year. Share the story *Birthday Presents* by Cynthia Rylant (Orchard Books) to help illustrate this concept for your youngsters. After reading the book, ask youngsters to talk about the many changes—physical, mental, and emotional—they have experienced since they were babies.

Then send home copies of the note on page 28 asking each family to provide a baby picture of their child. Create a bulletin board or wall display with the title "Birthday Babies." Display each baby picture side by side with a current photograph of the child. Write each child's birth date on a sentence strip and attach the strip below his pair of pictures. Give the display an interactive quality by stapling flaps of paper over the current photos. Students can try to guess the identity of each baby, then lift the flap to check. Little ones will delight in seeing the changes in themselves and their classmates since "babyhood"!

BIRTHDAY BABIES

May 7   August 15

October 2   September 21

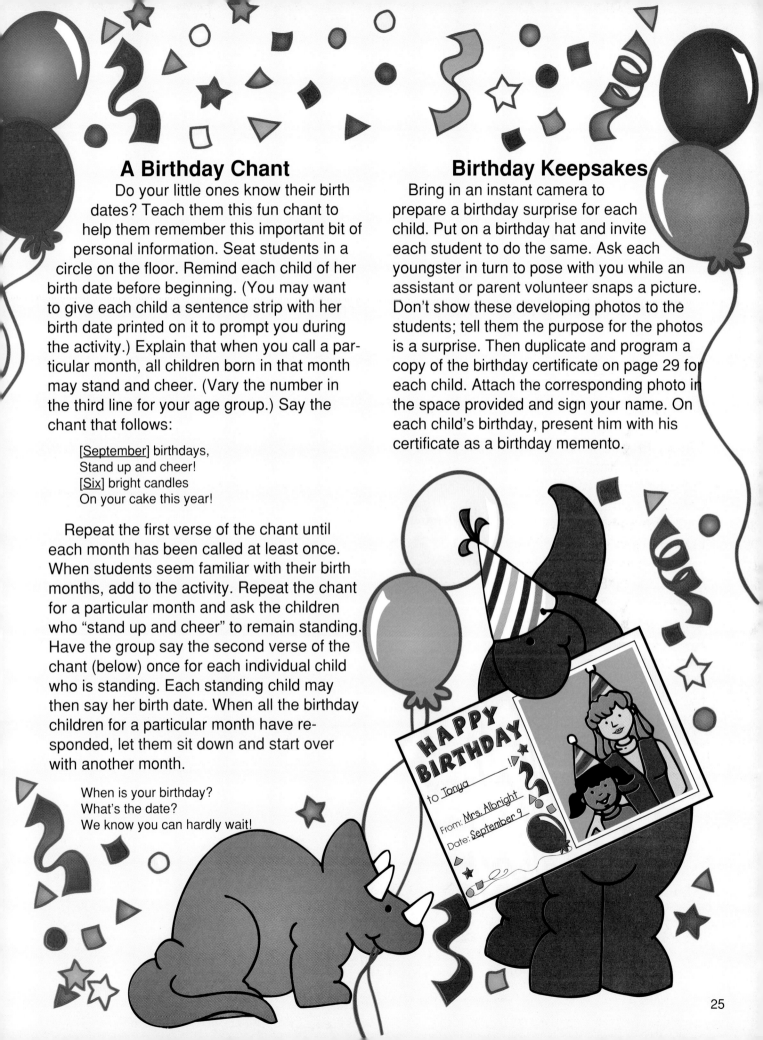

A Birthday Chant

Do your little ones know their birth dates? Teach them this fun chant to help them remember this important bit of personal information. Seat students in a circle on the floor. Remind each child of her birth date before beginning. (You may want to give each child a sentence strip with her birth date printed on it to prompt you during the activity.) Explain that when you call a particular month, all children born in that month may stand and cheer. (Vary the number in the third line for your age group.) Say the chant that follows:

> [September] birthdays,
> Stand up and cheer!
> [Six] bright candles
> On your cake this year!

Repeat the first verse of the chant until each month has been called at least once. When students seem familiar with their birth months, add to the activity. Repeat the chant for a particular month and ask the children who "stand up and cheer" to remain standing. Have the group say the second verse of the chant (below) once for each individual child who is standing. Each standing child may then say her birth date. When all the birthday children for a particular month have responded, let them sit down and start over with another month.

> When is your birthday?
> What's the date?
> We know you can hardly wait!

Birthday Keepsakes

Bring in an instant camera to prepare a birthday surprise for each child. Put on a birthday hat and invite each student to do the same. Ask each youngster in turn to pose with you while an assistant or parent volunteer snaps a picture. Don't show these developing photos to the students; tell them the purpose for the photos is a surprise. Then duplicate and program a copy of the birthday certificate on page 29 for each child. Attach the corresponding photo in the space provided and sign your name. On each child's birthday, present him with his certificate as a birthday memento.

A Cake Of Many Colors

What would a birthday celebration be without a cake? Read *The Birthday Cake* by Joy Cowley (The Wright Group), the story of a colossal cake fit for a queen. (This big book is available from The Wright Group. Call 1-800-523-2371 for ordering information.) The story's simple text follows two bakers as they build a cake with layers of different colors. After sharing the book, invite students to practice color recognition as they tell their own versions of the story on a flannelboard. Duplicate the cake-layer pattern on page 29 several times on tagboard. Color each cake layer a different color, including all the colors you'd like your students to learn. Laminate the cake layers for durability and cut them out. Affix the hook side of a piece of Velcro® to the back of each cutout. Have students build their multilayered cakes on a flannelboard, identifying each color as they work. For more advanced students, print the accompanying color words on sentence strips and attach the hook sides of pieces of Velcro® to the backs of those as well. Have students place the correct color word beside each cake layer on the flannelboard.

Wrap It Up!

After you serve the cake, it's time for—presents, of course! Most children delight in opening gifts on their birthdays. But while many have experience at unwrapping gifts, they may find wrapping them more of a challenge. Stock a gift-wrapping center to encourage practice of fine-motor skills and coordination. Ask families to donate empty boxes, birthday-themed wrapping paper, bows, ribbon, and cellophane tape. Given scissors and a large work area, your little ones are bound to get all wrapped up in this activity!

It's In The Cards

Little ones like to receive birthday cards almost as much as they like birthday presents. Recycle some birthday cards for new uses in a Birthday Card Basket to help youngsters practice a variety of skills. Ask parents to send in old or unused birthday cards, or purchase some inexpensive cards with different designs. Cut off the back flaps and discard them. Laminate the card fronts for durability.

Students can sort the cards, circle letters or words on them using a grease pencil, copy the text, match them to correctly sized envelopes (if available), or use them for lacing practice. (To create a lacing card, punch holes around the perimeter of a card. Thread a shoelace through one hole and secure it with a knot.) If you have enough cards, write one child's name on the back of each card. Students can then "deliver" the cards by matching the child's name on the card to the name on her cubby or desk.

Birthday Matchups

Gather a variety of birthday items for this fun game to help students practice visual memory. In advance, collect matching pairs of several birthday-related objects. You may wish to include two party hats, two gift bows, two birthday invitations, two birthday candles, two party blowers, and two balloons. Tape each individual item to a separate square of tagboard. Show the students all the pairs before you begin. Then ask several volunteers to stand in front of the group. Give each volunteer a tagboard card to hold, instructing him to keep it turned so that the birthday item cannot be seen.

The remaining students then take turns guessing which two volunteers are holding each matching pair of items. During his turn, a child may call two volunteers' names. Those children turn their cards around so that everyone can see what items they are holding. If the items match, the teacher takes those cards. The child who guessed correctly may have a turn to hold a card in the next round. If the items do not match, the cards are turned back around and another child may guess.

Donna Cox—PreK
Waterbridge Elementary
Orlando, FL

¡Feliz Cumpleaños!

Party hats, cake and ice cream, a special meal—most families have their own special ways of celebrating birthdays. Introduce your young learners to the birthday traditions of one Mexican-American family by reading *Hello, Amigos!* by Tricia Brown (Henry Holt and Company). Help your students practice saying, "Happy birthday," in Spanish—*"Feliz cumpleaños."* Then have students help you fill a piñata purchased from a party supply store. Save the piñata for a birthday celebration to culminate the unit (see "It's Party Time!").

It's Party Time!

Put on the party hats once again and welcome youngsters to a birthday bash for everyone! Invite some parents to join you to help supervise the festivities. Purchase or have parent volunteers donate unfrosted cupcakes. Allow each child to frost a cupcake and add colored sprinkles and a birthday candle. If fire codes permit, light each child's candle and allow it to burn while everyone sings "Happy Birthday To You!" After your little revelers blow out the candles, let them eat the cupcakes with scoops of ice cream on the side. If your students helped to fill a piñata (see "¡Feliz Cumpleaños!"), consider inviting a special guest, such as your school principal, to break it open. Then settle things down by reading the silly story *Moira's Birthday* by Robert Munsch (Annick Press Ltd.). Conclude the party by giving each child a small present, such as a birthday sticker or stamp.

Birthday Announcement

Use with "Who's Having A Birthday?" on page 24.

Parent Note

Use with "You've Come A Long Way, Baby!" on page 24.

Dear Family,

    At school we are learning about birthdays. Could you help by sending in a photo of your child as a baby? If you have a picture taken on your child's actual birth date, that would be wonderful! Don't forget to label the photo on the back with your child's name. We'll return it as soon as we're done with our activity.

        Thank you!

HAPPY BIRTHDAY

to _____!

From: _____

Date: _____

Attach photo here.

©The Education Center, Inc. • *Big Book of Monthly Ideas* • TEC1486

Cake-Layer Pattern
Use with "A Cake Of Many Colors" on page 26.

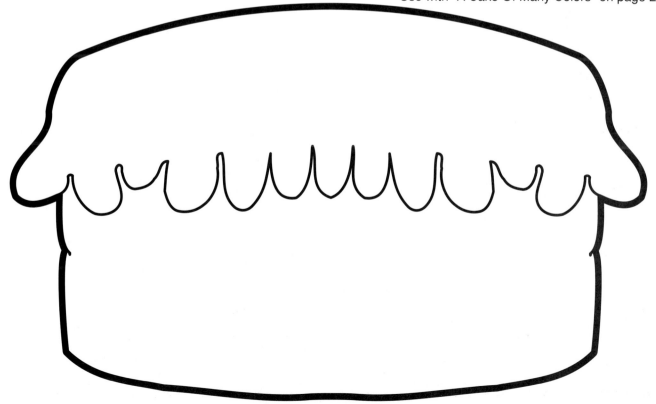

You've Got To Have Friends!

For many children, September means a new school year and new friends. With the ideas in this friendship unit, get your youngsters off to a great start by creating a classroom climate of kindness, sharing, and cooperation.

by Lucia Kemp Henry

Make A New Friend

Help your youngsters get to know each other with this simple cooperative activity. On white construction paper, reproduce the Puzzle Pals patterns on page 34 so that there will be one puzzle piece for each student. Use markers to color each puzzle pair with a distinctly different pattern or color. Laminate the patterns; then cut along the bold lines to cut each pair apart. Punch a hole near the top of each puzzle piece and thread a long piece of yarn through the hole. Tie the ends of the yarn to form a necklace.

Before school starts one morning, place a Puzzle Pal necklace in each child's cubby or at his seat. Encourage students to wear their necklaces. Give each youngster time to locate the wearer of the matching Puzzle Pal—his partner for the day. Ask each child to introduce his new friend to the class by saying, "This is my friend [insert child's name]." As this pair of students moves to a designated space (for forming a large circle), encourage everyone to sing "The More We Get Together." Repeat this entire cycle until every child has been introduced and all students are forming one large friendship circle.

The More We Get Together

The more we get together,
together, together.
The more we get together,
the happier we'll be.
'Cause your friends are my friends
And my friends are your friends.
The more we get together,
the happier we'll be!

What Is A Friend?

Help your youngsters think about what *friendship* means by asking them to brainstorm a list of descriptive words to complete the sentence, "A friend is...." Write the student-dictated words on cards, and display them on a wall or bulletin board. Using white construction-paper Friend Figures duplicated from pages 35 and 36, have each youngster create a self-portrait. Instruct each youngster to cut out his figure; then arrange the figures near the word cards so that they appear to be holding hands.

What Is A Friend?

A friend is ...
kind.
Daniel

Good Friends

To help children understand what kinds of behaviors make someone a good friend, teach your youngsters this poem. Later your little friendship experts may want to add some new stanzas of their own.

Good Friends

Good friends are so nice to have
When we work and play.
Good friends are awfully kind.
They help along the way.

Good friends say, "Hello," or "Hi!"
When they meet each day.
Good friends can take your coat
Or put your boots away.

Good friends like to help with blocks
When you have too many.
Good friends share their crayons, too,
When you don't have any!

Good friends help clean a mess
That's spilled upon the floor.
Good friends like to let you in
When you are at the door.

Good friends play a game of catch
Or make a jump rope turn.
Good friends show you how to play
If you want to learn.

Good friends say, "Thanks for your help!"
And say, "I'm sorry," too.
Good friends say, "I'm so glad
To have a friend like you!"

Jeremy shared his crayons with Ellie.

A Special Someone

After learning the "Good Friends" poem and seeing some of the behaviors in action, your students will be able to talk about what it means to be a friend. Take time each day to have youngsters tell you about friendly things they have seen people doing. Keep a list of these positive behaviors on chart paper and refer to them often. You can also review them as possible solutions to unresolved classroom conflicts.

Have your youngsters make a big book that features some of the friendly behaviors that they have seen or that they have performed. Ask each child to draw a picture that shows someone doing something "friendly." Write each youngster's description of her illustration in the remaining space on her paper. Staple all of the pages together beneath a construction-paper cover. Title this class booklet "Friends Do Special Things."

Friendship Songs

Begin and end your busy day with these songs about friendship.

Good Morning, Friends
(sung to the tune of "Row, Row, Row Your Boat")

Hi! Good morning, friends.
How are you today?
Let's each try to be a friend
To everyone today!

Good-Bye, Friends
(sung to the tune of "Are You Sleeping?")

Good-bye, friends. Good-bye, friends.
Time to go. Time to go.
Thank you, friends, for helping.
Thank you, friends, for sharing.
Love you so! Love you so!

Friendly Cooperative Fun!

Emphasizing cooperative games fosters friendship as well as fun! Try these whole-group games to focus on the importance of working together as a team.

Cooperative Hugs

Your classroom will be filled with friendly vibrations when your youngsters play this cooperative game. Begin by having your youngsters spread out within a large, open space. For safety's sake, be sure to emphasize that this is a walking game with no running allowed. Play a recording of some moderately paced instrumental music to accompany the game, or play an upbeat song with friendly lyrics such as the classic "You've Got To Have Friends" by Bette Midler. Play the music while youngsters dance around in place. When you stop the music, instruct *each child* to find *one person* to hug. Play the music again and have each pair of youngsters dance together. Stop the music again. This time have *each pair* of youngsters find *another pair* to hug. Then these *foursomes* can dance together until the music stops and they join *other foursomes* for a big hug. Continue in this manner until all your youngsters join together for one big friendly hug.

Make A Circle

This cooperative game is lots of fun to play and provides youngsters with an opportunity to develop their listening skills as well as their imaginations. Have youngsters spread out within a large, open space. Have them walk around quietly, listening for your signal. When you are ready, stand still and call, "Make a circle!" Your youngsters must move to where you are and join hands to make a circle around you. Do this several times—always moving to a different spot in the room.

When your students have mastered the basic circle-forming skill, throw in some simple variations. When you signal them, call something different such as, "Tiptoe into a circle!" or "Make a monkey circle!" (students move like monkeys once they are in the circle). Remind students that the circle must be formed around you each time.

The Friendship Train

This game is easy, but it takes quite a bit of cooperation to keep a string of little bodies all moving in the same direction! Have your youngsters spread out within a large, open area. Try this game a few times with an adult leader (the engine). Play some instrumental music softly in the background. Have the leader move toward one youngster. As the leader passes him, the youngster "hooks on" by placing his hands on her hips. Continuing from child to child, children continue to join the Friendship Train. The last child, or caboose, may then become the engine for the next game. If desired, make the game a bit more difficult by asking that youngsters build a train in boy-girl-boy-girl sequence.

Learning The Buddy System

Give each of your youngsters opportunities to work one-on-one with many different classmates by involving her in these partner activities.

Wear A Shirt

Gather a supply of long-sleeved, extra-large men's shirts. Ask for donations, or search yard sales and thrift shops for inexpensive castoffs. Make sure that you have enough shirts for every two youngsters. Group students in pairs and give one shirt to each pair. Explain that both people in each pair must "wear" the shirt together! Encourage students to come up with several different ways of doing this. After a while, have students select new partners and repeat the activity.

Buddy Crawl

Assign partners once again for this activity. Line up several sets of partners along one side of your play space. Instruct each pair to move to the opposite side of the play space together. Further explain that each person in each pair must be crawling and that the partners must remain in physical contact as they move. Youngsters can develop and try a number of different ways to accomplish this task. Some pairs may hold hands and crawl. Some may crawl side by side, keeping their torsos in contact. And some may crawl with one person leading while the other person crawls holding the leader's feet. Explain to students that this game is less of a race and more of a challenge to work together creatively.

Move A Hoop

Pair your students; then give each pair one plastic Hula-Hoop®. Ask each pair to step inside the hoop. Then instruct the pairs of children to move to a specified location. Explain that youngsters may move in any way, but they must both remain inside the hoop. Repeat the task a second time with the same partners to allow each pair to refine its communication and movement techniques. Later direct partners to jump, hop, skip, or otherwise move together inside the hoop to reach their destination.

Make A Shape

Provide each pair of children with a jump rope or six-foot length of heavy cord or rope. Hold up a sign bearing the outline of a square, circle, triangle, or rectangle. Have each pair work together to re-create the shape on the sign. Continue the activity, changing the outline to be copied.

Later you may want to include signs with more complex shapes such as an oval, a diamond, or a heart. Or you may want signs showing numerals or letters of the alphabet.

Friendship Puzzle Pals
Use with "Make A New Friend" on page 30.

Friend Figure

Use with "What Is A Friend? on page 30.

Apples Aplenty

Pick some or all of these "a-peel-ing" apple activities to share with your little ones. An apple a day will bring learning their way!

by Ada Hamrick

red   sweet
green   crunchy
round

A is for APPLE

Investigating Apples

Get right to the core of your apple study by bringing in a basketful of real apples. Include several different varieties. Invite youngsters to examine the apples up close. Encourage them to sort the apples by various attributes such as color, shape, or size. Cut open several of the apples, slicing some parallel and some perpendicular to the core. Have students examine the insides of the apples and discuss what they see and smell. Cut a few of the apples into pieces for your children to taste.

After the apple exploration, ask students to brainstorm words or phrases to describe apples. Responses might include *red, green, full of seeds, round, white inside, sweet,* or *crunchy.* Write the students' responses on a large apple shape cut from poster board or bulletin-board paper. Display the apple cutout throughout your study.

Math In Good Taste

While you have those apples handy, conduct a taste test to determine which color of apple is favored by your youngsters. Give each child three small pieces of apple: one from a red apple, one from a green apple, and one from a yellow apple. Ask her to taste each one and choose her favorite.

Construct a bulletin-board display to illustrate the results of the taste test. Cut three large, simple tree shapes from green and brown bulletin-board paper. Mount the trees on a bulletin board with a light blue paper background. Then duplicate the apple patterns on page 41 several times on red, green, and yellow construction paper. Cut out the apples and have each child choose an apple cutout in the color that corresponds to her favorite apple. Have her write her name on the cutout. After all the students have made their selections, place the yellow apple cutouts on one tree, the red apple cutouts on another tree, and the green apple cutouts on the third tree. Have students help you count the number of apples on each tree. Write the total for each tree on the trunk.

Then ask students to talk about the results. Mount a length of chart paper beside the apple trees. Write students' dictation as they discuss the results of the taste test. Encourage them to compare quantities of *more, less,* and *equal.*

Applesauce Stories

Incorporate cooking and language in this yummy activity. With one small group of students at a time, gather all the ingredients to create a simple blender applesauce recipe. For each group you will need a red apple, a green apple, a yellow apple, and small amounts of sugar, cinnamon, and water. Use a knife to peel and slice the three apples as students watch. Then let them assist you in placing the apple pieces in a blender and adding the sugar, cinnamon, and water. They'll be fascinated as they watch the blender turn the chunks of apple into creamy applesauce. Spoon the applesauce into individual cups for the students to eat.

Then have the group create a book illustrating the applesauce recipe. Assign each child one ingredient or tool that was used to prepare the recipe. Have him draw his item on a sheet of white drawing paper. Assist the children in placing the pictures in the correct order. Have them observe as you use a marker to write a label for the item on each page. Add a final page which reads "Applesauce!" Create a cover for the group's book with the title of their choice and all their names as authors. Repeat this process with the remaining groups of students.

Making Applesauce

by: Philip, Joey, Allyssa, Erica, and Jeannine

a red apple

a little water

An "Apple-tizing" Tune

What's the next best thing to munching on apples? Singing about them!

Apples, Apples
(sung to the tune of "Twinkle, Twinkle, Little Star")

Apples juicy, apples round;
On the tree or on the ground.

Apples yellow, apples red,
Apple pie and juice and bread!

Apples crunchy, apples sweet;
Apples are so good to eat!

Apples Everywhere

After giving students a chance to taste apples and applesauce, direct their attention to the many other products made from apples. Ask students to brainstorm a list of apple products. Then duplicate and send home the checklist on page 41 with each child. This family project will have parents and children working together to determine the apple products kept at their houses. Discuss the results when the checklists are returned. Hey! We eat apple butter at my house, too!

Name: Tina B.

Apples Everywhere!
Which of these apple products do you have at your house?

- ✔ apple juice
- ✔ apple pie
- ✔ applesauce
- ✔ apple butter
- ✔ apple-flavored cereal
- ✔ fresh apples
- ✔ apple jelly
- ✔ apple bread or muffins
- other:
  dried apple chips
  an apple doll

An Imaginary Trip To The Orchard

Where *do* all those delicious apples come from? Read *Picking Apples And Pumpkins* by Amy and Richard Hutchings (Scholastic Inc.) to familiarize your little ones with how apples are picked at an orchard. Then take your students on an imaginary apple-picking adventure!

Wake up! We're going apple picking today!	*Yawn, stretch, and pretend to hop out of bed.*
Let's drive to the farm.	*Pretend to steer car.*
Get your basket.	*Pretend to pick up apple basket.*
Let's go on the hayride to the orchard!	*Pretend to bump up and down in wagon.*
Wow! Look at all the apples! Let's pick some!	*Reach up and pretend to pick apples.*
Put them in the basket.	*Pretend to put apples in basket.*
Those apples are really high. Let's climb!	*Pretend to climb tree and pick apples.*
Let's use the apple picker.	*Pretend to use long pole to reach apples.*
Wow! Our basket is really full!	*Pretend to lift heavy basket.*
Let's pay for our apples.	*Pretend to give money.*
Let's drive home. That was fun!	*Pretend to steer car.*

Continue the activity if desired by having your little ones perform movements as they pretend to create apple pie.

Apple Trees All Year

For further learning about apple trees, share the story *The Seasons Of Arnold's Apple Tree* by Gail Gibbons (Harcourt Brace Jovanovich). Then have your students create accordion-folded booklets to demonstrate what they've learned about the seasonal changes in an apple tree.

For each child, accordion-fold a 12" x 18" sheet of white drawing paper to create four sections as shown. Label the front cover of each booklet with the title "The Seasons Of _____'s Apple Tree." Have each child personalize his book. To create the four trees inside the book, paint each child's hand and forearm with brown tempera paint. Have him press that hand and arm onto each of the four sections of the folded paper to create four trees. Label each tree as shown and have the child add the following art materials to complete each tree:

Winter... Do not add anything to the tree.

Spring... Glue crumpled pieces of light green and white tissue paper to the branches to represent leaves and flowers.

Summer... Sponge-paint green leaves on the branches and allow the paint to dry. Add apples by pressing a fingertip into red tempera paint, then making circular fingerprints on top of the green paint.

Fall... Tear pieces of red, yellow, and orange construction paper into small bits; then glue them to the branches and to the ground below the tree.

Have each child complete his booklet by dictating a sentence about the changes in the apple tree during each season. Print his dictation below each tree.

A Is For Apple

A study of apples provides a perfect opportunity to teach the letter *A* and its sounds. Demonstrate for students the formation of both the upper- and lower-case *A*. Then print the word *apple* on the chalkboard and point out to students that it begins with an *A*. Ask youngsters to list some other words with that same beginning sound. Discuss with students both the long and short sounds of *A*. Then create a gameboard to give students continued exposure to vocabulary with the initial *A* sounds.

Sketch out a simple tree shape on a sheet of poster board. Color the trunk brown and the leaves green; then cut out the tree. Duplicate two copies of page 42 on tagboard. Color the pictures and cut out the individual apple shapes to create six matching pairs. If desired, laminate the apples and gameboard for durability.

To play the game, two or more students mix up all the apples and place them facedown on the tree shape. In turn, each student flips over two apples attempting to find a match. If the two apples have matching pictures, he may "pick" them off the tree and keep them. If the pictures do not match, he must turn them back over. Play continues until all the pairs have been found. It's apple fun for everyone!

An Apple For The Teacher...Or Mom

These fabric apples will bring bushels of cheer to a special teacher, helper, or parent. To make an apple, have each child put some polyester fiber stuffing around a two-inch Styrofoam® ball. Have her place the padded ball in the center of a nine-inch circle of red patterned fabric and gather the fabric around the ball. Assist each child in securing the ends of the fabric with a rubber band. Have each child stick the stem of a silk leaf under the rubber band. Then have her wrap the gathered fabric with masking tape. Help her to wrap a strip of green fabric over the masking tape and glue it in place with fabric glue. Have each child present her gift to a special someone. My, oh my—who's the apple of your eye?

All About Apples

Polish off your apple study with these reproducible booklets that review facts about apples. Duplicate pages 43 and 44 for each child. Cut apart the booklet covers and pages, stack them in order, and staple the booklets together. Have each child complete his booklet as follows:

Cover: Color the tree. Glue several red-hot cinnamon candies onto the tree to represent apples.
Page 1: Color the apples appropriately.
Page 2: Glue real apple seeds in the spaces provided.
Page 3: Draw a picture of your favorite apple product in the space provided.

Encourage little ones to take their booklets home to share with their families.

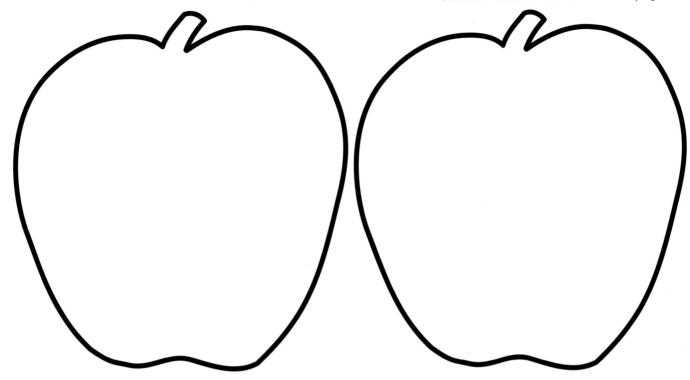

Name

Checklist

Apples Everywhere!

Which of these apple products do you have at your house?

- apple juice
- apple pie
- applesauce
- apple butter
- apple-flavored cereal
- fresh apples
- apple jelly
- apple bread or muffins
- other:

Note To The Teacher: Use with "Apples Everywhere" on page 38.

41

Patterns
Use with "A Is For *Apple*" on page 40.

ant

alligator

astronaut

acorn

acrobat

ape

All About Apples

by _____

Apples can be different colors.

1

Note To The Teacher: Use this booklet cover and page with "All About Apples" on page 40.

There are seeds inside an apple.

2

You can make lots of good things from apples. Here's a picture of what I like best!

3

Note To The Teacher: Use these booklet pages with "All About Apples" on page 40.

OCTOBER

Fire Safety Is A HOT Topic!

Preventing fire and related injury is one of the most important topics you will share with your children all year. Use the ideas in this unit to help your little ones learn critical safety skills.

ideas contributed by Deborah Burleson and Ada Hamrick

Talk About It

Anyone who has ever been mesmerized by a glowing fire in a fireplace can easily understand why fire would fascinate a young child. Begin your fire-safety unit by asking youngsters to name some places they have seen fire, such as on lighted birthday candles, at campfires, or during space-shuttle launches on television. Discuss with children how fire can benefit people by providing heat and energy. Point out that fire can be a wonderful thing when it is used carefully.

Then discuss the dangers of fire. Have any of the youngsters seen TV news stories about a house or forest fire? How do they think such a fire might start? Point out that when fire is not handled carefully, it can easily get out of control. It can damage property and hurt people and animals. Ask students to brainstorm a list of all the things they've heard about fire safety. This discussion will give you an idea of what your youngsters already know about fire safety and what you need to emphasize.

Playing It Safe

Use this activity to focus attention on an important safety rule—never play with matches! First read and discuss *Matches, Lighters, And Firecrackers Are Not Toys* by Dorothy Chlad (Childrens Press®). Then place several toys and a book of matches on a tabletop so that all the children can see them. Ask a volunteer to come forward and point to the item that doesn't belong. Ask him to explain his reasoning. Guide all the children to recognize the importance of not playing with matches. Repeat the activity with another selection of toys and a cigarette lighter. Then teach little ones this poem to help them remember what they've learned.

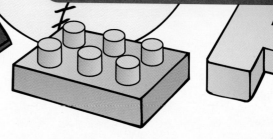

Don't play with a match –it's not a toy.
You could start a fire–boy, oh boy!
A lighter can be dangerous, too.
These are not toys for me or you.

Only a grown-up should light a match.
I'll stick with playing "house" or "catch."
So this is what I have to say:
I'm going to play it safe today!

—Ada Hamrick

The Sounds Of Sirens

Now that youngsters know what they can do to help themselves in the event of a fire, familiarize them with what will be going on around them if and when a fire occurs. The loud sounds made by fire engines, smoke alarms, and sirens can be very frightening for young children. Try this activity to get them accustomed to these sounds.

In advance, tape-record the sounds of a smoke alarm, a fire engine, or—if possible—your school's fire alarm. At circle time, discuss these sounds. Ask youngsters if they have heard any of these sounds; if so, what were their reactions? Give students a chance to express their fear or displeasure. Then explain the reasoning behind the high volume—to ensure that everyone knows there's an emergency. With the volume turned very low on your tape recorder, play the sounds you've recorded. What would happen if a real alarm were this quiet? Do students think they could hear it over the hubbub of a busy classroom? Would a quiet smoke alarm wake them from a sound sleep? Gradually increase the volume as you replay the tape several times, to get students used to the loudness of the sounds.

Fire-Drill Practice

Young children will need extra practice with your school's fire-drill procedures. If you made a recording of your school's fire alarm for "The Sounds Of Sirens" activity, use it for this classroom practice. Or ring a special bell to represent the fire alarm's sound.

Begin by discussing why fire drills are held at school. Then discuss the procedures your class will follow if the fire alarm is sounded. Have students line up; then walk them to the outside meeting place for your class. Demonstrate how you will count heads to be sure that everyone has arrived outside safely. Then return to the classroom. Ask students to pretend they are engaged in center-time activities. Explain that when you sound the pretend alarm, they should line up quickly and quietly. Do this several times. Then hold a practice fire drill—sounding the pretend alarm, lining up, and going outside to the meeting place. When you return to the classroom, reward your youngsters with a hearty congratulations and an assurance that they are ready for a real fire drill!

S-h-h-h-h

Let's Be Fire Fighters!

Now that your youngsters know what to do and what will happen in the event of a fire, give them some opportunities to demonstrate that knowledge. Begin by inviting children to participate in dramatic play. Transform your dramatic-play area into a fire station for a few weeks. Stock the area with child-sized raincoats and rubber boots, toy fire-fighter helmets (available at party-supply stores or through catalogs), a length of garden hose, a bell, and perhaps a stuffed Dalmatian. For an exciting central focus to the center, create a fire engine from a large appliance box. Have the children assist you in painting the box to resemble a fire engine, including a ladder along one side. Use a pizza pan as a steering wheel. Youngsters will delight in dressing as fire fighters, tossing the hose in the back of the truck, and speeding to a burning building to save the day!

Our Big Book Of Fire Safety

When we have a fire drill, we have to line up fast.

A Big Book Of Fire Safety

Create a class big book to show off students' knowledge about fire safety. Give each child a sheet of chart paper. Ask him to draw a picture that illustrates one thing he has learned about fire safety. Write his dictation at the bottom of the paper. Then make a front and back cover for the book from red poster board. Print the title "Our Big Book Of Fire Safety" on the front cover. Enlarge and duplicate the Dalmatian pattern on page 50, color and cut it out, and glue it to the cover. Punch holes in the front and back covers to correspond with the holes in your chart paper; then bind the pages between the covers with metal rings. Read the finished book to the class; then add it to your classroom library. This hot book is sure to spark a discussion about fire safety every time it's opened!

Something To Write Home About

Fire safety is a topic that must be addressed at home, as well as at school. Duplicate the parent letter on page 51 for each child to take home. Encourage the students to have their parents fill out the checklist at the bottom of the letter. Ask them to return it to school to indicate they've discussed important fire-safety issues at home. Give each child an opportunity to discuss his home fire-safety procedures.

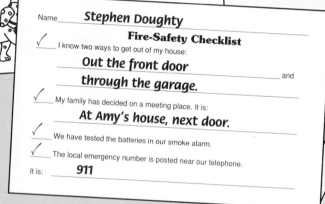

Dear Parent,

At school we have been discussing fire safety. Your child has learned some important safety skills, such as how to *stop, drop, and roll* if his clothes catch on fire and how to *crawl low* to avoid smoke inhalation during a fire. We've also practiced for a fire drill at school.

Please take some time to discuss important safety measures that apply at home. Knowledge of fire-safety procedures could save your child's life! After your discussion, please help your child fill out the checklist below and return it to school. We'll talk about each family's checklist to reinforce what the children have learned.

Name **Stephen Doughty**

Fire-Safety Checklist

✓ I know two ways to get out of my house:

Out the front door

through the garage. and

✓ My family has decided on a meeting place. It is:

At Amy's house, next door.

✓ We have tested the batteries in our smoke alarm.

✓ The local emergency number is posted near our telephone.

It is: **911**

Fire Chief Badges

Conclude your fire-safety unit by awarding each hardworking child a special fire chief's badge. Duplicate the badge patterns on page 50 on tagboard. For each child, cut out a badge shape. Invite the child to sponge-paint one side of the badge with silver tempera paint. After the badge dries, glue a child's school photo to its center. Using a permanent marker, print "Fire Chief" and the child's name on the badge. Use a piece of rolled masking tape to stick each child's badge to his shirt. Your youngsters will be glowing with pride!

Fire Chief

Maggie

Delightful Dalmatians

Have your youngsters noticed that wherever there are fire fighters, there seem to be Dalmatians? That's because the Dalmatian is the unofficial mascot—or good-luck charm—of fire fighters. Read about a Dalmatian in the book *Firehouse Dog* by Amy and Richard Hutchings (Scholastic Inc.) This selection with photo illustrations follows Hooper the dog and his fire-fighting friends through a day on the job.

After reading the story, invite youngsters to make firehouse dogs of their own. For each child, duplicate the Dalmatian pattern on page 50 on white construction paper. Have him color and cut out the pattern; then tape a craft stick to its back. Suggest that each child name his puppet. Then invite each child in turn to introduce his puppet and have it recite a fire-safety rule for the class. "Bow wow!" means "Never play with matches!"

Badge Pattern
Use with "Fire Chief Badges" on page 49.

Dalmatian Pattern
Use with "A Big Book Of Fire Safety" on page 48 and "Delightful Dalmatians" on page 49.

Fire Dog

Dear Parent,

At school we have been discussing fire safety. Your child has learned some important safety skills, such as how to *stop, drop,* and *roll* if his clothes catch on fire and how to *crawl low* to avoid smoke inhalation during a fire. We've also practiced for a fire drill at school.

Please take some time to discuss important safety measures that apply at home. Knowledge of fire-safety procedures could save your child's life! After your discussion, please help your child fill out the checklist below and return it to school. We'll talk about each family's checklist to reinforce what the children have learned.

Thank you!

- -

Name_____

Fire-Safety Checklist

_____ I know two ways to get out of my house:

_____ and

_____

_____ My family has decided on a meeting place. It is:

_____

_____ We have tested the batteries in our smoke alarm.

_____ The local emergency number is posted near our telephone.

It is: _____

- -

Note To The Teacher: Use this parent letter with "Something To Write Home About" on page 49.

Simply Spiders

Quick, precise engineers. Efficient hunters and travelers. Intimidating features. Virtually harmless to humans. What creatures are these? Spiders—simply spiders! Delight youngsters with the opportunity to learn more about spiders with this simply spidery unit.

ideas contributed by Carol McPeeters, Mackie Rhodes, and Sarah Tharpe-Winchell

The Human Spider

Begin your study of spiders by inviting students to imitate some arachnid actions. Have youngsters form a human spider to help them understand the coordination it takes for a spider to move on eight legs. Whether long and thin or short and stubby, a spider's legs are attached to its body in pairs. To help youngsters understand what a pair is, explain to them that they each have two legs—a pair. Then invite four volunteers of approximately the same height to become part of a human spider. Have the children hold their hands behind their backs. Then, facing outward, have them form a small circle. Lower a large beanbag chair—the body of the spider—into the middle of the circle. (If a beanbag chair is not available, use a large laundry bag stuffed with towels). Have the students lean their backs against the beanbag to support it between them. To keep the bag from slipping down, suggest that they use their hands to support it from the bottom. Challenge the human spider to move across the room, keeping all its legs attached to its body. Repeat the activity to give each child the opportunity to become part of the human spider. It may not be Spider-man®—but it moves just like a spider can!

Supper Time!

Do your students know that spiders eat only liquids? Spiders use their strawlike mouths to suck the body fluids from their victims. Entice your youngsters to sup like spiders with this tasty temptation. In advance purchase or prepare a class quantity of juice or a flavored drink. For each child, make a straw-sized hole just below the seal-strip on a resealable plastic sandwich bag. Push a straw into the hole so that it reaches the bottom of the bag. To support the bags during pouring, place them upright, one at a time, in the bottom of a cutaway cereal box. Fill each bag halfway with juice; then seal it tightly. At snacktime, encourage students to suck the liquid out of their bags as spiders do their meals. Have them discuss what happens to each bag as the liquid is drained from it. Explain that, like the bag, the spider's food also collapses as the liquid is sucked from it.

Dragline

A spider spins a silk thread, called a *dragline,* behind itself wherever it goes. It relies on the dragline to help it escape from danger by dropping quickly out of reach of the threat. The spider can climb back along its dragline after the threat has passed. To prepare a dragline for your little arachnid actors to use, tape one end of a 30-yard length of yarn to a toilet-paper tube. Wrap the yarn around the tube. Slide the tube onto a narrow belt. Then arrange an obstacle course using chairs, tables, stools, plastic cones, and other small furnishings. Loosely fasten the belt around the waist of a volunteer with the tube of yarn (the dragline) positioned near the middle of the child's back. Explain that the child will crawl on the floor pretending to be a spider as he negotiates the obstacle course. Have another child hold the loose end of the dragline at the beginning of the course. As the spider moves, his dragline will unroll, leaving a trail along the obstacle course. At the end of the course, remove the belt from the child's waist. Have him wind the yarn back onto the tube as he retraces his path.

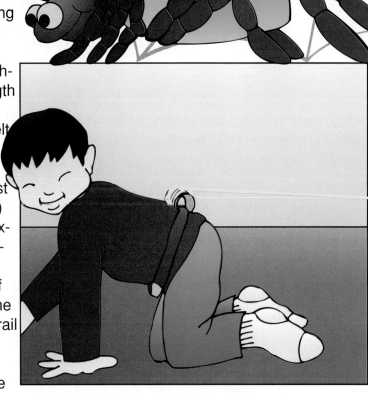

Spinning Surprises

Most female spiders spin a special kind of silk to enclose their eggs in an egg sac. Some spiders spin silk around their victims to prevent them from escaping. Have your youngsters spinning with delight with these super surprises. Provide a variety of rubber insects and small plastic eggs. Using arm-length pieces of yarn to represent silk, have each child wrap an insect or egg until it is covered. Secure the end of the yarn with a piece of tape. Place the wrapped items in a basket. Later encourage each student to make a selection from the basket, then unwrap the item. Ask him to try to guess the item before it is completely unwrapped.

The Scoop On Spiders

Did you know that...

... spiders are *arachnids,* not insects? Insects have six legs, while spiders have eight.

... all spiders spin silk? The spinnerets at the rear of their bodies spin the silk. Spiders use their silk as draglines, to make webs, to wrap their food, and to make egg sacs. Spiderlings use silk for *ballooning,* a special way of traveling through the air.

... most spiders have eight eyes? The number of eyes varies from species to species.

... all spiders have fangs? Poison flows through the tips of their fangs to stun their prey.

... most spiders are harmless? In North America, only six kinds of spiders are harmful to humans. These include four types of widows, the brown recluse, and the sack spider.

53

Spiders, Spiders Everywhere!

In corners and cracks, under rocks and grass—spiders can be found practically everywhere. But not all spiders are alike. Introduce your little ones to two kinds of common spiders—the house spider and the garden spider.

Spying On Spiders

Students will be ready to spy on some live spiders after reading *Spider Watching* by Vivian French (Candlewick Press). Using information from the book and this unit, engage students in a discussion about spiders. Then take a walk on both the inside and outside of your school building to look for spiders. If desired, have little ones use magnifying glasses for close-up examinations of the animals and their webs. As they make their discoveries, encourage youngsters to share their observations of spiders with the class.

Spiders At School

Provide youngsters with a firsthand opportunity to observe this fascinating creature by bringing a spider to school. Gently capture a spider using a small net, cup, or jar. If desired, capture both an indoor and an outdoor spider. Use a large jar with airholes in the lid to create a temporary home for the spider. Place the spider inside the jar along with a moist cotton ball, a small amount of gravel or sand, and a small branch. Encourage students to observe the spider without disturbing its home. Have them comment on its features and behavior. Ask them to look closely for the spider's dragline. Will the spider build a web? If it does, encourage children to describe the web. Keep in mind that spiders thrive in their natural environments—plan to release the spider the next day.

Spiders At Home

The house spider can be found almost anywhere indoors—in a corner, behind a door, above a window, or under the couch. The common garden spider can be found outdoors along the ground, in a tree, behind a bush, or on a fence. Where do you find spiders around *your* house? Pose this question to your students. After discussing the many places spiders can be found around a home, have students make a "Spiders At Home" booklet. Reproduce and cut apart a class quantity of pages 55 and 56. Have each student color the front and back covers to represent the outside of a house. For each booklet page, encourage him to write or dictate the name of a household item or location to complete each sentence. Then have him illustrate each sentence by drawing the items and pressing his fingers onto a stamp pad and then onto each page to create fingerprint spiders. Have the student draw eight legs on each spider. Invite the child to make a few fingerprint spiders on both covers, as well. Sequence the completed pages between the covers; then staple the booklet along the left side.

Spiders
At Home

Booklet Pages
Use with "Spiders At Home" on page 54.

A spider is **over** the _____.

A spider is **in** the _____.

A spider is **on** the _____.

A spider is **under** the _____.

Any Way You Slice It...

Pizza is a great theme! You can't top this spicy subject for capturing little ones' interest. And there's plenty of learning in every slice!

by Ada Hamrick

A pizza can be a circle.

We can be a circle.

Thank you for showing us how to make pizza.

Adrienne

Pizza Shapes

Begin this taste-tempting theme by bringing in two pizzas—one round and one rectangular. Ask youngsters to observe the shapes of the two pizzas; then take an instant photo of each one. Next cut the pizzas into slices as youngsters watch. Cut the round pizza into triangular pieces and the rectangular pizza into squares. Ask youngsters to identify each of these shapes. Then place an individual triangle and an individual square on separate serving plates and take an instant photo of each plate. Give each child a slice to enjoy.

After students finish eating, show the photos one at a time and review the four shapes—circle, rectangle, triangle, and square. Then divide the class into four groups. Assign each group a different shape to imitate. Have the students in the circle group lie down on a carpeted area to form a circle with their bodies. Take an instant photo of the group forming the circle. (You may need to stand on a chair to achieve the correct angle.) Ask the other groups to use their bodies to form their assigned shapes and take an instant photo of each one. Use all the photos to create a class book titled "Pizza Shapes." On sheets of construction paper, mount the photos of the corresponding shapes of pizzas and students; then program each page similarly to the one shown.

Visiting The Pizza Man

Many of your youngsters have probably visited a pizzeria or had pizza delivered to their homes. Learn more about the people who make and serve pizzas by reading the book *Pizza Man* by Marjorie Pillar (HarperCollins Children's Books). This photo-illustrated book with simple text will take youngsters through the day with a pizzeria worker as he does everything from mixing dough to assembling take-out boxes. Then plan a field trip to a local pizza restaurant or delivery center. You might even arrange to taste some free samples during your tour!

After your visit, be sure to assist the students in writing thank-you notes to the restaurant manager. To create a pizza-shaped note for each student, fold a sheet of tan construction paper in half. Trace a circle and cut it out, leaving a small strip of the fold uncut. Then ask each child to decorate the front of the note to resemble a pizza with her favorite toppings. Write the child's dictation for her thank-you message inside; then have her write her name below it. Now that's a note in good taste!

A Pizza Poem

This transparency tale will delight your youngsters. To prepare, use Vis-à-Vis® markers to illustrate seven transparencies for the overhead projector as shown. Be careful to make sure the illustrations line up when the transparencies are stacked, so that all the pizza toppings fall within the pizza outline and the smiles fall within the outlines of the faces. Stack them in order, with number 1 on the bottom and number 7 on the top. Use a hole puncher to punch two holes along the top edge of the stack. Bind the transparencies together with two metal rings. When you are ready to perform the poem for your little ones, set up the overhead projector and place only sheet number 1 on the lighted surface. As you read through the poem, flip over each sheet to overlap the previous one.

If you do not have access to an overhead projector, use clear sheet protectors in a three-ring binder. Cut open four sheet protectors along the outer and bottom edges. From one sheet protector, cut away one layer completely, to make a single thickness. Illustrate the seven resulting clear pages as shown. (Be sure that the illustrations overlap correctly.) Place the sheets in a three-ring binder. Perform the poem for your youngsters by holding the open binder and turning over the sheets one at a time, beginning with number 1 at the back and ending with number 7 at the front.

After learning the poem, little ones will enjoy using the transparencies as an individual or partner activity.

1

Five little children,
All in a row,
Ordered a pizza,
In a box—to go!

2
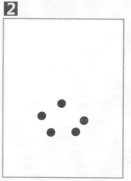
The first one said,
"Pepperoni tastes so fine!"

3

The second one said,
"I want mushrooms on mine!"

4

The third one said,
"I like sausage that's hot!"

5

The fourth one said,
"I want cheese—a lot!"

6

The fifth one said,
"Be sure to add some spice!"

7
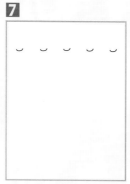
And they all had a pizza
That tasted mighty nice!

Pizza! Pizza! Write All About It!

All this talk about pizza will no doubt have your youngsters hungry for a slice or two. So plan a pizza party to conclude your pizza theme. Bring in one or two boxes of pizza mix, depending on your class size. Before preparing the pizza, read the simple rhyming story, *Pizza Party!* by Grace Maccarone (Scholastic Inc.). Then have little ones assist you in following the package directions to create a pizza for everyone to enjoy. Add whatever toppings you and your students would like.

Afterward have youngsters write a language-experience story about cooking and eating the pizza. Have the children dictate sentences for you to write on the chalkboard. Then help the children organize the sentences to reflect the correct sequence of events. Copy the sentences onto sheets of chart paper and have pairs of students illustrate each step.

Then have students help you make a cover for this giant-sized class book. Cut a piece of bulletin-board paper to match the size of your chart paper. Use a marker to outline a large pizza with a crust edge. Fill in the "sauce" portion of the pizza with red tempera paint and let it dry. Provide several cut vegetables, such as green peppers, onions, and mushrooms. Invite each youngster to dip a cut vegetable into a shallow container of tempera paint, then print with it on the pizza drawing. When the vegetable prints have dried, squiggle glue over the pizza illustration. Give the children short pieces of white or yellow yarn to "sprinkle" onto the pizza to resemble mozzarella cheese. After the glue has dried, cut out the letters for the title "Making Pizza" and glue them on the cover. Staple the cover to the chart-paper pages. Add the class book to your classroom library.

We put tomato sauce on our pizza.

Pizza Puzzles

Help students practice sorting skills with this appetizing center. Prepare several pizza-shaped puzzles by tracing and cutting 12-inch circles of manila paper. Use crayons or markers to decorate each circle to resemble a pizza. Draw lines across each cutout to resemble slices on a pizza. On each pizza, affix a sticker to each slice that fits into a common category. For example, one pizza might feature stickers with a farm theme; another pizza might have letters of the alphabet. Cut the slices apart on the lines. Laminate all the slices and store them in a delivery box donated by a local pizza shop. To use the center, a child removes all the slices from the box and sorts them by category; then he reassembles the pizzas.

Great "Pizzas" Of Literature

Curious George And The Pizza
by Margret Rey and Alan J. Shalleck
Houghton Mifflin Company

Little Nino's Pizzeria
by Karen Barbour
Harcourt Brace Jovanovich

How Pizza Came To Queens
by Dayal Kaur Khalsa
Scholastic Inc.

POP... POP...POPCORN!

Here's a topic that's just bursting with possibilities! Check out this sizzling selection of popcorn activities to get your little ones hoppin' and poppin' about learning!

by Ada Hamrick

A FEAST FOR THE SENSES

Can you hear the oil sizzling? Can you smell that delightful scent filling the air? Have your youngsters explore the five senses as they pop some popcorn. On the first day of your popcorn theme, bring in an electric skillet or popcorn popper, an extension cord, a king-size bedsheet, some popcorn kernels, and some oil. Spread the sheet in your circle area. Invite your students to sit well back from the edges of the sheet.* Then ask them to close their eyes as you prepare a surprise. Encourage the students to concentrate on what they can hear and smell while their eyes are shut.

Place the popper in the center of the sheet and turn on the heat. Pour in some oil. When the oil begins to sizzle, sprinkle in some popcorn kernels and periodically shake the pan. Leave the lid off. Invite students to open their eyes. Observe as your fascinated youngsters watch the popcorn hop right out of the pan onto the sheet! After a few kernels have popped, put the lid on the popper.

When all the kernels have popped, serve each child a small helping in a paper cup. (Add butter and salt, if you wish.) Ask students to concentrate on how the popcorn feels and tastes. After everyone has finished this snack, invite the children to describe the popcorn-popping experience. On a large sheet of chart paper, write the headings "Hear," "Smell," "See," "Feel," and "Taste." Have the students recount what they heard, smelled, saw, felt, and tasted during the experience. Encourage descriptive vocabulary as you write the students' sentences under each category.

Hear
I could hear the frying sound.

Smell
It smelled buttery.

See
I could see the corn pop.

Feel
It felt crunchy in my mouth.

Taste
It tasted salty.

*NOTE: Extra supervision will be helpful during this activity so that the children remain at a safe distance from popping kernels or oil. Explain that this science experiment is an exception and that popcorn poppers should never be used without lids.

POP MUSIC

Help youngsters recall the popcorn-popping experience when you teach this tune.

THE POPCORN SONG

(sung to the tune of "Down By The Station")

In the popcorn popper,
Kernels go ker-plink.
I can smell it cooking—
Almost done, I think!

See the popcorn popping,
Fluffy and so white.
Pop! Pop! Yum! Yum!
Tastes just right!

Kevin Piel Carly Juan Hannah

Sally LaJames

Carlos Josh

Beth

STRINGING THEM ALONG

A popcorn string is a wonderful thing—for small-motor practice! A few days in advance, pop a quart or two of popcorn, and allow it to sit uncovered. On the day of the activity, provide each student with a blunt, plastic needle that has been threaded with a length of dental floss. Invite your little ones to string the stale popcorn onto the floss. Place the finished strands on the trees near your classroom to provide food for birds.

Then create a paper popcorn string for your classroom. Provide each child with a large sheet of finger-paint paper and some white tempera paint. (Add a small amount of dishwashing liquid to the paint to make cleanup easier.) Invite each child to finger-paint on the paper; then let it dry. After the paint is dry, use a permanent marker to outline the shape of a puffy piece of popcorn on each paper. Ask each child to follow your line as best he can to cut out his piece of popcorn. Use the permanent marker to label each cutout with the child's name. Then have each child use a hole puncher to punch a hole at the top of his cutout. Thread a long length of brightly colored yarn through the hole in each piece, and knot the yarn at equal intervals to create a paper popcorn string. Display the string as a bulletin-board border or door decoration during your popcorn theme.

POPCORN PRETENDING

Get your youngsters moving when you invite them to imitate popcorn kernels in a giant popcorn popper. Use chalk or masking tape to outline a large square or circle on your classroom carpet. Encourage all your youngsters to find a space inside this imaginary popper as you "pour" the kernels into the pan. Have them crouch down to imitate the unpopped kernels. Pretend to insert a giant plug into the wall outlet. As the imaginary heat rises, ask students to pretend they are getting hotter and hotter. Encourage students to jostle around inside the popper as you "shake" the kernels in the pan. When each popcorn kernel is so hot that she can no longer stand it, have her "pop" into a standing position. When all the kernels have "popped," ask students to imagine that they are being coated with melted butter and sprinkled with salt. Then invite them to exit the popper one by one as you select and "gobble" each piece of popcorn.

KEEP ON MOVIN'...
with these musical selections:

"Popcorn"
Sung by Greg and Steve
We All Live Together Vol. 2
Youngheart Records

"Popcorn"
Sung by Raffi
The Corner Grocery Store
Troubadour Records

COLORFUL KERNELS

Provide fine-motor practice and help students practice sorting skills with some colored popcorn. Purchase a package of colored popcorn kernels and obtain an empty egg carton to create this center. In advance, paint the bottoms of the egg cups to correspond with the colors of the popcorn kernels. Allow the paint to dry. Place a small handful of colored popcorn kernels into a lidded container.

To use the center, a child opens the container of kernels and spreads them on a tabletop. He picks up each kernel and drops it into an egg cup painted with the corresponding color. If desired, have the child use a pair of tweezers to pick up the kernels. You may wish to make several sets of cartons and kernel containers so that more than one child can use the center at a time.

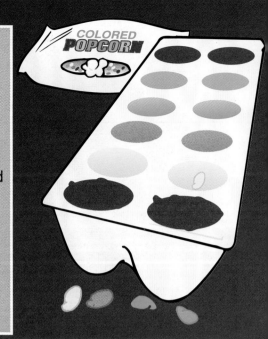

A "NUMMY" NUMBERS GAME

Help youngsters practice numeral identification with this game. Ask a local movie theater to donate a few small popcorn boxes. Then cut out a number of puffy popcorn shapes from heavy white paper. Program each cutout with a numeral that you'd like your students to learn to identify. Laminate the cutouts for durability.

To play the game, distribute a popcorn box to each student in a small group. Place all the popcorn cutouts facedown in a pile. The first player draws a cutout from the stack and attempts to identify the numeral printed on it. If correct, he may place the cutout in his box. If he is incorrect, he places the cutout at the bottom of the stack and the next child takes his turn. When all cards have been drawn, have each player count the popcorn pieces in his box. Vary the game by programming more cutouts with number words or sets or letters of the alphabet.

SNACKTIME, STORYTIME

Now that your little ones are popcorn experts, reward them with a snack of the fluffy white stuff! Pop a large batch of popcorn and give each child a cup of corn to munch. For added fun, provide a variety of toppings for students to sprinkle on their popcorn, such as butter flavoring, salt, Parmesan cheese, garlic salt, or cinnamon sugar. While students are munching, read aloud one of these "pop-ular" popcorn stories:

The Popcorn Dragon
Written by Jane Thayer
Illustrated by Lisa McCue
Published by Scholastic Inc.

The Popcorn Book
Written & Illustrated by Tomie de Paola
Published by Holiday House

BIG IDEAS FOR BOOK WEEK

Celebrate National Children's Book Week—the third week in November—with this collection of activities designed to capture the interest of your little bookworms.
ideas contributed by Valerie SchifferDanoff and Ada Hanley Goren

Ten Clever Classroom Reading Centers

Consider setting up an unusual reading center in your classroom. The extra effort will be worth it when you see the excitement generated as little ones visit the center to read and share books. Choose a center that will be appealing and provide a safe setting for the age level of your youngsters.

1. **"Read, Read, Read A Book"**—Bring in an old rowboat or canoe. Set it on top of a large blue sheet or shower curtain to simulate water. Fill the boat with fluffy pillows and books; then encourage youngsters to float away into the land of imagination.
2. **"Dive Into Books"**—Fill an inflatable kiddie pool with comfy pillows and inflatable swim rings or pool toys. Invite students to jump in and splash around with a good book!
3. **"Reading In Bed"**—Set up bunk beds, complete with pillows and "snuggly" blankets. Be sure to add some flashlights for reading under the covers!
4. **"Camp Out With A Good Book"**—Set up a tent with sleeping bags and a battery-operated lamp. Invite students to crawl inside and enjoy a backpack full of books.
5. **"Come Read With Me Down By The Sea"**—Set out some beach chairs, beach towels, and coolers filled with books. Add a bright lamp and a few pairs of child-sized sunglasses. Ahhh...there's nothing like a good book at the beach!

6. **"The Garden Of Reading"**—Surround a simple wooden bench with potted plants and hanging baskets. Have students "pick" books from large flowerpots and baskets. Children's appreciation for reading will be in full bloom!
7. **" 'Bear-y' Good Readers"**—Set up a few beanbag chairs and a large assortment of teddy bears. Encourage children to read to and with their furry friends.
8. **"Books In The Bathtub"**—Cut off one long side of an appliance box to create a bathtub. Paint the box white and partially fill it with Styrofoam® packing pieces. Add a vinyl tub pillow and a rubber ducky to complete the effect. Rub-a-dub-dub! Let's read books in the tub!
9. **"Relax And Read"**—Set up a freestanding canvas hammock and a few pillows to entice little ones to lie back and enjoy a good story.
10. **"Pack A Picnic Basket With Books"**—Bring in a child-sized picnic table or a checkered tablecloth to spread on the floor. Add a few picnic baskets full of good books, and let the reading feast begin!

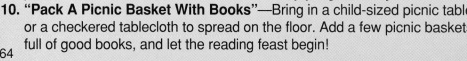

Get Ready, Get Set,...

During Book Week, you'll want to immerse your youngsters in books. So prepare by filling your classroom with a wide variety of books. Check out books from your school and public libraries, and put them *everywhere*—in your reading area, on your chalkboard ledge, in baskets, on tables, and in each of your centers. Include both fiction and nonfiction selections to appeal to the tastes of each of your students.

Then create a bookworm puppet to guide your class through their Book Week activities. Obtain a long, green sock and a pair of wiggle eyes. Fashion a pair of glasses for your puppet from a pipe cleaner. Hot-glue the wiggle eyes and glasses securely to the toe end of the sock. Slip the sock over one hand, and Buddy the Bookworm is ready to go!

A Bookworm's Booklet

National Children's Book Week is a good time to teach children how to care for books. Use your Buddy-the-Bookworm puppet to lead this discussion. Remind students of some basic rules for handling books, such as:
- Do not draw on books.
- Do not cut or tear a book's pages or covers.
- Turn the pages of a book carefully.
- Put books away when you are finished.

Then have little ones create fun reproducible booklets to help them remember some proper ways to care for books. Duplicate a copy of page 68 for each child. Have each youngster cut the booklet cover and pages apart on the bold lines, then color each of the illustrations. Assist each child in stacking the pages in the correct order and stapling them together along the left side. Then have each child use a hole puncher (making multiple punches) to create a hole, as indicated, through all four thicknesses of paper.

Before reading through the booklet, use a fine-tipped marker to draw a face on the tip of each child's right index finger. Have him insert his finger through the holes in his booklet. Now his personal bookworm is ready to read the booklet! Encourage little ones to share their booklets with family members at home.

I Am A Bookworm
by
Charles

The Family Connection

Invite family members to visit your classroom as guest readers during your Book Week festivities. Duplicate a copy of the parent letter on page 69 for each child to take home. If a parent can't come in person, she may be able to make a cassette recording of herself reading a favorite story. After receiving parents' responses, schedule visits from your guest readers and send home blank cassette tapes to those parents who volunteered to make recordings.

The parent letter also describes the activities in "The Book-Borrowing Bag" on this page and "Book Exchange" on page 67.

Mrs. Hamrick
Room #152
Conway Elementary

The Book-Borrowing Bag

Create a colorful, canvas tote bag that will help little ones safely transport classroom books between school and home. Purchase a medium-sized canvas tote bag with sturdy handles. Use fabric paints to create a cute bookworm design on one side of the bag. Then use a laundry marker to write your name, room number, and school name. Each day, encourage one child to choose a book from your classroom library to borrow. Place the book in the Book-Borrowing Bag and have the child take it home to share with family members. When he returns the book and bag on the next school day, another child may have a turn to borrow a book.

Where The Books Are

All this talk about books should have your youngsters hungry for more, more, more! Plan a field trip to the public library or a local bookstore. Prior to your visit, arrange for a librarian or bookstore employee to guide the students on a tour of the facility. During the tour, give children a chance to browse through the shelves of books. Provide them with information about proper behavior and procedures while in the library or store. If the tour includes a storytime, encourage students to sit quietly and listen carefully to the story. At the conclusion of the tour, have the class decide on a few books to check out from the library or purchase from the bookstore for your classroom.

After your field trip, encourage the children to role-play what they've experienced. Transform your dramatic play area into a library or bookstore for a week or two. Add a shelf of books and magazines and some other simple props, such as index cards (for library cards), a date stamp, or a toy cash register. Encourage youngsters to take turns role-playing the library or bookstore workers and the patrons.

A Book Week Bash

Culminate your Book Week unit with a classroom celebration. Invite parents to join you for a storybook parade, a festive book exchange, and some yummy Book Week bites!

Book Exchange

What's a party without presents? Invite each family (by way of the parent letter on page 69) to donate a book for the book exchange. Wrap a few extra books in case you don't receive enough donations. Place each child's festively wrapped book in a large basket or box. During the party, have each youngster choose a book to unwrap and take home. Or ask the children to donate their books to the class library, so that everyone can enjoy them.

A Storybook Parade

Little ones love to participate in parades! Encourage each child to show off his favorite book in a special Book Week promenade. Use a large, zippered plastic bag and a 30-inch length of yarn to make a storybook necklace for each child. Punch a hole in each side of the bag, just below the zippered closure. Thread each end of the yarn through a hole and tie it securely. Invite each child to place his favorite paperback book into the zippered bag, then slip the necklace over his head so that the book's cover faces outward as the bag rests on his chest. Then have youngsters line up and parade through your school, showing off their book choices to the other students, teachers, and parent visitors.

Cinderella
written and illustrated by Cathie Carter

Bite A Book

Once you're back in the classroom, conclude the festivities with a special snack. Have the children create book-shaped snacks with cover illustrations of their favorite bookworm—Buddy! Give each child two graham-cracker squares (to serve as the book's front and back covers). Invite her to use a plastic knife to spread canned white frosting (to represent the book's white pages) on one cracker, then top it with the other cracker. Then have her squeeze a thick line of green decorator tube icing onto the book's cover to create a likeness of Buddy the Bookworm. To make Buddy's glasses, have her place two pieces of Cheerios® cereal and two short pieces of a pretzel stick at the top end of her green icing worm, as shown. Then invite each child to bite into a good book—her Book Week snack!

67

Booklet Cover And Pages

Use with "A Bookworm's Booklet" on page 65.

I treat books gently. 2

I Am A Bookworm

by

©The Education Center, Inc.

I put books away. 3

I keep books clean. 1

Dear Family,

We will be celebrating National Children's Book Week during the week of November _____. We have planned some very special activities, and we'd like to invite you to participate in one or more of the following ways:

_____ Would you like to be a guest reader in our classroom? Please indicate if you can join us to read a story aloud to the children.

_____ If you are unable to visit us in person, would you like to make a cassette recording of one of your child's favorite stories? We'd love to hear your voice in our listening center! Please indicate your interest, so I can send you a blank cassette tape.

_____ Could you send in a book for our book exchange? Please choose a book your child is willing to donate. Wrap it in gift paper and ribbon, and send it to school on _____.
(date)
Each child will have the opportunity to choose a book donated by a classmate.

Also, each child will be bringing home our Book-Borrowing Bag with a book from our classroom library. Please share the book with your child and return it in the bag on the next school day. Enjoy reading with your child!

Please return this form by _____ to indicate your participation.
(date)

Thank you!

- -

Note To The Teacher: Use this with "The Family Connection" and "The Book-Borrowing Bag" on page 66 and "Book Exchange" on page 67.

Think Thanks!

These treats, trimmings, and times to reflect will have youngsters thinking thanks for the many terrific things in their lives.

ideas contributed by Deborah Burleson, Lucia Kemp Henry, and Mackie Rhodes

A-Tisket, A-Tasket, We're Gonna Fill A Basket!

Weave a home-school connection by inviting parents and students to donate food for a giving basket. In advance, arrange to distribute food donations to a charitable organization or a needy family. Obtain a large basket or decorate a box to resemble a basket. Embellish the basket with ribbon, bows, and other trimmings. Then duplicate the parent letter on page 74 for each child.

Ask students to think about the many foods they eat each day. Encourage them to name some of their favorite foods. Do they feel thankful when they eat their favorites? Tell them that some children and their families do not have very much food or very many different foods to eat. Then show them the basket and explain that it is a giving basket—that the class will collect food in the basket to give to people in need. The food will be given to a family or families in time for Thanksgiving. Ask the students to tell their families about the giving basket. Provide each student with a copy of the parent letter to take home. As each child brings in a donation, tell him how much his contribution to the giving basket is appreciated. To keep youngsters interested in filling the basket, use the contents of the basket for the activities in "Taking Inventory."

Taking Inventory

Keep little ones "ac-count-able" for the contents of the giving basket in "A-Tisket, A-Tasket, We're Gonna Fill A Basket" by having them take a daily inventory. Each day encourage a small group of students to empty the basket. Have them sort the items from the basket into different categories. Encourage the students to use various criteria for sorting, such as *food types* (beans, tomatoes, corn) or *package types* (cans, boxes, bags). List the different categories chosen by the group on a sheet of chart paper. Have the youngsters count the number of items in each category. Write the total of each one beside its corresponding category on the chart. Afterwards help the students place the items back into the basket one at a time, counting each one aloud. Write the total number of items at the bottom of the chart paper and circle that number. Each day compare the total number of items to the number from the previous day. On the last collection day, count all of the items aloud with the class. Return the items to the giving basket; then thank each child for helping to fill and keep count of the foods in the basket. After the basket of food is delivered, be sure to share with students the thanks offered by its recipients.

Books To Be Thankful For

Treat youngsters to these literature picks to highlight the spirit of Thanksgiving. Then send a copy of the bookmark on page 74 home with each child to encourage reading together as a family.

Over The River And Through The Woods
illustrated by John Steven Gurney (Scholastic Inc.)

Following some joyous choruses of this Thanksgiving favorite, invite little ones to create their own version of a horse-drawn sleigh. First read the song aloud; then sing it with your students several times. Have a wagon available for youngsters to use as a sleigh. Or make a sleigh from a large box with a rope handle looped through two holes at one end. Arrange an obstacle course using cones, furniture, and a Hula-Hoop® or two to represent features of the terrain described in the song. Encourage small groups of children to ride and maneuver the makeshift sleigh through the obstacle course. Suggest that the children take turns pulling and riding in the sleigh. Give each small group of children an opportunity to use the sleigh.

A
Healthy
Serving
Of Thanks!
by Amber

Thanksgiving At The Tappletons'
by Eileen Spinelli (J. B. Lippincott Junior Books)

After hearing this humorous story about one family's Thanksgiving fiasco, youngsters will delight in creating these paper-plate books. Read the book aloud to students, helping them identify the absurdities in the story. Then, on four separate white paper plates, have each child draw a picture of a person or an activity for which he is thankful. Encourage him to write or dictate a sentence about each picture. Arrange the illustrated plates between two paper-plate covers so that the illustrations are all right-side-up. Use a hole puncher to make two holes through the plates along the rims near the tops of the pictures. Thread a short length of yarn through each set of holes and tie it. On the front cover, write the title "A Healthy Serving Of Thanks!" Encourage students to take their books home to share with their families.

Thanksgiving Treat
by Catherine Stock (Macmillan Publishing Company)

Your students will be ready to lend a helping hand with their own families' Thanksgiving Day preparations after hearing this story. Prior to reading the story, duplicate page 75 on white construction paper for each child. Prepare a tray of tempera paint mixed with a small amount of dishwashing liquid. Read the story aloud to your youngsters. Afterwards engage them in a discussion about the many things their families do to prepare for Thanksgiving. List these things on a sheet of chart paper. Ask students to name some of the things they can do to be helpful during the preparations. Then have each child dip his hand in the tray of paint and make a handprint on his copy of page 75. When the paint dries, encourage each child to take his paper home and have his family help him complete the sentence. Remind students to try to be helpful on Thanksgiving Day.

Dear Parent

On Thanksgiving Day, I can help ____

Thanksgiving Trimmings And Treats

Youngsters will enjoy preparing these decorations and dishes for a little taste of Thanksgiving.

Popping With Thanks

"Thanks!" will be popping up everywhere when youngsters make these pop-up cards to express their appreciation for the people and things in their lives. For each child, duplicate the pop-up card pattern on page 76 and trim along the straight dotted line. Have him color the letters in the word "Thanks!" Encourage the child to cut pictures from magazines and catalogs to represent things or people for which he is thankful. Have him glue the pictures in the boxes indicated on his paper. Then cut each child's paper on the curved dotted line. Help the child glue the edges of his paper onto a sheet of construction paper, being careful not to glue the pop-up section. When the glue dries, fold the construction paper in half, pulling the pop-up section forward. On the front of the card, write "For these things, [child's name] gives...." When the card is opened, "Thanks!" will pop up at the cardholder. Encourage students to share their cards with one another, then with family members at home.

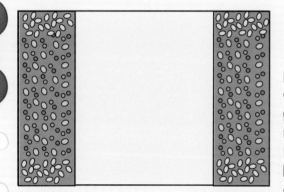

Seeded Placemats

As youngsters create these seed design placemats, remind them of the role the Native Americans played in teaching the Pilgrims how to plant and grow crops. In advance, collect a variety of seeds to represent plants that the Native Americans helped Pilgrims to grow, such as seeds from corn, pumpkins, beans, and sunflowers. For each child, cut a 9" x 12" sheet of construction paper in half. To make a placemat, glue each paper-half to the end of a 12" x 18" sheet of construction paper in a contrasting color. Then have the student create designs or patterns by gluing seeds to the sides of his placemat. Put the completed placemats aside for later use in "A Taste Of Thanksgiving" on page 73.

Pleasing Place Cards

Invite your students to use some foods commonly eaten by the early settlers and Native Americans to make place cards for your Thanksgiving table. To prepare, put dried or fresh cranberries and popped popcorn into separate containers. For each child, cut a 6" x 9" piece of tagboard. Refer to the provided diagram to crease the tagboard cards as indicated. Then write each student's name on his card as shown. Have him glue some popcorn and cranberries around his name. When the glue dries, fold the place card along the creases, and tape the end in place. Set the completed place cards aside to be used in "A Taste Of Thanksgiving" on page 73.

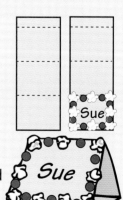

A Taste Of Thanksgiving

Have youngsters help create some of these tasty treats; then add a few of your own favorites to provide a tantalizing taste of Thanksgiving. Set tables with the placemats and place cards made in "Seeded Placemats" and "Pleasing Place Cards" on page 72. Serve each child a cup of cranberry juice with his plate of treats. Enjoy!

Fry Bread

2 cups self-rising flour
1 cup milk
cooking oil

Mix the flour and milk in a large bowl, adding flour as necessary to form a dough. Flatten small amounts of the dough into patties. Using a wok or an electric skillet set at 400°F, brown the bread patties in hot oil. Drain the cooked bread on a paper towel. Serve the warm bread with butter, jam, or cinnamon sugar. Makes approximately 24 small servings of bread.

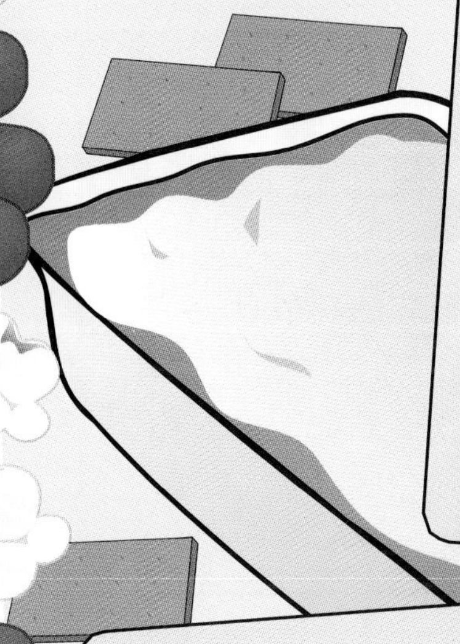

Sweet Potato Pudding

4 or 5 medium eggs, slightly beaten
4 cups canned sweet potatoes
1 cup brown sugar or honey
1 12-oz. can evaporated milk
1 1/2 teaspoons cinnamon
1 teaspoon salt
1 teaspoon ginger
1/2 teaspoon ground cloves
marshmallows (optional)

Combine all the ingredients, except the marshmallows, and mix well. Pour the mixture into a buttered dish. Bake at 350°F for 45 minutes to 1 hour—until a knife inserted in the center comes out clean. If desired, top the mixture with marshmallows; then return it to the oven until the marshmallows are browned. When cooled, serve the pudding with graham crackers.

Cranapple Cubes

1 16-ounce can cranberry sauce
1 cup chunky applesauce
1 cup plain yogurt

Pour the ingredients into a large bowl and mix them together with a mixer set on low speed for one minute. Pour the mixture into ice-cube trays. Cover the trays with foil; then push a Popsicle® stick through the foil into each cup. Place the trays in a freezer overnight. Pop the cranapple cubes out of the trays and serve them.

Parent Letter

Use with "A-Tisket, A-Tasket, We're Gonna Fill A Basket!" on page 70.

Dear Parent,

As part of our focus on Thanksgiving, our class is collecting nonperishable food items to fill a giving basket. The basket of food will be donated to a needy family in time for Thanksgiving. As the food is collected, our class will inventory the contents of the basket to practice our counting and categorizing skills. Your contribution in this effort will be greatly appreciated. If you can, please send a nonperishable food item to school with your child by _____.

(date)

      Thank you!

Bookmark

Use with "Books To Be Thankful For" on page 71.

Books To Be Thankful For

Have your family take some time this Thanksgiving to appreciate a good book together!

Albert's Thanksgiving
Written by Leslie Tryon
Published by Atheneum Books for Young Readers

Daisy's Crazy Thanksgiving
Written by Margery Cuyler
Published by Henry Holt and Company, Inc.

Thanksgiving At Our House
Written by Wendy Watson
Published by Clarion Books

© The Education Center, Inc.

Books To Be Thankful For

Have your family take some time this Thanksgiving to appreciate a good book together!

Albert's Thanksgiving
Written by Leslie Tryon
Published by Atheneum Books for Young Readers

Daisy's Crazy Thanksgiving
Written by Margery Cuyler
Published by Henry Holt and Company, Inc.

Thanksgiving At Our House
Written by Wendy Watson
Published by Clarion Books

©The Education Center, Inc.

Dear Parent,

Thanksgiving Day brings a lot of excitement, along with the large amount of work necessary to prepare for your family celebration. Before the preparations begin, please decide with your child a way in which he can help. Then complete the sentence. Encourage your child to help during the preparations as stated.

A Helping Hand

On Thanksgiving Day, I can help_____

_____.

Note To The Teacher: Use with *Thanksgiving Treat* on page 71. Have the child make his handprint at the bottom of the page.

Pop-Up Card Pattern
Use with "Popping With Thanks" on page 72.

The First American Thanksgiving

Share information about the customs and lifestyles of the Native American people of the eastern woodlands and the early Pilgrim settlers with your youngsters. Then delight them with activities that highlight the friendship forged between these two groups and the resulting celebration—the first American Thanksgiving!

ideas contributed by Deborah Burleson, Lucia Kemp Henry, and Mackie Rhodes

A Longhouse Is A Lot Of House!

In this measurement activity, youngsters will go to great lengths to experience the distance covered by a Native American longhouse. In advance measure and mark a distance of 100 feet along your school's sidewalk or playing field. During group time, explain that many of the Native Americans of the eastern woodlands lived in homes called *longhouses.* The houses were given their name because they were long—sometimes 100 feet or longer! Take students to the premeasured area so they can see just how long 100 feet is. Invite them to lie down head-to-toe to form a line along the marked distance. While they are lying on the ground, count to determine how many children it takes to cover a distance of 100 feet. If necessary, ask children who were counted first to lie down at the other end of the line until the entire distance is covered. Then have students discuss what they think it would be like to live in a longhouse.

A Typical Day

Use this call-response song to familiarize little ones with some of the routine activities of Native Americans in the early 1600s. Before singing each call verse, whisper the action from that verse to a different child. Encourage the child to perform movements to represent that action while the class sings his name in the response. Repeat the song until every student has had a turn to perform a movement.

Who Is In The Longhouse?
(sung to the tune of "Mary Wore A Red Dress")

Who is [in the longhouse, longhouse, longhouse]?
Who is [in the longhouse],
[Sweeping the floor]?

[Child's name] is [in the longhouse, longhouse, longhouse]?
[Child's name] is [in the longhouse],
[Sweeping the floor]!

Each time the song is repeated, replace the underlined phrase with one of the italicized phrases below. Then choose one of the action phrases that follow for the last line of each verse.

- *in the longhouse* .... building a fire; eating corn
- *by the warm fire* .... cooking beans; sewing clothes
- *in the village* .... playing ball; weaving baskets
- *in the big field* .... planting seeds; gathering squash
- *at the river* .... catching fish; taking a bath
- *in the forest* .... chopping wood; gathering nuts

77

Shake It To The Beat

Have students make their own versions of a Native American rattle and water drum.

To make a rattle for each child, collect a small frozen-juice can and its lid. Put a variety of bean and corn seeds into a container. Then prepare a  tray of paint and several different sponge shapes. Have each child sponge-paint designs on a strip of construction paper cut to fit around his can. When the paint dries, glue the paper around the can. Have the student place a few spoonfuls of the seed mixture in his can; then glue the lid in place. When the glue dries, encourage student partners to take turns creating and reproducing simple rhythmic patterns using their rattles.

To prepare a water drum, collect a large shortening or margarine container with a plastic lid for each child. Encourage each youngster to use crayons or markers to create designs and patterns on a sheet of construction paper cut to fit around his container. Wrap the paper snugly around the container; then glue it in place. Clip  clothespins around the container's rim to hold the paper until the glue dries. Then partially fill each container with water and place the lid on it. In turn have each youngster beat his drum for the class. Encourage students to listen to and compare the different pitches created by the drums.

Story Belt

Have your students create their own Native American *wampum* belts—belts made of shell beads. To make imitation wampum beads, mix one-half cup of rubbing alcohol, a few drops of food coloring, and one cup of small pasta shells in a separate container for each color desired. When they are thoroughly covered with the colored mixture, remove them from the liquid; then spread them out on paper towels to dry overnight. Explain to students that the Native Americans sewed wampum beads onto belts to record stories. Invite each child to make her own wampum belt on a 4" x 18" strip of tagboard by gluing the colored shells onto her strip in the form of characters or designs. When the glue dries, have the child write or dictate a sentence about her wampum belt on a strip of paper. Glue the paper strip to the back of her belt. Use a hole puncher to make a hole in each end of the belt. Thread a length of yarn through each hole in the belt and tie it securely. Tie the belt around the child's waist. Invite each youngster in turn to tell the class about her wampum belt.

The sun helps things grow.   Amber

A Trip To Remember

Use a class-made model of the *Mayflower* and lots of descriptive language to help your youngsters imagine the Pilgrim children's voyage to the New World. To learn about some of the Pilgrims' experiences, use the sections regarding the *Mayflower* and the Pilgrims' voyage in *...If You Sailed On The Mayflower In 1620* or *The Pilgrims' First Thanksgiving,* both by Ann McGovern (Scholastic Inc.).

To make a model of the *Mayflower,* obtain a large appliance box, two brooms, and four poster boards. In advance use a utility knife to cut the box to resemble a ship. Provide several trays of tempera paint and some paintbrushes. Have one small group of children at a time paint the box. When the paint dries, cut one slit near the top of a box end and another slit at the bottom directly below the first slit. In the same manner, cut slits on the opposite end of the box. Create a mast for a sail by sliding a broom handle through one slit, then through the other, at each box end. To make a sail for each mast, staple two sheets of white poster board together along three edges. Then slip the open ends of the poster boards over the brooms. Print the name *"Mayflower"* on the side of the ship with a wide permanent marker.

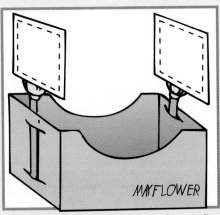

Using the information from the books, describe what the voyage must have been like for the children on the *Mayflower.* Then invite small groups of students to role-play Pilgrim children sailing to the New World.

Miniature Mayflower

Have little ones make miniature models of the *Mayflower* to take home and share with their families. Collect a class supply of walnut-shell halves and small baby-food jars with lids. For each child, cut a small sail from white construction paper; then cut a circle slightly smaller than the opening of the jar from blue construction paper to represent the sea. Have the child glue the sail cutout to one end of a 1 1/2" length of craft stick. Give the child a small amount of play dough to press into the walnut shell. Then have him push the craft stick into the play dough. Help the child glue the walnut half to the sea cutout so that it resembles a ship on water. When that glue dries, have the child place a few drops of glue in the bottom of his baby-food jar. Help him place the entire ship-and-water assembly into the jar over the glue; then have him place the lid on the jar. When the glue in their miniature models is dry, encourage youngsters to take the models home and tell their families what they have learned about the *Mayflower's* voyage.

Land, Ho!

When your students make these body posters, they will get caught up in the excitement of learning more about the Pilgrims. In advance cut four child-length pieces of white butcher paper. Have the students discuss how the Pilgrim children must have felt when the *Mayflower* finally made landfall in the New World. Ask them to talk about some of the things the children may have done at that time. Did they jump up and down with joy? Did they run excitedly along the beach? After the discussion, divide the students into four groups. Have one child from each  group lie on the sheet of butcher paper. Encourage him to position his body to represent a Pilgrim child who is jumping, running, or showing excitement. Trace that child's body onto the paper with a marker. Then have students examine pictures of Pilgrim children and their clothing in *The Pilgrims' First Thanksgiving* by Ann McGovern (Scholastic Inc.). Ask each group to work together to embellish their Pilgrim-body outline with facial features and clothing using a variety of craft items. Invite each group to dictate what they think their Pilgrim child would have said when the ship landed. Write the dictated sentences on speech bubbles. Then display each poster and its speech bubble with the title "Land, Ho!"

All In A Pilgrim's Day

Youngsters will delight in pretending to perform Pilgrim jobs with this song that describes some of the typical activities of the early settlers. Before singing the song, read aloud or paraphrase Kate Waters's *Sarah Morton's Day: A Day In The Life Of A Pilgrim Girl* and *Samuel Eaton's Day: A Day In The Life Of A Pilgrim Boy* (both published by Scholastic Inc.). While singing the song, encourage students to perform actions to represent the job described in each verse.

This Is The Way We Stir The Pudding

*(sung to the tune of
"Here We Go 'Round The Mulberry Bush")*

This is the way we [stir the pudding, stir the pudding, stir the pudding].
This is the way we [stir the pudding]
All in a Pilgrim's day!

Each time the song is repeated, replace the underlined words with one of the following: *knead the bread, feed the hens, milk the goats, fetch the water, gather the wood, hoe the garden, pull the corn, husk the corn, catch a fish,* and *pick up nuts.*

DECEMBER

Hooray For Hanukkah!

Brighten dark, wintry days with these activities centered around the Festival of Lights—Hanukkah. Invite your little ones to participate in some of the warm and wonderful traditions of this ancient holiday.

by Ada Hanley Goren

What's It All About?

The Jewish holiday of Hanukkah recalls a miracle that happened more than two thousand years ago in Jerusalem. After a three-year battle for religious freedom, a band of rebel Jews defeated the Syrian king who had attempted to force the Jewish people to worship Greek gods. The defeat enabled the Jews to reclaim their Temple and rededicate it to their one God. But they had only a small amount of purified oil to light the *menorah,* a special lamp which was supposed to burn day and night in the Temple as a symbol of holiness. Miraculously, that small amount of oil lasted not one, but *eight* days! Thus, Hanukkah became an eight-day celebration recalling this miracle and the victory for religious freedom.

While your little ones are too young to grasp the full meaning of this holiday and its historical perspective, you may be able to paraphrase part of the story to suit their understanding and interest level. They *will* be able to relate to the delightful traditions associated with Hanukkah. Read *Hanukkah!* by Roni Schotter (Little Brown and Company, Inc.) to introduce a family celebration of the Festival of Lights.

Light The Lights

The menorah is the central symbol of Hanukkah. If possible, bring one in for the children to examine. Point out the eight candles (one for each night of Hanukkah) plus the helper candle, the *shammash.* Explain that on each night of Hanukkah, the shammash is lit, then used to light the other candles. One candle is lit on the first night, two on the second, and so on. On the eighth night, all eight candles and the shammash are lit.

After looking at a real menorah, have students dramatize the lighting of the candles. First create nine flame shapes from tagboard. Decorate each one with glue and gold glitter; then attach a craft stick to the back of each one. Invite eight children to sit in a row, each one holding a flame puppet. Give a flame to one more child—the shammash. Then teach your youngsters this song, substituting the appropriate number words in each of eight verses. The shammash "lights the candles" by using his puppet to tap each of the eight children's flames at the proper points in the song. Instruct each child playing the part of a candle to stand up when she is "lit" and sit down when she goes "out". Repeat the activity until everyone has had a turn.

Share Your Light
(sung to the tune of "Twinkle, Twinkle, Little Star")

Shammash candle, share your light
With [one] candle the [first] night.
Shine so brightly in the dark,
Share with all your little spark.
Then out you go to rest and then,
Tomorrow night you'll glow again!

In the last verse, change the last line to "Next year you will glow again!"

Make A Menorah

Have each youngster create his own menorah with some easy-to-find materials. Purchase several boxes of standard-size birthday candles (you'll need nine candles per child) and ask each family to send in a roll of Lifesavers® candy. (You may want to provide a few extra rolls of Lifesavers® for little ones to snack on as they create their projects.)

Give each child a 1" x 8" strip of poster board. Ask each youngster to spread a thick coat of glue down the center of his poster-board strip. Then have him count out nine candies and glue them to the strip in a straight line. Have him glue the two additional candies atop the Lifesavers® candy in the center of the strip, creating a tall holder to set off the shammash candle. Allow the glue to dry thoroughly. When the glue has set, give each child nine birthday candles to place in his finished menorah. Squeeze a drop of glue into the hole of each Lifesavers® candy to secure each candle.

If you'd like, create these menorahs in the traditional colors of Hanukkah—blue and white. Request that families send in rolls of white, mint-flavored Lifesavers® and use blue birthday candles.

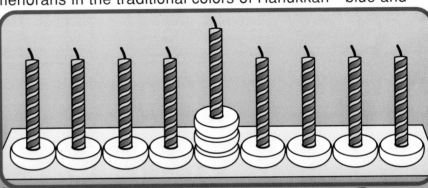

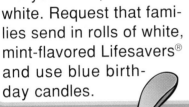

Potato Latkes

(makes approximately 20 latkes)

12 medium potatoes, peeled and grated
2 small onions, grated
4 eggs, beaten
4 Tbsp. all-purpose flour

1/2 tsp. baking powder
2 tsp. salt
Vegetable oil

Rinse the grated potatoes in a colander. Squeeze the potatoes between paper towels to remove excess moisture. Then combine the potatoes, onion, eggs, flour, baking powder, and salt in a large bowl. Heat oil in an electric skillet over medium-high heat. Drop 1/4 cup of the mixture at a time into the hot oil. Use a fork to flatten each round. When the latkes turn brown around the edges, flip them over and fry until crisp. Drain on paper towels before serving.

A Hanukkah Treat

Introduce youngsters to a favorite holiday dish enjoyed by many Jewish Americans—*latkes*. Latkes are potato pancakes fried in oil. The cooking oil is a reminder of the miraculous oil in the Hanukkah story.

Begin by sharing the sweet story *Inside-Out Grandma* by Joan Rothenberg (Hyperion Books For Children). Grandma explains how wearing her clothing inside-out will help her remember to buy oil to fry latkes for Hanukkah. After reading the story, have your little ones help you prepare potato latkes following the recipe shown. Served with applesauce and sour cream, latkes are certainly a tasty tradition!

Spin The Dreidel

A dreidel is a special top marked with a Hebrew letter on each of its four sides. Jewish children often play dreidel as part of Hanukkah festivities. Teach your little ones this simple game for fun and math practice too. In advance prepare a simple dreidel using a pint-sized milk carton. Completely open the top of the carton to rinse it out. When it's dry, tape the top closed, leaving a center opening large enough to slide an unsharpened pencil through. Insert the pencil, poking it through the center bottom of the carton. (The dreidel will spin on the eraser end of the pencil.) Duplicate the four Hebrew letters on page 86; then cut apart the four squares. Glue one letter to each side of the carton, being sure to place the bottom of each letter toward the eraser end of the pencil.

Introduce the dreidel to your youngsters and explain the game to them. Each child begins with a supply of counters such as dried beans, pennies, nuts, or foil-wrapped chocolate coins. For each round of the game, each participant puts one of his counters into a central pot. Then each player takes a turn spinning the top and putting in or taking out counters from the pot, according to the letter that lands face up on the dreidel. Explain the meaning of each letter as you show children the dreidel. Each time the pot is emptied, each player puts in one of his counters to replenish it. Young children will need help with the concept of *half*, so be prepared to supervise the game and give help when necessary.

נ *nun*—take nothing

ג *gimmel*—take everything

ה *hay*—take half

ש *shin*—put one in

Letter Painting

Give students more experience with the Hebrew letters on the dreidel with this painting project that strengthens visual-motor skills. Enlarge the Hebrew letters on page 86 and post the copies near your painting easel. Have children take turns using wide paintbrushes and tempera paint to copy the letters onto large sheets of art paper. Children with more highly developed fine-motor skills will enjoy using smaller brushes—such as those that come with watercolors—to copy the letters.

In The Spirit

An important part of the Hanukkah holiday in Israel is giving to charity. Bring some of that Hanukkah spirit into your classroom by conducting a canned food drive. Duplicate the parent note on page 86; then send a copy home to each family. Collect the canned goods during the eight days of Hanukkah. Don't miss out on opportunities for counting and sorting the canned goods as they arrive in your classroom! You may even want to make a poster to illustrate progress toward a preset goal. At the conclusion of the drive, donate the cans to a local food bank or shelter.

Dear Family,
At school we have been learning about the traditions of Hanukkah. We've learned that in Israel, gifts to charity are an important part of this special holiday. In accordance with that tradition, we will be collecting canned and boxed food items during the eight days of Hanukkah. All the food we collect will be given to ___Urban Ministries___ at the end of our food drive. Please send in any contribution you can make by ___Dec. 10___.

Thank you and Happy Hanukkah!

Hanukkah Stories To Share

Read aloud one or more of these books about the Festival of Lights. Consider serving a Hanukkah treat for students to enjoy as they listen. Children in Israel enjoy jelly-filled doughnuts, known as *sufganiot*, during the holiday. So bring in a box of jelly doughnuts (or doughnut holes) for your little ones to eat while they listen to these Hanukkah tales.

The Chanukkah Guest
Written by Eric A. Kimmel
Published by Scholastic Inc.

Light The Lights! A Story About Celebrating Hanukkah And Christmas
Written by Margaret Moorman
Published by Scholastic Inc.

Arielle and the Hanukkah Surprise
Written by Devra Speregen and
   Shirley Newberger
Published by Scholastic Inc.

Grandma's Latkes
Written by Malka Drucker
Published by Harcourt Brace Jovanovich

Dreidel Letters

Use with "Spin The Dreidel" and "Letter Painting" on page 84.

nun—take nothing

gimmel—take everything

hay—take half

shin—put one in

Parent Note

Use with "In The Spirit" on page 85.

- -

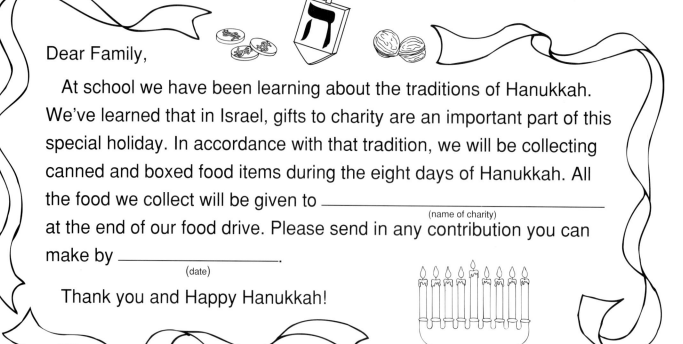

Dear Family,

At school we have been learning about the traditions of Hanukkah. We've learned that in Israel, gifts to charity are an important part of this special holiday. In accordance with that tradition, we will be collecting canned and boxed food items during the eight days of Hanukkah. All the food we collect will be given to _____
(name of charity)
at the end of our food drive. Please send in any contribution you can make by _____.
(date)

Thank you and Happy Hanukkah!

The ABCs Of Christmas

A is for art
B is for baking
C is for Christmas fun in the making!

You'll find everything from *A* to *Z* in this collection of activities for the holiday season.
ideas contributed by Deborah Burleson and Ada Hanley Goren

A Is for Angels

Gather some paper punches with unique shapes—such as hearts or stars—to make these heavenly art projects. Duplicate the angel pattern on page 95 on white construction paper for each child. Invite each youngster to cut out her pattern, then make several rows of punches along the hem of her angel's skirt. To complete her angel, have her draw an angelic face and add trims such as sequins, star stickers, or scraps of lace and paper doilies. Display the finished angels in your classroom windows with some clouds made from polyester fiber stuffing.

B Is For Baked Goods

Ahhh…Christmas means the delightful scent of freshly baked cookies! Invite youngsters to help you bake a batch of Santa cookies. Purchase a few rolls of refrigerated sugar-cookie dough. Roll the dough out on a floured surface to a thickness of about 1/2 inch. Use a biscuit cutter to cut a circle from the dough for each child. Knead the remaining dough together; roll it out and use a knife to cut it into squares. Then cut each square into triangles, making one triangle for each child. Place each child's circle on a sheet of waxed paper labeled with his name; then place a triangle at the top of each circle to resemble Santa's hat. Encourage each child to press two M&M's® into his cookie to resemble Santa's eyes. Bake the cookies as directed. After the cookies have cooled, have each child spread red frosting onto the hat portion of his cookie. Then use a can of whipped cream for the finishing touches—a pom-pom for Santa's hat and a fluffy white beard!

C Is For Candy Canes

A few boxes of candy canes will make for delicious math practice! Purchase (or ask parents to donate) a few boxes of candy canes in various colors and sizes. Use the candy canes to help little ones practice their sorting, patterning, and counting skills. Conclude your lessons by inviting each youngster to choose a candy cane to eat at snacktime or after school.

D Is For "Dear Santa"

Invite each youngster to relate his Christmas wishes to Santa with this fun oral-language activity. To prepare, ask each family to send in a blank cassette tape. Then teach your little ones this Christmas rhyme:

> Dear Santa, I've been good!
> As good as good can be!
> So tell me, will you—pretty please—
> Bring these gifts to me?

Then ask each youngster, in turn, to make a recording of his message to Santa. Have him recite the rhyme, then list his Christmas wishes on his cassette tape. Send each child's tape home to become a treasured keepsake for Mom and Dad.

F Is For Fruitcake

Are your little ones fruitcake fans or foes? Bring in a fruitcake to provide students with a taste of the holiday and some math practice, too. Prior to sampling the fruitcake, prepare a simple yes/no graph like the one shown. Then invite each child to taste a small piece of the fruitcake. Have him register his reaction by writing his name under the "yes" or "no" column of the graph or by attaching a name card under the appropriate column. Then count the names in each column and compare the results.

Do You Like Fruitcake?	
Yes ☺	No ☹
Ashley	Carlos
Devon	Angela
	Ruthie

E Is For Elves

Santa may need some help fulfilling all those Christmas wishes! Encourage youngsters to make some mischievous elves, Santa's traditional helpers. Provide each child with a coffee filter, a construction-paper triangle (approximately 3" x 3" x 3"), glue, crayons, and scissors. Demonstrate how to fold the coffee filter in half, then in half again. Ask each child to glue the folded edges of her coffee filter together. Then have her glue her triangle over the point of the folded filter to create an elfin hat. Encourage each child to draw a face on her elf; then have her create a beard by cutting slits along the rounded edge of the coffee filter. Write each child's name on the back of her finished elf. Later, when the children have left the room, hide the elves in various locations. When they discover the elves' disappearance, engage the children in a hunt for these mischievous fellows.

G Is For Gift Wrap

What fun it is to unwrap gifts at the holidays! But youngsters will have fun wrapping gifts as well. Set up a gift-wrapping center in your classroom for fine-motor practice. Ask parents to donate an assortment of boxes, rolls of wrapping paper, ribbons, bows, and tape. Given a few pairs of scissors, your little ones will be ready to wrap!

H Is For Ho, Ho, Ho!

Use Santa's favorite phrase to help youngsters develop auditory memory skills. First ask your students to join you in producing a hearty "Ho, ho, ho!" Then ask them to listen as you produce the phrase in a different way, such as in a whisper. Ask the children to repeat the phrase in a similar fashion. Continue, each time producing the phrase with a different volume, cadence, or inflection and asking the children to repeat after you. Then let each youngster, in turn, produce a "ho, ho, ho" in his own way for his classmates to repeat.

J Is For Jingle Bells

Ring in the holiday with a favorite Christmas carol—"Jingle Bells." Add real jingle bells for a musical accompaniment. For each child, hot-glue three small jingle bells to a length of wide, heavy ribbon. Present these to your little carolers; then invite them to join you in singing and ringing "Jingle Bells."

I Is For Icicles

Although cold, snowy weather doesn't exist everywhere during the holiday season, people traditionally think of icy winter weather at Christmastime. Add an icy touch of winter to your classroom when you invite youngsters to make icicles to decorate their cubbies or tables. Have each child finger-paint with white tempera on a sheet of art paper. Before the paint dries, encourage each child to sprinkle his paper with clear or iridescent glitter. After the paint is dry, cut one long edge of each child's paper into jagged icicle shapes. Then mount the straight edge at the top of each child's cubby or on one edge of his table. Brrr…it's cold in here!

K Is For Kris Kringle

Do your youngsters know who Kris Kringle is? Chances are, they know him by the name of Santa Claus. Take some time to discuss Christmas traditions in other countries. Explain that children the world over know Santa (or a Santa figure) by other names. Kris Kringle is a German version of Santa. In Holland, Sinterklaas arrives on horseback to leave gifts in children's shoes. In France, the gift-giver is known as Père Noël. And in England, Father Christmas leaves goodies in children's socks hung on their bedposts. Ask youngsters if they have heard any other names for Santa Claus.

L Is For Lights

Lovely lights create warm feelings on cold winter nights during Christmas and many other winter holidays around the world. Invite your little ones to enjoy the glow of colored lights when they use a Lite-Brite® to create holiday designs. If you don't already have a Lite-Brite® in your classroom, purchase or borrow one. (Supervise young children as they use the Lite-Brite® to prevent them from placing the colored pegs in their mouths.) Encourage youngsters to make their own Christmas designs, such as a tree, a candy cane, or a star. Then watch students glow with pride when their designs are displayed for their classmates to see!

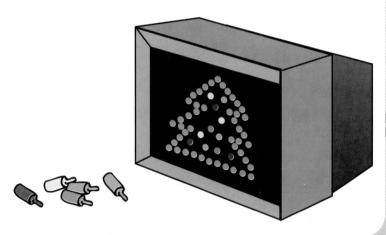

M Is For Mistletoe

Explain the tradition of mistletoe to your youngsters. Tell them that when mistletoe is hung over a doorway, those caught standing below it must kiss! Then involve your little ones in a Musical Mistletoe game. Seat children in a circle and play some Christmas music as the students pass a small sprig of artificial greenery from child to child. When you stop the music, encourage the child holding the imitation mistletoe to blow a kiss to the classmate of her choice. Then she may hand the greenery to that child, who may begin passing it for the next round of music.

N Is For Noel

Besides being part of a popular Christmas carol, do your youngsters know what *Noel* is? It means "Christmas" in French. Familiarize your students with how to say "Merry Christmas" in several different languages:

- in French: *Joyeux Noel* (zhwah-YUH noh-EL)
- in Spanish: *Feliz Navidad* (fay-LEEZ nah-vee-DAHD)
- in Italian: *Buon Natale* (bwohn nah-TAH-lay)

Finish up by teaching the sign language for "Merry Christmas." Invite little ones to extend Christmas greetings to classroom visitors in the language of their choice!

Merry

Brush side of M upward against chest; repeat.

Christmas

Right-hand C arcs to right.

Is For Ornaments

Encourage little ones to create special ornaments for a classroom tree or their own trees at home. For each child, provide glue, a small paper doily, a foil cupcake liner, and an assortment of craft gems and sequins in holiday shapes. Have each child flatten his cupcake liner, then glue it to the center of his doily. Invite him to glue a few sequins and craft gems of his choice to the center of the cupcake liner. Punch a hole at the top of each child's finished ornament. Thread a six-inch length of yarn or ribbon through the hole; then tie it into a loop for hanging this oh-so-lovely ornament!

Is For Quiet

Chances are, with all the excitement of the season, little ones will find it hard to settle down. If a rest time is not a regular part of your daily routine, schedule a quiet time during each school day of the holiday season. Invite youngsters to listen to Christmas story cassettes or peaceful selections of holiday music as they relax and recharge their batteries.

Is For Pictures

Document all the holiday happenings in your classroom by snapping lots of photos during activities or your class party. Get the photos developed quickly or use an instant camera. Then create a special memento for each of your students' families. For each child, select a photo that features him prominently. Create a simple frame for each photo by cutting a piece of tagboard slightly larger than the photo. Cut a piece of holiday gift wrap in the same size and glue it over the tagboard. Laminate the frame; then glue the child's photo to the center and attach a strip of magnetic tape to the back. Finish off the frame by affixing a small, stick-on gift bow to one corner.

If you have duplicate copies made of your photos, place the extra set into a photo album for your youngsters and classroom visitors to enjoy.

magnetic tape

BACK

Is For Reindeer

If the holiday wiggles have gotten hold of your youngsters, help them use some excess energy with a Reindeer Romp! Play a recording of a lively holiday selection—perhaps "Rudolph The Red-Nosed Reindeer"—and invite youngsters to prance, trot, gallop, and "fly" like reindeer around an open space. Encourage each child to form a pair of antlers by holding her hands—with fingers spread—above her ears.

S Is For Stars

Stars are a popular symbol of the holidays. Share Julia Noonan's illustrated version of the traditional song "Twinkle, Twinkle, Little Star" at storytime. The Christmas Eve setting of this lovely book (published by Scholastic Inc.) will warm your youngsters' hearts. After reading the story, engage the students in creating their own twinkling stars. For each child, duplicate the star pattern on page 96 on tagboard. Have each child cut out his star, then glue on a variety of shiny art materials, such as aluminum foil, tinsel garland, foil star stickers, and glitter. If desired, have each child glue his finished star near the top of one end of a toilet-tissue tube. Voilà—a twinkling tree-topper!

T Is For Treats

Looking for something new for your holiday party? Enlist parents' help in preparing treat bags for each of your students. Purchase a class quantity of holiday gift bags. (Check your local drug store or paper-goods store for inexpensive bags.) Label each bag with a different child's name. Then duplicate the parent note on page 96 for each child to take home. As parents' donations arrive at school, distribute them among the treat bags. On the day of your class party, present each child with a treat bag to open and enjoy.

U Is For "Under The Tree"

Teach your youngsters this rhyme about one of their favorite holiday places.

Under The Tree

What do I see
Under the tree?
Boxes with paper and bows.

Some that are big,
Some that are small,
Some are for me, I suppose!

V Is For Visitors

Visiting friends and neighbors is a popular pastime during the holiday season. Enjoy some classroom visitors when you invite your students' families to join you for a Christmas Open House. To prepare, decorate your classroom with holiday art created by your youngsters. Then send home a copy of the programmed invitation on page 97 with each child. Serve hot chocolate, coffee, or cider, as well as some Christmas cookies. Play some holiday music and take time to chat with parents and exchange holiday greetings. Parents will enjoy the chance to touch base with you at midyear and to see their children's beautiful work on display.

W Is For Wreath

The increasing popularity of wreaths as decorations means they're not just for Christmas anymore! But your little ones will enjoy creating holiday wreaths with the traditional red and green colors of Christmas. For each child, cut out the center of a sturdy green paper plate. Give each child several wrapped peppermint discs and invite her to glue them on her paper-plate wreath. Then assist her in tying a 24-inch length of red ribbon into a bow. Have her glue the center of the bow to the bottom of her wreath. After all the glue has dried, use a hole puncher to punch a small hole at the top of the wreath. Thread one-half of a pipe cleaner through the hole and twist it into a loop to create a hanger for the finished wreath.

X Is For Xs And Os

Invite each youngster to create a greeting card for mom and dad, signed with *X*s and *O*s—kisses and hugs! To prepare, purchase a few sponges in holiday designs (or cut your own designs from kitchen sponges). Provide shallow trays of tempera paint in a variety of colors. Give each child a sheet of 9" x 12" construction paper. Show him how to fold his paper in half card-style. Then invite him to press the sponges of his choice first into the paint, then onto his card front to create a holiday design. When the paint has dried, open the card and write his dictated holiday message for his family on the inside. Then have each child sign his name below his message, followed by a few *X*s and *O*s.

Merry Christmas Mom and Dad!

Zach
X O X O X

Is For Yule Log

Tell your students that people in many countries follow a Christmas custom of placing a special, large log in their fireplace. They burn this *yule log* on Christmas Eve, then save the ashes to bring them good luck in the coming year. Your students will feel lucky when you invite them to help you make a special snack in the shape of a yule log.

Yule Log Cake
(makes enough for 2 cakes)

1 box chocolate cake mix   cocoa
4 eggs   Cool Whip® (one 6-ounce container per cake)
1/2 cup water

In a large bowl, beat the eggs with an electric mixer on high speed for 5 minutes. Add the water and cake mix and beat on low speed until moistened. Divide the batter in half. Follow the directions below for each half of the batter to make two cakes. (Or set half the batter aside if you wish to make only one.)

Spray a jelly-roll pan with nonstick cooking spray. Line the pan with waxed paper; then spray the lining with cooking spray. Spread the cake batter on the pan, creating a thin layer. Bake the cake at 350°F for about 13 minutes.

Spread a clean cloth towel on a table. Sift four tablespoons of the cocoa onto the towel to form a 10" x 15" rectangle. While the cake is still very warm, loosen the edges from the pan. Turn the cake out onto the cocoa-dusted towel and peel off the waxed paper. Starting at the narrow end, roll the cake and towel together and let the cake cool completely. Then gently unroll the cake. Spread the Cool Whip® over the cake; then reroll it without the towel.

Serve a slice of the finished cake to each child. Invite him to shake additional cocoa (to represent the ashes of the yule log) over his serving before eating it.

Is For Zzzzzzz's

There's almost nothing as challenging for a young child as going to sleep on Christmas Eve. Help your youngsters with this formidable task by holding a practice bedtime at school. On one of the last school days before the holiday, make rest time a special event. Serve cups of hot cocoa as you read aloud a favorite version of "The Night Before Christmas." Then invite little ones to curl up on their rest mats and sleep to a recording of quiet Christmas music. Complete the effect of this practice Christmas Eve by filling a tiny felt stocking with a few goodies—such as small candies or stickers—for each child to enjoy when she awakens.

Star Pattern
Use with "*S* Is For Stars" on page 92.

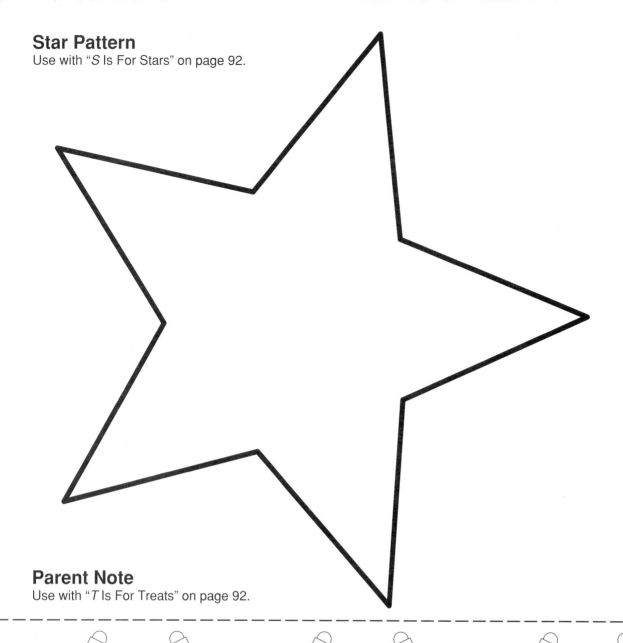

Parent Note
Use with "*T* Is For Treats" on page 92.

Dear Family:

Happy Holidays! Our holiday party will be here soon! I will be putting together treat bags for the children to enjoy at the party. If you would like to help, please send in a class quantity of a small treat such as stickers; candy; small, inexpensive toys; or handcrafted gifts. We have _____ children in the class, and I will need any donated items by _____.
                                                                        (date)

Thank you for your support at this busy time of year!

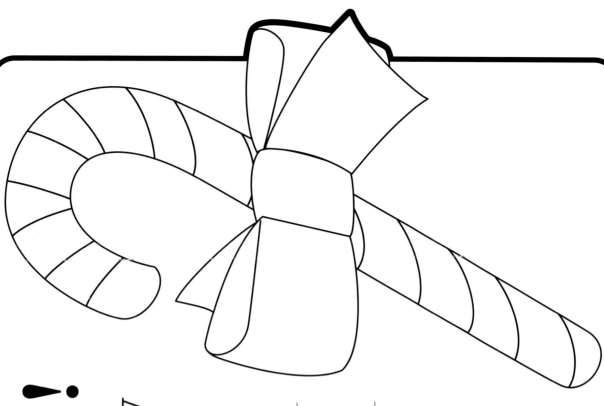

Please Come! To A Holiday Open House

When? _____

Where? _____

Come exchange holiday greetings with parents, teachers, and students! We look forward to seeing you!

Note To The Teacher: Use with "V Is For Visitors" on page 93.

KWANZAA!

Kwanzaa is a weeklong celebration of the values and traditions of the African-American culture. Use the ideas and activities in this multidisciplinary unit to help your youngsters develop an awareness of the symbols and principles of this cultural celebration.

ideas contributed by Mackie Rhodes and Dayle Timmons

A TIME TO CELEBRATE

In 1966 Dr. Maulana Karenga began a new holiday in an effort to create awareness of—and to preserve—African values and traditions. This holiday became known as *Kwanzaa*—the Swahili word for "first fruits." Kwanzaa is observed for seven days, from December 26 to January 1. Many of the elements of Kwanzaa are based on traditional African celebrations in which family and friends gather and give thanks, remember their ancestors, evaluate their lives, and plan for the future. Singing, dancing, feasting, and gift-giving are also part of the celebration.

To help youngsters understand the American connection to the African origins of Kwanzaa, assist them in locating the United States and Africa on a globe; then tape a piece of yarn to the globe, connecting these two locations. Explain that the African-Americans now living in the United States are related to people of Africa from long ago. Some may even have family members living in Africa today. Leave the yarn on the globe during your Kwanzaa study. Encourage students to independently explore the globe and the locations of the United States and Africa.

READ ALL ABOUT IT!

Refer to some of these books for more information about Kwanzaa. Then use the activities on the following pages to teach your little ones more about this special celebration.

The Gifts Of Kwanzaa
Written by Synthia Saint James
Published by Albert Whitman & Company

My First Kwanzaa Book
Written by Deborah M. Newton Chocolate
Published by Scholastic Inc.

Imani's Gift At Kwanzaa
Written by Denise Burden-Patmon
Published by Simon & Schuster

Kwanzaa
Written by Janet Riehecky
Published by Childrens Press®

Kwanzaa
Written by Deborah M. Newton Chocolate
Published by Childrens Press®

Kwanzaa
Written by A. P. Porter
Published by Carolrhoda Books, Inc.

SYMBOLS OF THE CELEBRATION

Set up a Kwanzaa table to serve as the central focus of your study on this important holiday. Cover the table with a red, green, black, or African-print cloth. Place a woven mat over the cloth. Then put a pedestal-style cup, dried corn on the cob, a bowl of fruit and vegetables, a candleholder with seven candles, and a few gift-wrapped boxes on the mat. If desired place a note-card printed with the Swahili word beside the object which represents each symbol (see "Say It In Swahili").

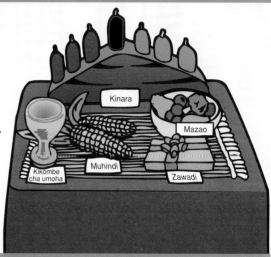

SAY IT IN SWAHILI

Teach your little ones some of the Swahili words related to the Kwanzaa celebration. Print each of the words on a separate sentence strip; then draw or glue a picture of what the word represents. For instance, write the word *mazao* and draw a few fruits and vegetables. As you show students each of the word cards, encourage them to use the picture cues along with the beginning sounds to recall the words. Youngsters will be proud to share their Swahili vocabulary with their friends and family.

- *Mkeka* (em-KAY-kah)—a straw mat
- *Kikombe cha umoha* (kee-KOM-bay chah oo-MOH-jah)—the unity cup
- *Kinara* (kee-NAH-rah)—a candleholder for seven candles
- *Mishumaa saba* (mee-shoo-MAH SAH-bah)—the seven candles of Kwanzaa: three red on the left of the kinara, one black in the middle, and three green on the right
- *Mazao* (mah-ZAH-o)—fruits and vegetables
- *Muhindi* (moo-HEEN-dee)—ears of corn
- *Zawadi* (zah-WAH-dee)—gifts

THREE COLORS OF KWANZAA

Kwanzaa is represented by three colors—black, red, and green. Black represents the color of the people. Red stands for their struggles. Green symbolizes their hope. Encourage your children to participate in some color sorting and counting with this activity using the colors of Kwanzaa. Gather an assortment of black, red, and green pom-poms. Beside each of seven bowls, place a numeral card labeled with a different numeral from one to seven. To play, have a child use a pair of tongs to pick up and place a corresponding number of same-colored pom-poms into a bowl.

A KWANZAA MAT

A handwoven straw mat called a *mkeka* is placed on the Kwanzaa table to represent the past and the foundation of the African-American people. To prepare for youngsters to make their own mkekas, cut a supply of green and red construction paper into three-inch squares. Give each child a large sheet of black construction paper. Explain to students that a mkeka is a mat that has been made by hand. It is a symbol of tradition and history. Have each child glue a pattern onto his black paper using the green and red squares. When the glue has dried, affix a label printed with "mkeka—an African woven mat" on the back of each child's mat. Encourage the child to take his mkeka home to share with his family.

THE UNITY CUP

The *kikombe cha umoha*—sometimes referred to as kikombe—is the unity cup of Kwanzaa. During each night of this celebration, each family member takes a drink from the cup to symbolize that they are one people. Invite each student to decorate a kikombe for her family. Purchase a classroom quantity of clear, plastic champagne glasses. Cover a table with newspaper; then have each child put on a paint smock. With her glass placed upside-down on the newspaper, encourage the child to use red, black, and green fabric paints to create a design on the bowl of her glass. After the paint dries, attach a label printed with "kikombe—the unity cup" to each student's glass. Ask each child to take her kikombe home to be used as a unity cup during a special family celebration.

A HARVEST TO REMEMBER

Another symbol of Kwanzaa is the *mazao*—a bowl of fruits and vegetables used to represent the harvest. Encourage your youngsters to cultivate their thinking skills with this tactile activity. Place a variety of real or plastic fruits and vegetables in a large bowl or basket. In turn have each student put on a blindfold or close his eyes. Ask him to reach into the bowl and pick out a food. Have the child feel the shape and texture of the item, then guess what food he is holding. After he makes his guess, have him remove his blindfold to see if he is correct.

CORN FOR THE CHILDREN

During the Kwanzaa celebration, one ear of corn—*muhindi*—is used to represent each child in the family. Give your students an opportunity to explore the number of children in their own families as they create an ear of corn to represent each one. To prepare, shuck and clean several ears of corn; then cut each one in half. Prepare several trays of yellow tempera paint. Give each child one sheet each of white and green construction paper. Have the child dip the corn into the paint, then roll it over his white paper to create corn prints. After the paint dries, help the child cut a corn shape from his paper to represent each child in his family. Then help him cut corn husks from his green paper to glue to each of his corn cutouts. Have him glue his ears of corn to a large sheet of black, red, or green construction paper labeled with his name. During group time, show each child's paper to the class. Encourage the students to count the ears of corn on the paper to determine how many children are in that child's family.

THE LIGHTS OF KWANZAA

Candles play an important role in the celebration of Kwanzaa. The *kinara,* the candleholder used during this celebration, is a symbol for the ancestors of African-Americans. Seven candles, or *mishumaa saba,* are placed in the kinara. On the left side of the kinara are three red candles. A black candle stands in the middle, and three green candles are placed to the right of it. On the first night of Kwanzaa, the black candle is lit, and is then lit first each following night of the celebration. On the second night, a red candle is lit, followed by a green candle on the third night. An additional candle is lit each night, alternating the red and green candles until all are burning on the final night of Kwanzaa. Try one or both of the following kinara activities to bring learning opportunities to light for your little ones.

Provide each child with a portion of play dough and seven birthday candles (in the traditional Kwanzaa colors, if possible). Encourage youngsters to design kinaras from their play dough and candles. As they create, prompt them to describe their designs and to count the candles.

Youngsters will enjoy making these wearable kinaras. Have each child color a design on a sentence strip. Fit the strip around the child's head and trim the excess, but do not attach the ends together. Have the child cut strips of red, green, and black construction paper representing the Kwanzaa candles; then have him glue the strips to his headband. If desired, have him glue a yellow, tissue-paper flame to each strip. After the glue dries, staple the ends of each child's headband together.

A KWANZAA FEAST

The sixth night of Kwanzaa is a time for feasting and celebrating through music, storytelling, gift-giving, and thanksgiving. Traditional foods and family favorites are served during the feast, called *karamu* in Swahili. To prepare for a class karamu, ask parent volunteers to prepare some of these recipes or any of their favorite dishes. Decorate the classroom in the colors of Kwanzaa—red, green, and black. Then invite youngsters and parents to participate in the feast and celebration. Have students wear their kinara headbands made in "The Lights Of Kwanzaa" on page 101. After the feast, encourage students to dance and play instruments to African music.

HOPPIN' JOHN

2 cups instant white rice
2 cups water
2 cubes of chicken bouillon
    (or 6–8 slices of bacon,
    diced)
1 small onion, finely
    chopped
2 16-oz. cans black-eyed
    peas
1/2 cup finely chopped
    celery (optional)

Mix all the ingredients together in a pan. Bring the mixture to a boil. Cover and simmer for 20 minutes. Makes approximately 16 small servings.

SWEET POTATO PIE

2 large sweet potatoes
3 eggs
1 Tbsp. vanilla
1/4 cup butter
3/4 cup sugar
1/4 tsp. cinnamon
frozen pie crust, thawed

Scrub the potatoes; then bake them at 350°F on a cookie sheet for 1 1/2 hours. Peel the baked potatoes and place them in a bowl. Add the remaining ingredients, mixing them together with a potato masher or fork. When the ingredients are thoroughly combined, pour the mixture into a prepared pie crust. Bake at 350°F for 30–45 minutes or until the center is set.

BANANA BAKE

6 large, peeled bananas
3 Tbsp. butter
3 Tbsp. brown sugar
2 tsp. cinnamon

Cut each banana in half lengthwise. Place the halves cut-side-up in a baking dish. Put the butter in a pan and melt over low heat. Mix the sugar and cinnamon into the melted butter; then pour the mixture over the tops of the bananas. Cover with foil and bake at 350°F for 45 minutes. When the bananas cool, cut each in two and serve. Makes 24 small servings.

Smitten With Mittens

No matter where you live, January is probably one of the coldest months of the year. Keep your youngsters' hands busy and warm with these marvelous mitten ideas!

ideas contributed by Ada Hanley Goren and Janna Omwake

A Mitten Mixer

Introduce the topic of mittens with a cooperative activity. A few days prior to beginning your mitten unit, gather enough pairs of mittens to have a pair for every two children. Or duplicate the pair-of-mittens pattern on page 108 onto various colors of construction paper; then cut out and decorate pairs to make enough for each child to have one mitten.

As students enter your classroom on the first day of your mittens unit, give each child a mitten—real or paper—to hold. When everyone has arrived, ask each child to find the youngster holding the mate to his mitten. Then explain this fun cooperative activity. Ask each student to sit facing his partner and pretend he is looking into a mirror. Have each child in a pair take a turn as the leader. Ask the leader to perform a series of movements (of his choice) using his mitten—such as placing the mitten on his nose, tapping his head with the mitten, or putting the mitten on his hand and waving. His partner performs the same motions, simulating a mirror image. Continue the activity until each child has had a turn to be the leader a few times.

Why Mittens?

Discuss with youngsters why people wear mittens. Ask them to brainstorm a list of other winter clothing that protects people from the cold. Then try this hands-on experience. In advance, prepare a tray of ice cubes and gather a few pairs of real mittens. Working with a few children at a time, hand each child an ice cube: first in her bare hands, then while she is wearing a pair of mittens. Ask her to describe the difference in the way her hands felt while holding the ice with and without the mittens. After all the children have participated in the ice-cube activity, teach them this song about the purpose of mittens.

Mittens Feel So Nice
(sung to the tune of "Row, Row, Row Your Boat")

Warm, warm, warm and snug—
Mittens feel so nice!
So grab a pair in chilly air
Or in the snow and ice!

Mittens Vs. Gloves

Do your youngsters prefer to wear mittens or gloves? Create a class graph to find out! Prepare a large sheet of bulletin-board paper with the title "Do You Like Mittens Or Gloves?" Write the headings "Mittens" and "Gloves" on the left side of the graph. Distribute a half-sheet of construction paper to each child. Explain that if she prefers to wear gloves, she should trace around each finger and thumb on one hand; then have her cut on her outline to create a glove-shaped cutout. If she prefers to wear mittens, have her trace a mitten shape around her four fingers and thumb; then ask her to cut out that shape. Have each child label her cutout with her name, then affix it to the appropriate row on the graph using rolled masking tape or Sticky-Tac. Together with your youngsters, count the votes on each line to determine the class preference. Use the graph to discuss the concepts of *more* and *fewer*.

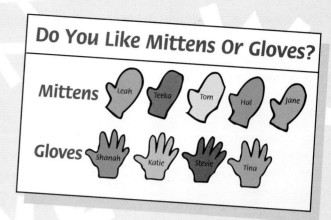

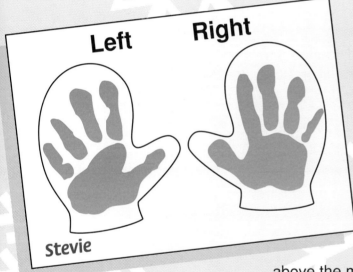

One For The Left And One For The Right

This handy-dandy activity will help youngsters learn to identify *left* and *right*. Duplicate the pair-of-mittens pattern on page 108 on construction paper for each child. Then prepare a shallow tray of tempera paint with a little dish detergent mixed into it. Working with one or two children at a time, invite each student to press one hand at a time into the paint, then onto the mitten outline that corresponds to that hand (left or right). As each child makes his handprints, remind him which hand is his left and which is his right. Point out the words "Left" and "Right" printed above the mittens. Encourage the children to take the completed papers home and display them on their refrigerators or in their rooms as visual reminders of left and right.

Mitten Munchies

Emphasize the idea of a *pair* when you invite little ones to make mitten-shaped snacks. Cut two mitten-shaped slices of bread for each child. (A mitten-shaped cookie cutter would be helpful for this task.) Ask each child to arrange his two mitten shapes with the thumbs together, to make a mirror-image pair. Then invite him to spread peanut butter or cream cheese on top of each bread shape. Provide decorations for the mittens, such as carrot rounds, thinly sliced celery, raisins, and coconut. Encourage each child to decorate his two mittens identically to create a matching pair. Then invite him to munch those mittens—either one at a time or as a mitten sandwich!

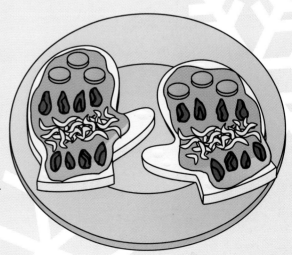

A Favorite Story

No unit on mittens would be complete without a reading of *The Mitten* adapted by Jan Brett (G. P. Putnam's Sons). Share this beautifully illustrated adaptation of an old Ukrainian folktale with your youngsters. Then use the animal patterns on page 109 to create a storytelling set for little ones to use. (Before beginning, you may wish to make some color copies of page 109 for use in other activities. See "Nicki Says" on this page.) After duplicating the pattern on page 110 for later use, mount page 109 on a sheet of tagboard. Cut out the individual animals; then laminate all the pieces for durability. Create a mitten shape by cutting two small sheets of poster board into identical mitten shapes. Staple or glue their edges together, leaving the cuff edge open so that students can insert the animal cutouts. Store the cutouts inside the poster-board mitten; then place the mitten and a copy of the book in your reading center for youngsters to use in retelling the story.

Nicki Says

Use the animal patterns on page 109 to help students practice positional concepts. Prepare the cutouts as directed for the activity described in "A Favorite Story." Then use either a real or a poster-board mitten for this small-group version of Simon Says. Use the name of the boy from the story—Nicki—in place of Simon. Place the cutouts and the mitten on a tabletop. Give a direction to one child in a small group, such as, "Nicki says, 'Put the bear *on* the mitten,' or "Nicki says, 'Make the badger hop *over* the mitten.' " Then have the child follow your direction using the named animal pattern—but only if Nicki says so! Continue until each child in the group has had the opportunity to demonstrate his understanding of several positional words. Then repeat the activity with the remaining groups.

As a variation, make a few color copies of page 109. Prepare multiple sets of the animal cutouts. After working with the children in a small group as described, divide the group into sets of partners. Give each pair of students a set of animal cutouts and a mitten. Have each child, in turn, give directions for his partner to follow using the cutouts and mitten. The children will love trying to trick one another by omitting the phrase "Nicki says."

106

A Mitten Without Knittin'

After hearing about Baba's fine knitting in *The Mitten* by Jan Brett (see "A Favorite Story" on page 106), your little ones will want to craft their own mittens. While you probably don't want to conduct a knitting lesson in your early-childhood classroom, you can invite youngsters to imitate sewing with this fine-motor activity. In advance, purchase several sheets of plastic canvas from a craft store. Cut each sheet of canvas into seven-inch squares, making one square for each child. Then use one of the mitten patterns from page 108 to make a template from tagboard. Use a permanent marker to trace around the mitten template on each plastic canvas square. Then provide each child with a large, plastic safety needle and various colors of yarn.

Demonstrate how to thread a needle and to stitch yarn in and out of the holes in the canvas. Encourage each youngster to "sew" around the outline of her mitten, then create designs inside the mitten outline with various colors of yarn. As a variation—one that is particularly good for younger preschoolers—let the students "sew" with long pipe cleaners. These are stiffer and easier for little fingers to manipulate. The result will be an interesting, fuzzy texture and some marvelous mittens!

A Class Book Of Mittens

Encourage little ones to use descriptive words with this class book activity. For each child, duplicate the class book page on page 110. Make one additional copy to use as a template for the book's covers. Have each child use either her own real mittens or a pair of paper mittens that she has decorated for the source of her description. Then have each child pose with her mittens as you snap a photo. Ask each child to glue the developed photo to her book page; then ask her to provide three descriptive words or phrases about her mittens for you to write on the blanks. Have her cut around the outline to create a mitten-shaped book page.

Use the extra book page as a template to trace front and back covers on poster board. Cut out the covers; then stack the students' pages between the covers and bind the book with two metal rings at the side. Print the title "Our Mitten Book" on the front cover and place the book in your classroom reading area for children to enjoy.

My mittens are
_____ warm _____,
_____ fuzzy _____,
and _____ yellow _____.

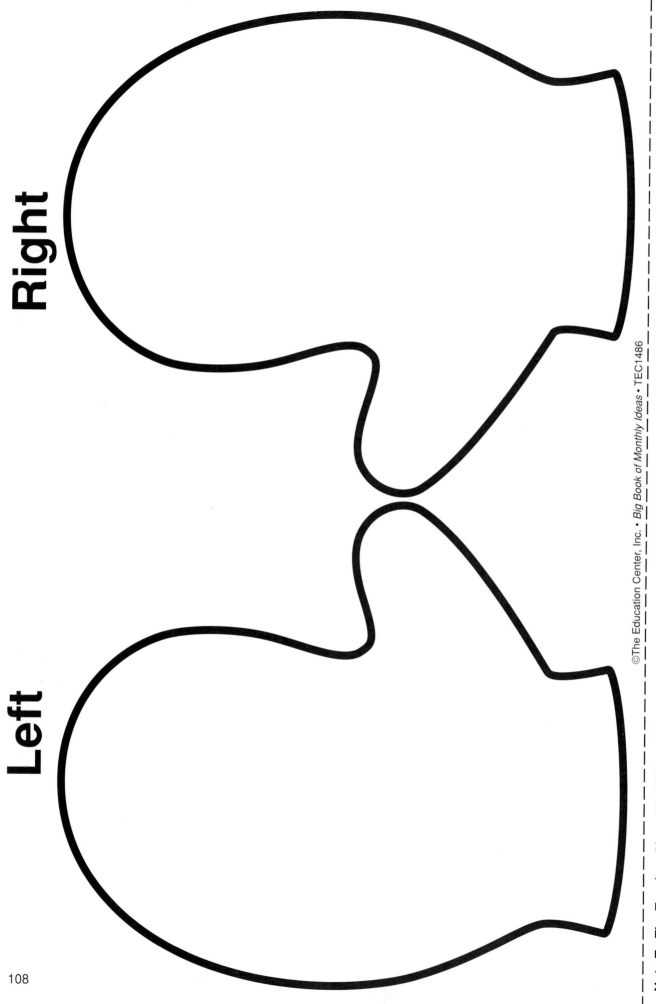

Right

Left

108

Note To The Teacher: Use with "A Mitten Mixer" on page 104, "One For The Left And One For The Right" on page 105, and "A Mitten Without Knittin'" on page 107.

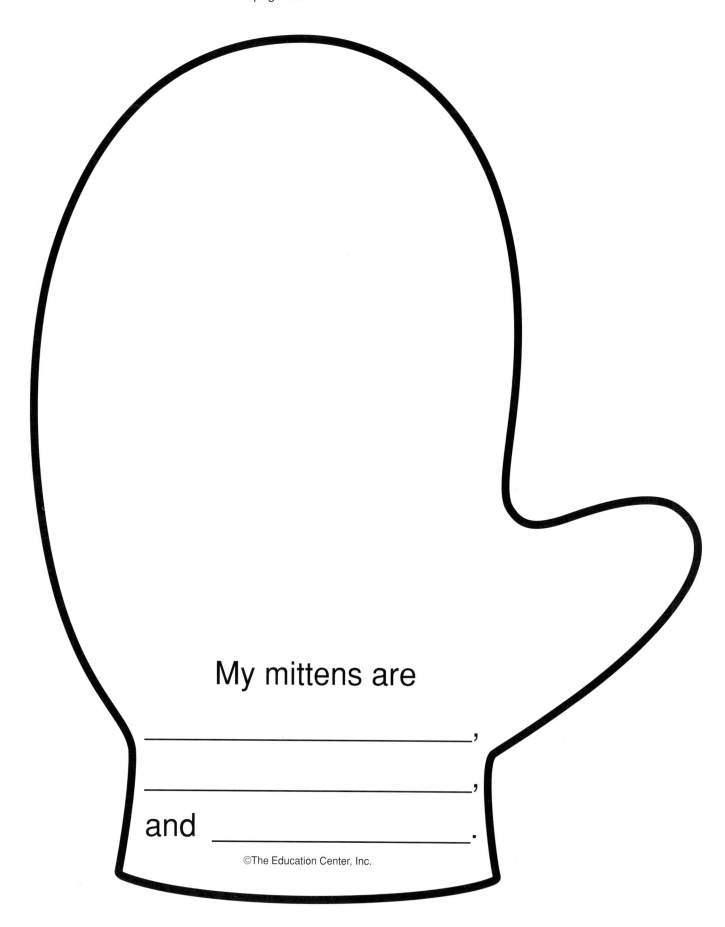

My mittens are

_____,

_____,

and _____.

©The Education Center, Inc.

Hand In Hand:
A Celebration Of Martin Luther King's Birthday

Dr. Martin Luther King, Jr., was a famous Black American who had a dream that someday all people would learn to love each other and live in harmony. His birthday is celebrated as a national holiday on the third Monday of January so that Americans will remember how his life touched the lives of millions. Place Dr. King's important message in the hands and hearts of your little ones with these ideas emphasizing love and friendship.

ideas contributed by Dayle Timmons

Dr. King's Dream

Give youngsters some basic information about who Dr. Martin Luther King, Jr., was and why we celebrate his birthday (see "Reading About Martin Luther King, Jr." on page 114 for some sources). Then read them this excerpt from his famous "I Have A Dream" speech:

"I have a dream that one day...little black boys and black girls will be able to join hands with little white boys and girls and walk together as sisters and brothers."

Explain to the children that Dr. King didn't mean a dream such as the ones we have when we are sleeping—but that the word *dream* can also mean a hope or a wish. Dr. King's hope was that all people would someday live together in harmony and friendship. Ask your students to stand in a circle; then teach them the first verse of this song.

He Had A Dream
(sung to the tune of "He's Got The Whole World In His Hands")

Verse 1

Martin Luther King, Jr., had a dream.
Martin Luther King, Jr., had a dream.
Martin Luther King, Jr., had a dream.
He had the whole world in his dream.
(Make a big circle with both hands.)

Verse 2

He had [Courtney] and [Wesley] in his dream.
He had [Kelly] and [Amanda] in his dream.
He had [Jimmie] and [Therese] in his dream.
He had the whole world in his dream.

After children have learned the first verse, sing the second verse, substituting two children's names in each line. Sing the children's names in the same order as they are standing in the circle, and explain that as each child hears her name, she should join hands with the children next to her. Continue in this manner until you have named everyone in the circle. Then sing the original verse again while everyone is holding hands.

111

Rainbow Of Dreams

Tell youngsters that Martin Luther King, Jr., gave a famous speech about his hope—or dream—for the future. Millions of people heard or have read his words about what the world might be like if people lived together in harmony. Invite youngsters to share their own dreams with all who visit your classroom when they help create this beautiful display. Duplicate page 115 for each child. Ask each student to draw a self-portrait in the open space at the bottom of his page. Then have him dictate his dream for the future for you to write in the dream cloud. Mount each child's paper on a sheet of construction paper.

To make a colorful centerpiece for the display, use a pencil to lightly outline the arc and stripes of a rainbow on a large sheet of white bulletin-board paper. Gather red, orange, yellow, green, blue, and purple tempera paints and a paintbrush for each color. Working with one child at a time, paint the child's hands; then direct him to press his hands onto the outlined rainbow. Have each child contribute a few handprints until the rainbow is complete with an arc in each color. Allow the paint to dry; then mount the rainbow on a bulletin board. Add the children's papers and a title strip that reads "Rainbow Of Dreams."

A "Hand-some" Wreath

In honor of Dr. King's birthday, decorate your classroom door with this lovely wreath. First cut a large circle from a sheet of poster board. Cut out the center of the circle to create a base for the wreath. Trace around each one of each child's hands on a different color of construction paper—black, white, or a multicultural, skin-toned shade. Assist the children in cutting out their hand shapes. Then encourage each child to glue his hand cutouts to the poster-board base. Invite each child to glue a red, construction-paper heart on the wreath. Finish the wreath by tying on a fluffy bow created with red, white, and black gift-wrapping ribbon.

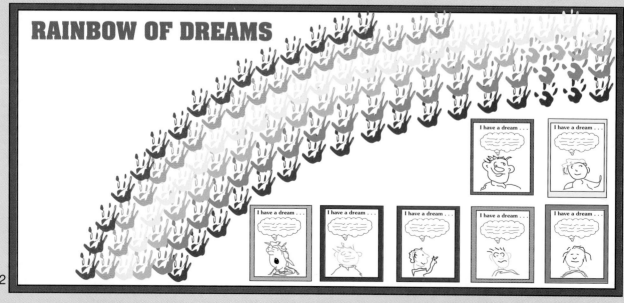

112

My Hand, Your Hand

In the spirit of Martin Luther King's beliefs, make a class book to show off the sameness that we all share, as well as the uniqueness of individuals. Take youngsters to your school's or center's copy machine. Ask each child to place one hand palm-down on the glass; then invite him to use his other hand to press the "copy" button to make a photocopy of his hand. Return to the classroom and assist each child in carefully cutting out his photocopied hand. Have each child glue his cutout to a sheet of white paper. On each child's paper, write "[Child's name]'s hand" below his cutout. Then give each child a small, red, construction-paper heart to glue on his hand picture. Stack all the pages and bind them between black construction-paper covers. On the front cover, use a white crayon to print the title "We'll Walk Hand In Hand." This book will become a hands-down favorite in your classroom reading center!

Joshua's hand

Heart Art

Reread Dr. King's words from his "I Have A Dream" speech (on page 111). Then invite each child to create this symbolic art project. Working with one small group at a time, give each child two sheets of construction paper—one light blue and one red. Use a paintbrush to paint a child's hands—one with black tempera paint and the other with white. Have the student make a paint handprint on each side of her sheet of light blue construction paper as shown. Then have her wash her hands. Provide her with a pair of scissors and demonstrate how to fold and cut her sheet of red construction paper to make a heart. Encourage her to glue the cut-out heart between her two handprints. Talk with the group about what the finished pictures symbolize—Dr. King's vision of love and friendship between people of different races.

Birthday Bracelets

After all the holding, painting, tracing, and copying of hands, youngsters have probably surmised that their hands are a special part of this unit of study. So accentuate those hands with some special bracelets! To prepare, ask parents to donate a large supply of black and white buttons or beads. Cut a supply of small, red, construction-paper hearts; then punch a hole through the center of each heart. Cut a six-inch length of black or white yarn for each child. Dip one end of each length of yarn into glue and allow it to dry and harden overnight.

To make a bracelet, invite each child to string some black and some white beads or buttons and some paper hearts onto her yarn. Tie the ends of each child's length of yarn to fit her wrist. Encourage the children to wear their bracelets during a class celebration of Dr. King's birthday (see "Happy Birthday, Dr. King!" on page 114).

Happy Birthday, Dr. King!

Honor Martin Luther King, Jr., on this special day with a classroom birthday celebration! Dr. King's favorite foods were old-fashioned Southern favorites—such as fried chicken, sweet potatoes, black-eyed peas, and cornbread—so ask a few parents to donate these dishes for the celebration. Prepare some white and some chocolate cupcakes for students to decorate, as well.

Have each child ice the cupcake of her choice with either chocolate or vanilla frosting. Then invite her to add a few heart-shaped candies to the top of her cupcake. Lead youngsters in singing "Happy Birthday" to Dr. King before enjoying this festive feast!

Reading About
Martin Luther King, Jr.

Although there have been many, many books written about Dr. King's life, only a few are appropriate for very young children. You may need to paraphrase the text of these selections for younger children, but these books will provide illustrations that will help youngsters get a sense of who Martin Luther King was and what he believed.

Happy Birthday, Martin Luther King
Written by Jean Marzollo
Published by Scholastic Inc.

A Picture Book Of Martin Luther King, Jr.
Written by David A. Adler
Published by Scholastic Inc.

Martin Luther King Day
Written by Linda Lowery
Published by Carolrhoda Books

My Dream of Martin Luther King
Written by Faith Ringgold
Published by Crown Publishers, Inc.

I Have A Dream...

Note To The Teacher: Use with "Rainbow Of Dreams" on page 112.

Calling All Community Helpers!

Invite youngsters to learn all about the workers who serve their communities with this unit focusing on real experiences and dramatic play.

ideas contributed by Ada Hanley Goren and Ann Saunders

Classroom Careers

Chances are that you routinely assign classroom jobs to your students. Help youngsters make the connection between their responsibilities in the classroom and jobs performed by workers in the real world. As you talk about the responsibilities associated with each of your classroom jobs, ask youngsters if they can think of a real job that is similar. Then announce new job titles and show youngsters the equipment they'll be using to perform each job. Take some suggestions from the list below or make up some of your own.

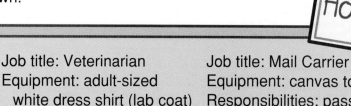

Meteorologist
Caroline Hodnett

Job title: Veterinarian
Equipment: adult-sized white dress shirt (lab coat)
Responsibilities: cares for class pets

Job title: Mail Carrier
Equipment: canvas tote bag
Responsibilities: passes out papers and supplies

Job title: Farmer
Equipment: gardening gloves
Responsibilities: cares for classroom plants

Job title: Waitperson
Equipment: tray
Responsibilities: helps to serve snacks and meals

Job title: Tour Guide
Equipment: special visor
Responsibilities: leads the class to each destination outside the classroom (line leader)

Job title: Secretary
Equipment: special pencil
Responsibilities: helps take attendance and lunch count

Now that you've revamped your classroom jobs, use the cards on pages 120 and 122 to create a new job board. First duplicate page 121 for later use. Then mount pages 120 and 122 on sheets of tagboard. Cut the cards apart; then laminate all the cards for durability and repeated programming. Program the blank cards with jobs specific to your classroom. Each time you make new job assignments, print a child's name on each card with a wipe-off marker. Post the cards on a bulletin board or in a pocket chart with the title "We're On The Job!"

Community Helpers Up Close

After providing an overview of many different community helpers, focus students' attention on some individual jobs in the workforce.

Police Officer

If you haven't invited a police officer to speak to your class, discuss this important job. Emphasize the police officer's role in promoting the *safety* of citizens. Then invite youngsters to role-play an interaction with a police officer. Have one student pretend to be lost, and have another child (equipped with a pad and pencil) play the part of a helpful police officer. Encourage the lost child to give important personal information to help the officer locate his parents. Ask younger children to give their full names. Older children may be able to recite their addresses or phone numbers. Have the police officer "write" this information on his pad, then pretend to use it to help the child find his family.

After every child has had a turn to role-play an officer or a lost child, conclude your activity by awarding each youngster an honorary treat—an edible police badge! Roll out refrigerated sugar-cookie dough on a floured surface; then have each child use a star-shaped cookie cutter to cut out a cookie badge. Then give him some dough scraps and ask him to roll five small balls of dough. Have him press one ball of dough onto each point of his star. Bake the cookies as directed on the package. Cool the cookies; then invite each child to frost his cookie with white icing. Have him place a silver, ball-shaped cake decoration on each of his cookie's rounded points. Then encourage your youngsters to bite into those badges!

Firefighter

Many youngsters are fascinated with the job of a firefighter. Share the pictures from a photo-illustrated book about firefighters on the job—such as *Fire Fighters* by Robert Maass (Scholastic Inc.)—to stimulate a discussion about this important job. Then follow up your discussion with this red-hot art project! Invite each youngster to draw a picture of a house on a sheet of paper. Encourage each child to glue torn pieces of red, orange, and yellow construction paper onto her house picture to represent the flames of a fire. After the glue has dried, invite students to role-play the job of firefighters. Place a protective covering over the paint tray of an easel and on the floor below the easel. Working with one child at a time, attach her picture to the easel. If desired, provide a child-sized raincoat, rubber boots, and firefighter's helmet for the child to wear. Give her a spray bottle filled with a mixture of white tempera paint and water. Explain that the bottle represents a fire extinguisher and her job is to "put out the fire" on her paper. While she "extinguishes" the house fire, have her classmates imitate the sound of a fire engine's siren. Then give the next child a turn to spray away!

Charles

Doctor

Learning about health-care professionals will be in the bag with this activity! Begin by sharing the photo-illustrated book *When I See My Doctor...* by Susan Kuklin (Bradbury Press) to

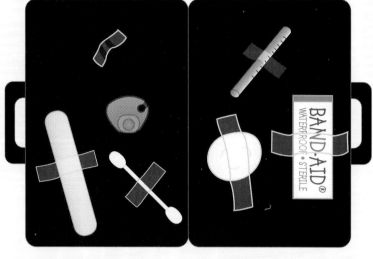

stimulate a discussion about the jobs of doctors and nurses. Invite your students to share their experiences about visits to the doctor's office. Then take a closer look at the tools that are used by health-care workers. If possible, show the children some real medical equipment borrowed from a parent or a local medical office. Then invite each child to create his own doctor's bag.

For each child, fold and cut a 12" x 18" sheet of black construction paper as shown. Have each child glue a red, construction-paper cross to the outside of his bag. Use a white crayon to write "Dr. [child's name]" above the cross. Then provide each of your diminutive doctors with some tools to store in his bag.

Create pretend thermometers by cutting clear plastic straws into halves; then use a permanent black marker to make lines on one side of each straw half. Provide each child with a pretend stethoscope—a length of yarn threaded through two holes punched in opposite sides of an egg-carton cup and tied into a necklace. Have each child open (unfold) his doctor's bag and tape his thermometer and stethoscope—as well as a cotton ball, an adhesive bandage, a tongue depressor, and a cotton swab—to the inside of his bag. Invite each child to take his bag home to share with his family.

Carpenter

Switch youngsters' attention to another type of tools—those used by a carpenter. Share the book *A Carpenter* by Douglas Florian (Greenwillow Books) for a simple look at the job

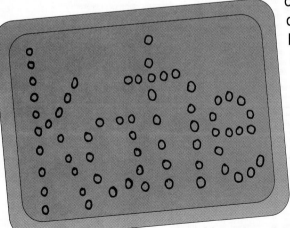

of a carpenter and the tools he uses. Display some of the tools shown in the book. Ask youngsters to brainstorm some ways to use the tools safely. Show them a pair of safety goggles and ask if anyone knows what they are used for. Then invite youngsters to make their own imitation safety goggles. Provide each child with two pipe cleaners and a set of two rings cut from a six-pack beverage holder. Demonstrate how to twist a pipe cleaner around the outer edge of each plastic ring to form a pair of goggles. Help each student bend the pipe cleaners to fit around her ears.

Now that the children have safety goggles to wear, it's tool time! Invite small groups of youngsters to don their goggles and use plastic hammers to pound golf tees into Styrofoam® meat trays. Encourage youngsters to hammer designs, shapes, letters, numbers, or their names into their trays. Carpet squares placed beneath the trays will muffle the pounding, but not the fun!

Storekeeper

Your youngsters have probably visited many different kinds of stores. Ask them to brainstorm a list of as many kinds of stores as they can think of for you to write on the chalkboard or a sheet of chart paper. Then read the story *On Market Street* by Arnold Lobel (Scholastic Inc.) for a mention of even more merchandise! Ask your students to decide what types of merchandise they'd like to sell if they were storekeepers.

Duplicate the class-book page on page 121 for each child. On his page, have each student draw pictures or glue cut-out pictures of items he'd like to sell in his store. Write his dictation on the blank line. Use two 12" x 18" sheets of construction paper to create front and back covers for the book. Stack the pages together; then center the stack along the bottom long edge of one of the sheets of construction paper. Staple the stack in place along the top edge of the pages. Position the other sheet of construction paper on top of the first, aligning and stapling together each side edge and the top edge. Cut the top sheet of construction paper to fold open as shown; then draw handles on the resulting doors. Print the title "Our Store Story" across the top of the cover. Read the finished book to your youngsters, and then place it in your classroom library for further enjoyment by your young entrepreneurs!

Truck Driver

How do all those shoes, toys, flowers, and groceries get to the stores where they're sold? In trucks, of course! Teach youngsters more about trucks and truck drivers when you show the video *Close Up And Very Personal: Big Rigs* (available from Stage Fright Productions, 1-800-979-6800). After viewing the video, engage your youngsters in towing some goods cross-classroom with this fun math activity.

To prepare, place several toy dump trucks or trailer trucks in your block area. Place an equal number of boxes or baskets on the other side of the classroom. On the side of each truck, tape a slip of paper with a numeral printed on it. On the side of each box or basket, tape a slip of paper with a numeral that corresponds to one shown on one of the trucks.

Then invite a few children to each choose a truck to "drive." Instruct each child to identify the number on his truck. Then have him place that number of blocks (or other small manipulatives, depending on the size of your toy trucks) in his truck. Each student may then "drive" his truck across the room to its destination—the box or basket with the corresponding number. Once there, have the drivers unload their cargo. Have them count the blocks to make sure they're delivering the whole order! Then have those drivers make a return trip to the block area so a new set of truck drivers can make their deliveries!

Job Assignment Cards

Use with "Classroom Careers" on page 116.

Farmer

Veterinarian

Waitperson

Mail Carrier

Secretary

Tour Guide

If I had a store, I would sell _____.

Note To The Teacher: Use this page with "Storekeeper" on page 119.

Job Assignment Cards

Use with "Classroom Careers" on page 116.

Librarian

Custodian

Meteorologist

FEBRUARY

Be Mine!

TIP-TOP TEETH

If National Children's Dental Health Month has you searching for ideas your students can sink their teeth into, try this multidisciplinary unit. Begin with a grand entrance and a song-and-dance routine, and soon your little ones will be anxious to spruce up their pearly whites.

ideas contributed by Linda Gordetsky

Happy Smiles Brush Through Here!

HAPPY SMILES BRUSH THROUGH HERE!

Greet your students with a giant toothbrush door decoration to announce your dental health studies. For bristles, cut white plastic garbage bags into strips and tape them to the top of your classroom door frame. Cut out bulletin-board paper to complete a giant toothbrush. Program it with a dental health slogan. Each morning, students will enjoy "brushing" through the doorway, and you'll be sure to see happy smiles as they do!

BRUSHING UP!

Tape-record your class singing the following tune. While you play the tape, assist your children in forming a circle and choosing motions that correspond to each line of the song. When you come to the chorus each time, do the usual "Hokey-Pokey" moves.

BRUSHY, BRUSHY
(sung to the tune of "The Hokey-Pokey")

You put your toothpaste on.
Watch it squeeze right out.
Put your toothpaste on,
And squish it all about.

Chorus:
You do the Brushy, Brushy,
And you move it all around.
That's what it's all about.
Brushy, Brushy!

You put your toothbrush in.
Don't take your toothbrush out.
You put your toothbrush in,
And you scrub it all about.

Chorus:
You do the Brushy, Brushy,
And you move it all around.
That's what it's all about.
Brushy, Brushy!

Now put some water in.
Don't let the water out.
Now put some water in,
And swish it all about.

Chorus:
You do the Brushy, Brushy,
And you move it all around.
That's what it's all about.
Rinse out!

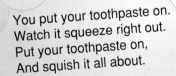

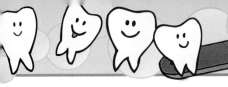

CHECKUP

Before beginning this exploration activity, have each youngster wash his hands thoroughly. Provide a metal or Mylar® mirror for each child in your group. Direct students to open wide and take a peek at their teeth. Guide them in discussing and discovering things about their teeth by asking a series of questions. For example, you might ask students what color their teeth are, how many there are, and whether any teeth are loose or missing. You might also discuss the body parts that are adjacent to the teeth, such as the gums, lips, and tongue. As your discussion progresses, write what students know about teeth on an experience chart.

FABULOUS FOODS

Introduce your youngsters to the facts that some foods are helpful to teeth and some foods can be harmful. Explain that some foods can be beneficial because they can actually help clean the surfaces of teeth and because they can give the body necessary nutrients to promote the growth of strong, healthy teeth. Give some examples, such as milk, apples, and cheese. Then ask students to name other foods that might be good for teeth.

Then provide students with magazines and safety scissors, and ask them to cut out pictures of all kinds of foods. When all your students have contributed to the collection, hold up one picture at a time and ask students to comment on whether the food shown is primarily beneficial or harmful to teeth. Without explaining what you are doing, attach each picture to a piece of chart paper that has been divided into two columns so that all the healthful foods are on one side and all the harmful ones are on the other. When you have attached all the pictures, ask students what they notice about each column of pictures. Title each column as the children suggest.

MR. BIG MOUTH

Mr. Big Mouth can be an invaluable tool in teaching about dental health. To make Mr. Big Mouth, tape shut the flaps of a sturdy cardboard box. Flip the box upside down; then paint two eyes and a mouth on it as shown, taking care to leave at least enough of an opening in the mouth so that a child's arm will fit through it. Cut away the opening between the upper and lower teeth. Cut narrow channels between the teeth, so that real floss or string will fit between them.

Each day during your dental health studies, put a different array of foods in a basket before the children arrive. Some should be foods that are good for the teeth and some foods that are not. Have children take turns choosing a food from the basket. If he has pulled out a food that is beneficial for teeth, have him "feed" it to Mr. Big Mouth. If the food is not good for teeth, have him continue pulling items from the basket until a healthful alternative is selected. See "Floss And Brush" on page 127 for another way to use Mr. Big Mouth.

OUR FRIEND THE DENTIST

The Berenstain Bears Visit The Dentist by Stan & Jan Berenstain (Random House, Inc.) is a delightful complement to your dental health studies. (*Just Going To The Dentist* by Mercer Mayer [Western Publishing Company, Inc.] is also a good choice for introducing this activity.) Read the story aloud—paraphrasing for younger children if necessary. Follow up the story with a discussion about dental care workers, emphasizing the concept that a dentist helps keep our teeth strong and healthy. Also explain that when our teeth are in need of repairs, the dentist can take care of that too.

If desired, use the patterns on page 131 to create a headband for the dentist, one with flowers for the mother, and one with a cap's bill for the child in the song below. After students have learned the song, have them wear the appropriate headbands and act out the drama described in the song. Repeat this activity until every child has had a turn to play a role.

THERE'S NOTHING LIKE BEING THERE!

Give students an opportunity to visit a local dentist's office and talk to the personnel there. You may even stage the entire trip as an appointment for a doll or stuffed animal that has a particularly toothy grin. If you choose this alternative, the children could check the patient in at the front desk and seat him in the dentist's chair when they enter the examination room. The dentist may even pretend to give the patient's teeth a quick exam. Regardless of whether a mock patient is involved or not, photograph the students during their field trip. Back in your classroom, share with students a factual book, such as *When I See My Dentist…* by Susan Kuklin (Bradbury Press) or *My Dentist* by Harlow Rockwell (Greenwillow Books). Give students opportunities to tell which scenes from the book remind them of things they saw at the dentist's office.

OUCH, MY TOOTH!

(sung to the tune of "There's A Hole In The Bucket")

My tooth hurts, dear Mama, dear Mama, dear Mama.
My tooth hurts, dear Mama. I must say it hurts.

We'll go to the dentist, dear Tommy, dear Tommy.
We'll go to the dentist. I'll call her right now.

She sees a small hole in one bright shiny tooth.
She sees a small hole in one bright shiny tooth.

Oh, how did it get there, dear Dentist, dear Dentist?
Oh, how did it get there—that hole in my tooth?

You ate too much candy and cookies and soda.
You ate too much sugar—and needed to brush.

You made it feel better, dear Dentist, dear Dentist.
You made it feel better. I promise to brush!

My, What A Toothy Grin!

Read aloud Taro Gomi's *The Crocodile And The Dentist* (Scholastic Inc.). When the giggles subside, have students use context clues to complete the following sentences: "Once there was a little ___ who woke up with a toothache. His mother called the ___ who said, 'You may have a ___. You must ___ more often and stop eating so much ___.' " Then let student volunteers take turns saying something related to teeth, but omitting words for their classmates to supply.

> "Brush them and floss them and take them to the dentist, and they will stay with you. Ignore them and they'll go away."
> —American Dental Association

Floss And Brush

Prepare Mr. Big Mouth (see page 125) for this activity by stuffing some green and brown tissue-paper pieces between some of his teeth. Read students the quote shown from the American Dental Association. Find out what your children think that it means. Turn their attention to Mr. Big Mouth's teeth. Ask them to comment on what they see. What would they suggest to do to care for these yucky teeth?

Using string, demonstrate proper flossing methods—using a gentle up-and-down motion to rub the sides of Mr. Big Mouth's teeth. Explain that flossing precedes brushing and that children should always have parental assistance when flossing their own teeth. Choose a child to wear the dentist headband (see "Our Friend The Dentist" on page 126), and help him floss Mr. Big Mouth's teeth with string to remove the buildup between his teeth. Then replace the tissue-paper pieces and have the dentist choose another student to take a turn wearing the dentist's headband and flossing Mr. Big Mouth's teeth. After giving several children a turn, show students what real dental floss looks like and explain that imitation floss was used to floss Mr. Big Mouth's teeth.

Explain to students that after teeth are flossed, they must be brushed. Using short, *gentle* strokes, brush the fronts and backs of Mr. Big Mouth's teeth. Scrub gently on chewing surfaces. Give students who have not yet had an opportunity to care for Mr. Big Mouth's teeth a turn to brush his pearly whites.

Tempting Tooth Tales

Tempt parents to join in reading some dental delights by providing a list of related children's books. Duplicate the toothbrush bookmark pattern on page 129. Assist each child in cutting out her copy of the pattern; then assist her in folding the paper so that the writing is folded to the inside, using the partial dotted lines as guides. Show each student how to fringe the widest part of her cutout to resemble the bristles on a toothbrush. Provide art supplies so that each student can decorate the handle of her toothbrush with her favorite colors. Encourage each child to show her toothbrush to her parents and read some tooth tales with them also.

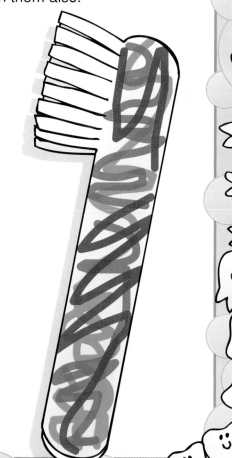

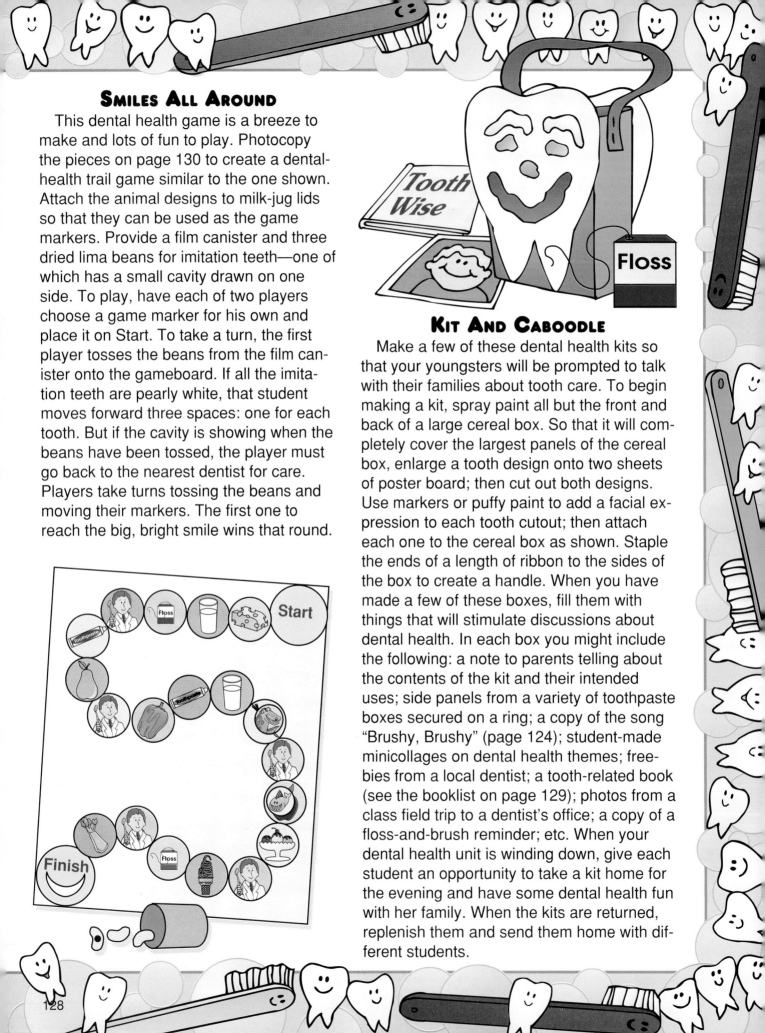

SMILES ALL AROUND

This dental health game is a breeze to make and lots of fun to play. Photocopy the pieces on page 130 to create a dental-health trail game similar to the one shown. Attach the animal designs to milk-jug lids so that they can be used as the game markers. Provide a film canister and three dried lima beans for imitation teeth—one of which has a small cavity drawn on one side. To play, have each of two players choose a game marker for his own and place it on Start. To take a turn, the first player tosses the beans from the film canister onto the gameboard. If all the imitation teeth are pearly white, that student moves forward three spaces: one for each tooth. But if the cavity is showing when the beans have been tossed, the player must go back to the nearest dentist for care. Players take turns tossing the beans and moving their markers. The first one to reach the big, bright smile wins that round.

KIT AND CABOODLE

Make a few of these dental health kits so that your youngsters will be prompted to talk with their families about tooth care. To begin making a kit, spray paint all but the front and back of a large cereal box. So that it will completely cover the largest panels of the cereal box, enlarge a tooth design onto two sheets of poster board; then cut out both designs. Use markers or puffy paint to add a facial expression to each tooth cutout; then attach each one to the cereal box as shown. Staple the ends of a length of ribbon to the sides of the box to create a handle. When you have made a few of these boxes, fill them with things that will stimulate discussions about dental health. In each box you might include the following: a note to parents telling about the contents of the kit and their intended uses; side panels from a variety of toothpaste boxes secured on a ring; a copy of the song "Brushy, Brushy" (page 124); student-made minicollages on dental health themes; freebies from a local dentist; a tooth-related book (see the booklist on page 129); photos from a class field trip to a dentist's office; a copy of a floss-and-brush reminder; etc. When your dental health unit is winding down, give each student an opportunity to take a kit home for the evening and have some dental health fun with her family. When the kits are returned, replenish them and send them home with different students.

Toothbrush Bookmark Pattern

Use with "Tempting Tooth Tales" on page 127.

Dear Parent,

At school we have been studying dental health. Your child has learned that flossing, brushing, proper nutrition, and regular dental checkups are needed to keep teeth strong and healthy. Read a few of these books with your child to reinforce our dental health lessons. Use this toothbrush as a bookmark.

The Berenstain Bears Visit The Dentist
By Stan & Jan Berenstain
Random House, Inc.

Bill And Pete Go Down The Nile
By Tomie dePaola
G. P. Putnam's Sons

The Crocodile And The Dentist
By Taro Gomi
Scholastic Inc.

Doctor De Soto
By William Steig
Scholastic Inc.

Little Rabbit's Loose Tooth
By Lucy Bate
Scholastic Inc.

My Dentist
By Harlow Rockwell
Greenwillow Books

My Tooth Is About To Fall Out
By Grace Maccarone
Scholastic Inc.

Gameboard Pieces

Use with "Smiles All Around" on page 128.

Headband Patterns

Use with "Our Friend The Dentist" on page 126. Use the dentist headband pattern with "Floss And Brush" on page 127.

"VALEN-TASTIC"!

Excite your little ones during this time of affection with lots of activities dealing with the magic of Valentine's Day. You'll love using the following collection of ideas to practice skills from across the curriculum.

by Angie Kutzer

COOPERATIVE CARDS

Spread a little love around your school with this assembly-line activity. To prepare, make several heart-shaped tagboard patterns and gather pencils, construction paper, scissors, stickers, and an assortment of art supplies such as glue, lace, and markers. With your students, make a list of people around your school to whom they would like to send valentines—office workers, custodians, administrators, and book buddies. After reading the story *Valentine Cats* by Jean Marzollo (Scholastic Inc.), divide your class into five groups: tracers, cutters, writers, artists, and postal workers. Have the tracers trace the heart patterns onto construction paper. Continuing on down the assembly line, have the cutters cut out the tracings and the writers copy "We Love You!" onto the heart cutouts. Encourage the artists to decorate the cutouts before passing them along to the postal workers to be folded and stamped (with stickers or rubber stamps). When all the cards are finished, accompany your students throughout the school to distribute them. Now *that's* special delivery!

HAPPY HUNTING

Have a happy heart hunt. While the children are away, hide at least three heart cutouts for each child. When the children return, ask them to each find three hearts. Encourage youngsters to gather on the carpet as soon as they have found the hearts. To practice one-to-one correspondence, have each child return his heart cutouts to you one by one as he names a loved one for each heart. To conclude this activity, pass each child a heart as you mention one of his lovable characteristics. Love makes the world go 'round!

VALENTINE DRAMATICS

Encourage oral communication skills by having groups of six students perform the following rhyming skit. You will need to gather a few props before you teach the rhyme. Give Child One a valentine with candy attached. (Child Two doesn't need anything.) Give Child Three a handful of valentines. Give Child Four five valentines and Child Five a valentine gift bag. The child playing the part of Teacher needs a teacher prop (pointer, glasses, etc.). Align five chairs in a row facing your students. Have children one through five sit in the chairs in numerical order.

Introduce your children to the rhyme by reading it aloud and demonstrating the motions. Rehearse the rhyme a few times so that your students can begin to join in. Now you're ready! Have your entire class say the rhyme as the Teacher stands behind the chairs and taps each actor when it is his turn to perform the motions. When they're finished, the first group goes back to the audience so that more stars can shine!

FIVE LITTLE CHILDREN ON VALENTINE'S DAY
(to the rhythm of "Five Little Jack-O'-Lanterns")

Five little children sitting at their seats— *(Children sit and look down.)*
The first one said, "My valentine has treats!" *(First one shows his valentine to group.)*
The second one said, "I don't have a valentine." *(Second one pokes out his lip and whines.)*
The third one said, "Here, have some of mine!" *(Third one happily hands second child some cards.)*

The fourth one said, "Aren't valentines fun!" *(Fourth one tosses valentines in air.)*
The fifth one said, "Hey, look! I have a ton!" *(Fifth one looks inside bag with fourth child.)*
"[Kissing sound]" went the teacher and *(Teacher blows kiss to audience.)*
"[Kissing sound]" went the crowd. *(Audience blows kisses back to teacher.)*
Five little children stood up and took a bow. *(Children take a bow.)*

VALENTINE SHAPES

Change piggies to valentines in this fun rhyme for the flannelboard. Cut out the valentines on page 135 and attach a piece of felt to the back of each. With your students, review the traditional nursery rhyme "This Little Piggy Went To Market." Show each valentine character to your children, ask them to name its shape, and have them find things around the room with the same shape. End the activity by reciting the rhyme at the right several times while children take turns manipulating the valentine pieces on a flannelboard. Leave the pieces on the board and encourage your children to perform the rhyme during center time.

This little valentine is a circle.
This little valentine is square.
This little valentine is a triangle.
This little valentine has hair!
This little valentine said,
     "Happy Valentine's Day!"
To everyone, everywhere!

CHOOSE A MATE

There are several histories regarding the beginning of Valentine's Day. The earliest one recorded in English tells of birds choosing their mates on this day. Relay this information to your youngsters and get ready to fly! Use the following adaptation to the traditional circle and singing game of Bluebird. Students hold hands in a circle with arms up, making arches between the children. One child is selected as the first bird. He "flies" in and out of the arches while everyone sings the song. At the end of the verse, he taps another child and they both begin to fly while the song is sung again. Continue until there is a classroom full of lovebirds!

REDBIRD
(sung to the tune of "Bluebird")
Redbird, Redbird, through my window,
Redbird, Redbird, through my window,
Redbird, Redbird, through my window,
Oh, won't you be my friend?
(Oh, we are all good friends! *[last time through]*)

Three!

ROLL, COUNT, AND EAT!

Seasonal candies like conversation hearts, valentine-colored M&M's®, or cinnamon hearts can provide excellent counting practice for your little ones. Pair up your students. Give each pair a plate containing two spoonfuls of candy and a die. The children will take turns rolling the die, naming the number rolled, counting the same number of candies, and eating them! The partners see to it that numbers are named correctly and that candy is counted correctly.

MY TEACHER LOVES ME!

Wondering what to do for your little ones this Valentine's Day? Give them a keepsake that will last a lifetime—a special photo of the two of you. In advance have a parent volunteer, another teacher, or an assistant take a photo of you with each child. Once the pictures are developed, use a heart-shaped cookie cutter and a pen to trace around each one. Then cut out the shapes. On Valentine's Day, duplicate page 136 on white construction paper for each child. To make a valentine, have each child color, cut, and assemble the puzzle to reveal the mystery message. Help him glue the puzzle to another piece of construction paper and read the message. Later, while your students are out of the room, go by and mount each heart-shaped photo on the correct card; then sign and date it. The children are sure to put this photo card in their scrapbooks to enjoy for years to come!

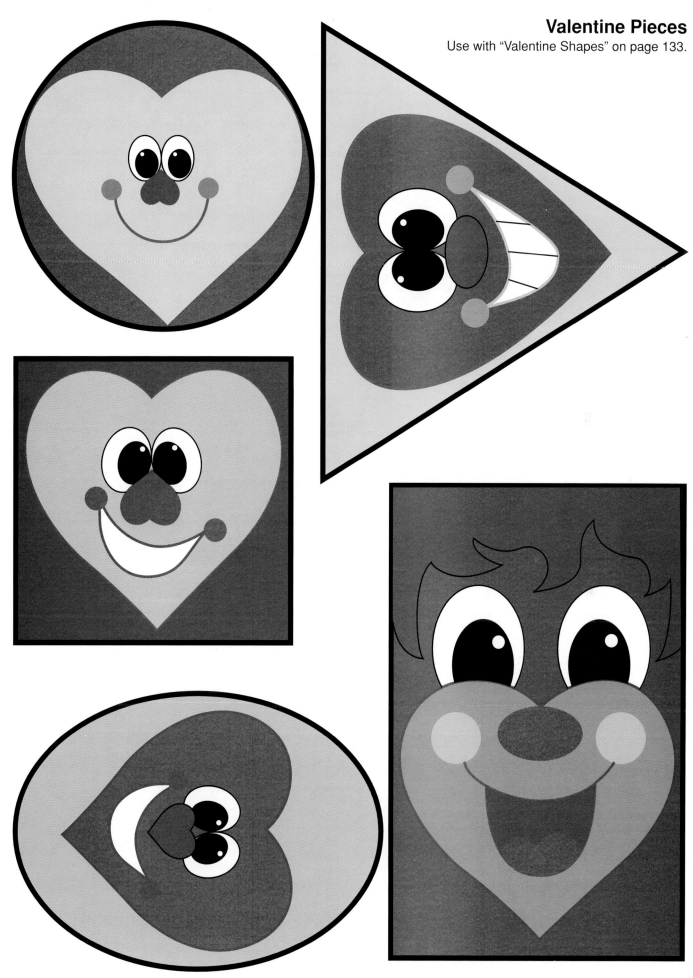

Teacher Valentine

Use with "My Teacher Loves Me!" on page 134.

Hip, Hip, Hooray! It's The 100th Day!

If you and your kindergartners have been keeping track of the school days since the beginning of the year, it's time to celebrate a mathematical milestone—the 100th day of school! Use these activities to help your young learners grasp the concept of "100." One hundred days of school? Cool!

ideas contributed by Ada Hanley Goren and Vicki Pacchetti

Dressed For The Occasion

You can count on this sweatshirt to be the perfect attire for your 100th Day activities—and your students can count on it, too! Before the 100th day of school, purchase an over-sized, solid-colored sweatshirt, two shades of fabric paint, and 100 pom-poms (preferably ten each of ten different colors). Beginning at one shoulder, use hot glue or fabric glue to attach the pom-poms (like colors together) in a line that wraps around and around the shirt until all the pom-poms have been used. After the glue dries, use one shade of fabric paint to write the numeral "1" below the first pom-pom. Continue labeling each pom-pom in numerical order, switching to the other paint color to write each numeral divisible by ten (10, 20, 30, etc.). Wear the finished sweatshirt as part of your 100th Day celebration.

Count On It!

A study of the number 100 naturally lends itself to practice with counting—especially counting by tens. For this activity, you'll need several copies of the counting chart on page 140. First make one copy of the chart. Beginning with the numeral 1 in the top left corner, write the numerals 1–100 in the boxes. Make an enlarged copy of this chart to use with the whole class. Then duplicate a class supply of the numbered chart on colored paper. Finally duplicate a class supply of the original, blank chart on white copy paper. Cut the colored-paper copies into strips as shown. Leave the blank charts intact.

Show the students the enlarged chart. Review the numbers 1–100. Point out the numbers divisible by ten; then ask youngsters to look for other number patterns on the chart. As a class, practice counting aloud to 100, first by ones, then by tens. Point to each number on the chart as it is recited. Then give each child a blank chart, a set of number strips, and a glue stick. Ask him to glue the strips onto the counting chart in the correct order. When he has finished, have him refer to the enlarged chart to check his work.

100-Piece Creations

Provide a variety of manipulatives in quantities of 100 to get students involved in some creative, cooperative fun! Have youngsters help you count out 100 pattern blocks, 100 wooden blocks, or 100 pieces from any other suitable manipulative set in your classroom. Then divide the class into small groups and ask each group to take a turn creating a design or a structure using the 100 blocks or pieces. Take an instant photo of each group's finished project before inviting the next group to take its turn. Extend this activity by providing one or more 100-piece jigsaw puzzles for students to put together.

Take It Outside!

Take youngsters on a trip to the playground for some gross-motor experiences with the number 100. Lead the children in a variety of group activities, such as counting 100 trips down the slide, taking 100 steps from a designated point, or doing 100 jumping jacks. Finish off the outdoor fun with a 100-yard dash. Whew! Learning about 100 is exhausting!

Estimation Stations

Set up several estimation stations for math—100th Day style! If desired, divide your class into three groups and have the groups rotate from station to station.

Station One: Create three trains of plastic, snap-together cubes. Make one train exactly 100 cubes in length. Make each of the other two trains fewer than or more than 100 cubes in length. Invite each student to place his name card in a pile next to the train he believes to be exactly 100 cubes long. After everyone has estimated, count the cubes in each train to find out which one is made up of exactly 100 cubes. Read the name cards to identify the students who guessed correctly.

Station Two: Invite an adult volunteer to pose the question, "How long is 100 seconds?" Have her watch the clock and say, "Go!" when she begins her 100-second count. Direct each child to sit down when she thinks 100 seconds have passed. Have the volunteer ring a bell when 100 seconds have actually passed. Wow! 100 seconds is longer than you think!

Station Three: Collect five same-size, lidded jars. Place a different filler—such as peanuts, paper clips, cotton balls, M&M's®, and buttons—into each jar, filling one jar with exactly 100 items and putting fewer than or more than 100 items in each of the other jars. Place the lid on each jar; then glue a construction-paper square of a different color to each jar lid. Place the jars and a sheet of construction paper in each corresponding color on a tabletop. As students visit this station, have them examine the five jars and estimate which one contains exactly 100 items. Have each child write her name on the sheet of paper that corresponds to the jar-lid color of her choice. After everyone has made an estimate, count the contents of each jar together to determine which jar contains exactly 100 items. Then read and count the names on the paper to determine how many children guessed correctly.

100th Day Headbands

These headbands are right at your finger-tips—or actually at your students' fingertips! Encourage each child to make 100 fingerprints to decorate a headband for your 100th Day celebration. For each child, cut a 3" x 24" strip of heavy white paper. Also cut a class supply—by hand or with a die-cutting machine—of the numeral 100 from brightly colored construction paper. Then purchase or borrow ten stamp pads in ten different colors.

Have each child glue his cutout numerals to the center of his white paper strip. Then have him press each of his fingers and thumbs—one at a time—onto a different stamp pad. On his white paper strip, have him make ten prints with each of his ten fingers. The result? 100 fancy fingerprints on one handsome headband! Fit each child's headband to his head and staple the ends together. All dressed? Let's celebrate!

A Colorful Counting Cake

What would a celebration be without a cake? Make this special cake in the shape of the number 100 to mark this very special school day. Have youngsters assist you in preparing the batter as directed on a package of cake mix. Divide the batter evenly among one square and two round cake pans. Bake the three cakes for approximately 25 minutes. Cool the cakes; then cut the square cake in half. Use one-half of the square cake as the number 1 and discard the other half. On a large tray or a sheet of cardboard covered with foil, place the square cake-half next to the two round cakes to form the number 100. Use canned cake frosting and decorator tube icing to delineate the numbers more clearly. Then have youngsters help you add the finishing touch—100 M&M's® candies! Invite each child to put on a few M&M's®; count together continuously until you reach 100. Encourage each youngster to enjoy a slice of this colorful counting cake as you share one of the stories listed in "Stories You Can Count On."

Stories You Can Count On

Extra! Extra! Read all about it—the number 100, that is! Share one or more of these just-right-for-the-100th-day-of-school stories with your little ones.

The Wolf's Chicken Stew
Written by Keiko Kasza
Published by G. P. Putnam's Sons

The 100th Day Of School
Written by Angela Shelf Medearis
Published by Scholastic Inc.

I Can Count To 100...Can You?
Written by Katherine Howard
Published by Random House, Inc.

Count To 100!

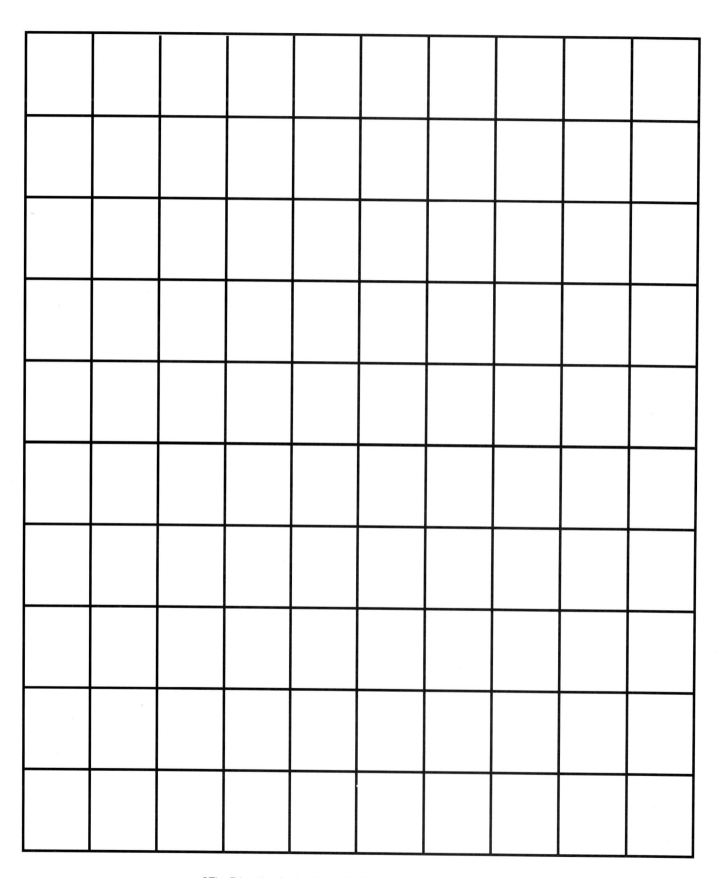

Note To The Teacher: Use with "Count On It!" on page 137.

HERE COMES SPRING!

Planting, building, cleaning, chirping, growing, wakening...it must be spring! Use the following activities to chase away those winter doldrums and spark an epidemic of spring fever. Your little ones will be amazed at the changes happening all around.

ideas contributed by Barbara Backer and Angie Kutzer

SPRING'S MYSTERIES

Introduce your spring unit with this guessing game. To prepare, cover a box with gift wrap or Con-Tact® covering in a springtime print. Put a collection of spring-related objects inside the box—such as a bird's feather, a small blossom, an umbrella, and a pack of seeds. During group time, tell your students that they are going to guess what the next unit of study will be. Have a child come forward and pick one clue from the box. Direct him to show it to the group. Ask for the object's name; then ask if anyone has a guess for the unit's topic. Have another child pick a clue from the box. Question the children again. Repeat this procedure until all of the objects have been chosen and named. End the activity by affirming children's guesses that it's all about spring!

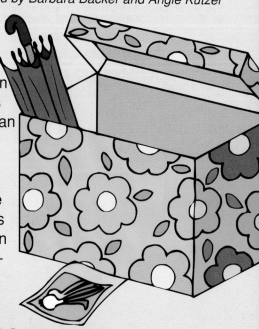

SPRING THINGS
kites
bunnies
robins
flowers
green leaves

SPRING THINGS

Channel all of the excitement aroused during "Spring's Mysteries" into a brainstorming session. In advance cut a large sun shape from bulletin-board paper. Read *When Spring Comes* by Robert Maass (Henry Holt And Company) to your group, and discuss the many characteristics of this season. List these spring words and phrases on the sun cutout along with the title "Spring Things." Keep this list handy so that students can add to it during the rest of the unit.

LOOKING FOR SPRING

Once your little ones have made a good listing of spring things, grab your camera and take your group outdoors to search for signs of spring. Take an instant picture of each child holding or pointing to an item that indicates spring has arrived. Return to the classroom, attach the pictures to a sheet of chart paper, and take dictation about each child's find. Hang this refreshing chart out in the hallway to remind everyone that spring has sprung!

"I found a pretty flower."

Payton

TIME TO PLANT!

Spring means warm, moist soil—perfect for planting! Use the story *The Garden In Our Yard* by Greg Henry Quinn (Scholastic Inc.) to help your little ones understand the yearly cycle of a garden. Use the reproducible on page 145 to encourage your students to "plant" their own gardens. Have each child draw what she would like to grow in a garden. Write her completion to the sentence, "I will plant _____ in my garden." Provide real seeds for your children to glue in the "dirt" at the bottoms of their pages. Combine these pictures in a class book titled "Our Gardens." Imaginations are sure to sprout up all kinds of garden goodies!

A CLASS OF GRASS

Give your budding gardeners some hands-on experience with plant growth. Divide the number of children in your group in half and obtain that many large, Styrofoam® take-out boxes. Cut on the hinge of each box, separating the lids from the plates. You will also need a bag of potting soil, a few misting bottles, and a bag of grass seed. Distribute a lid or plate to each child. Have him scoop some soil out of the bag and lightly pack it in his tray. Then direct him to sprinkle two or three handfuls of seed over the dirt and to pat the seeds lightly into the soil. Pass around the filled misting bottles so that your little ones can water their seeds.

While waiting for the grass to grow, invite your youngsters to add some interest to their grass gardens. Have each child draw a house on construction paper, tape the house to a craft stick, and place it at the edge of his tray so that the grass will now resemble a front yard. Once the grass has grown quite a bit, give your little ones that spring experience that's not so cheerful to grown-ups— mowing the lawn! Encourage them to crank up their scissors and start trimming!

Note: Depending on the variety of seed, the grass should sprout in seven to ten days.

"TREE-RIFIC" SPRING

Explore the area outside your classroom to find a tree that has definite seasonal changes. On the same day each week, lead your children out to observe while you take a picture of the tree. Pin the photo to your classroom calendar and discuss with your youngsters how the tree has changed each week. Take these pictures until the tree completes its spring transformation. After the last discussion, use the photos in a pocket chart for a "tree-mendous" sequencing opportunity!

SCRUB-A-DUB!

Spring's warmer weather allows people to spruce up their homes and surroundings after the harshness of winter. Celebrate the new season by having a spring-cleaning day with your youngsters. They will enjoy sweeping sidewalks, scrubbing outside walls with soft brushes, and picking up litter and twigs. On an especially warm spring day, provide sponges and buckets of water for cleaning toy vehicles. Wash away winter and spiff up for spring!

A BUILDING BOOM

Construction also swings into high gear during spring's warm weather. Take a walk with your little ones to see if there is any new construction in your area. If so, walk by often to discuss the progress being made and to observe any machinery in action. Bring the skills of building to your class by setting up indoor and outdoor construction centers.

For an outdoor center, provide tools sized correctly for young children, wood scraps, safety goggles, and preschool nails (one inch long with broad, flat heads). Draw spring designs on thick tree-stump pieces for students to trace by hammering nails. Before opening the center, model safety rules and establish a limit to the number of workers at the center at one time. (As always, supervision is the best precaution.)

For an indoor center, provide containers of pretzel sticks, gumdrops, large marshmallows, toothpicks, Gummy candies, and caramel cubes. Encourage your little ones to construct a few edible edifices. Hard hats are desired, but not required!

MANUFACTURING MELODY

Teach your little ones the following song to sing as they pantomime motions or build structures at the centers described in "A Building Boom":

BUILDING A NEW HOUSE!
(sung to the tune of "Jimmy Crack Corn")

Look at them hit and pound the nails.
Look at them tote the cement pails.
Look at them paint the tall porch rails.
They're building a new house!

Name _____

I will plant _____ in my garden.

Note To The Teacher: Use with "Time To Plant!" on page 143.

WILD And

No "lion"! "Ewe" and your little ones will enjoy springing into March with these thematic lion and lamb activities!

So It's Been Said

Introduce your youngsters to the wacky weather of March by explaining the old saying, "March comes in like a lion and goes out like a lamb." Discuss with your students characteristics of lions (wild and loud) and lambs (quiet and gentle). Then explain that March's weather is wild and ferocious like a lion one day, then gentle and quiet like a lamb the next. Track the changes in March's weather with a duplicated supply of calendar tags using the patterns on page 150. (Or use lion and lamb rubber stamps or stickers for this activity.) Each day during March, discuss the weather and have students decide if it's a "lion day" (cold and windy) or a "lamb day" (warm and sunny). Have a student volunteer use a removable glue stick to attach the appropriate tag to the date on the classroom calendar.

March
Did we have more lion days or more lamb days?
Lions 🦁🦁🦁🦁🦁🦁🦁🦁🦁🦁🦁🦁🦁🦁🦁🦁
Lambs 🐑🐑🐑🐑🐑🐑🐑🐑🐑🐑🐑🐑🐑🐑🐑
We had __16__ lion days.
We had __15__ lamb days.
We had more __lion__ days.

At the end of the month, have children remove the calendar tags and sort them into two groups—lions and lambs. Then create a graph similar to the one shown. Ask students to count the calendar tags in each row. Were there more lion or lamb days in March?

Lions And Lambs Math

Get your students roaring about math with some activities that provide additional uses for the lion and lamb patterns at the top of page 150.

A Pride Of Patterns

Supply each child with a 2 1/2" x 9" strip of paper programmed with a pattern (as shown) and a copy of the lion and lamb reproducibles. Have each student continue the pattern by gluing the reproducibles to his strip. Ask more advanced children to create their own lion and lamb patterns.

A Flock Of Numbers

Improve your students' one-to-one correspondence skills with this nifty number book. Use seven sheets of construction paper to create a book with a cover and six pages. On the front cover, write "Our Lion And Lamb Counting Book." Starting with page one, write "0 Lambs," followed by "1 Lion" on the back of that page. Continue to alternate lions and lambs as the numbers increase to ten.

Then duplicate and cut apart ten copies of the lion and lamb patterns on page 150. On each page, have students identify the numeral and the animal name; then have student volunteers glue the correct number of lions or lambs to the page.

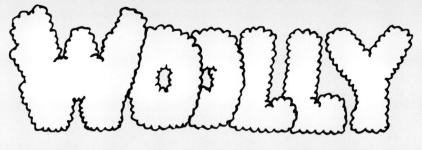

ideas contributed by Mary Sue Chatfield, Ada Hanley Goren, and Sharon Murphy

Lion And Lamb Lore

Lion Facts
- Lions are members of the cat family.
- They are large and very strong.
- Only male lions have the thick hair called *manes* on their heads and necks.
- Lions live on grassy plains in groups called *prides*.
- A male is called a *lion,* a female is called a *lioness,* and a baby is called a *cub.*
- Cubs drink a lioness's milk until they are 1 1/2 months old.
- Adults eat zebra, antelope, buffalo, deer, and gazelles.

Lamb Facts
- Lambs are members of the sheep family.
- A male sheep is called a *ram,* a female is called a *ewe,* and a baby is called a *lamb.*
- Sheep live in groups called *flocks* and are usually found in pastures, on farms, and sometimes on dry plains (because they can live without water for long periods of time).
- People raise sheep mainly for food and for their woolly coats.
- Lambs drink their mother's milk.
- Sheep eat grass, grains, hay, wood, and shrubs.

After sharing these facts, divide your little ones into groups of five and invite them to adapt the familiar rhyme "This Little Piggy Went To Market" to fit a lion or a lamb. First explain to your students that—in the original rhyme—the first two lines tell where a pig might go, lines three and four tell what a pig might eat, and line five tells the sound a pig makes. Provide help to each group as children work to create either a lion or a lamb rhyme similar to the ones shown. Write each line from each group's rhyme on a lion or lamb cutout or a sheet from a shaped notepad (one line per page). Have each student illustrate one line of her group's poem. Then add covers and staple each group's illustrations together to form booklets.

This little lamb went to the pasture.
This little lamb stayed in the barn.
This little lamb had milk to drink.
This little lamb had grass.
This little lamb cried, "Baa, baa, baa,"
   all the way home.

This little lion went out on the plain.
This little lion stayed with its mother.
This little lion had wildebeest.
This little lion had gazelle.
This little lion cried, "Meow, meow, meow,"
   all the way home.

Lovable Lambs

Invite students to read, draw, and write about lambs with this idea. To begin, share with your little ones *Mary Had A Little Lamb* by Sarah J. Hale (Scholastic Inc., 1992). This book gives the familiar nursery rhyme a contemporary interpretation with its beautiful photographs. After a first read-through, encourage your youngsters to read (or sing) the first part of it by themselves. Repeated readings will help them become familiar with the additional verses. Next provide each student with a simple cutout of a lamb. Have students use glue, cotton balls, and construction paper to cover and decorate their lambs as shown.

Near the bottom of an 8 1/2" x 11" piece of white paper, write "_____ had a little lamb"; then duplicate a class supply. Photograph each student holding his lamb. When the photographs have been developed, glue each picture to one of the duplicated sheets. Have each child write his name on the blank. Then have him dictate a second line telling something about his lamb. (Ask more advanced students to dictate some facts they have learned about lambs.) Compile the pages into a class book titled "We All Have Little Lambs."

Lion And Lamb Lyrics

Get your youngsters in tune with the names of lion and lamb family members with some flannelboard cutouts and singing. Duplicate and color the flannelboard patterns on page 150. Laminate the designs before cutting out each one. Attach the hook side of a piece of Velcro® to the back of each design. Now you're ready to get your flannelboard out and start singing these rhymes to the tune of "Row, Row, Row Your Boat."

Sheep, sheep, sheep, I see.
Daddy's called a *ram*.
See the mother called a *ewe*,
With her baby lamb.

Lions, lions, lions, I see.
Together in a pride.
Mother's called a *lioness*;
Cubs are by her side.

Masks Worth Roaring About

You'll get a roaring response as you nurture students' creative sides with these lion masks. Supply each child with a paper plate (with the inside circle cut out) and ten 3-inch squares each of yellow and brown tissue paper. Instruct each student to place his pointer finger in the middle of a tissue square and wrap the tissue paper around his finger. Next have him dip his folded tissue in glue and place it on the paper plate. Have him alternate the colors of tissue paper as he continues the pattern around the paper-plate circle. Help each youngster draw and cut out two ears from brown construction paper; then staple them to the top of his paper plate. Use glue or a staple to attach a craft stick. Paint your youngsters' noses with black face paint and have them put on their masks. Then lead your pride of lions on a parade throughout the school!

Wild Or Tame?

Reinforce students' classification skills with the lion and lamb theme and two Hula-Hoop® rings. To begin, discuss the words *domesticated* and *wild*. Lambs are domesticated animals. They are cared for by farmers who are responsible for providing food, water, and shelter for them. Lions have to find their own food, water, and shelter; therefore they are considered wild animals. Have your students look through magazines to gather pictures of many different animals. Then place two Hula-Hoop® rings on the floor in an overlapping position and label the hoops as shown. As each child shares an animal picture, invite the class to help her decide into which category the picture should be placed. Help your students determine which animals might fall into the overlapping category (such as birds, rabbits, mice, and snakes). Continue this activity until each child has had a chance to share and place a picture.

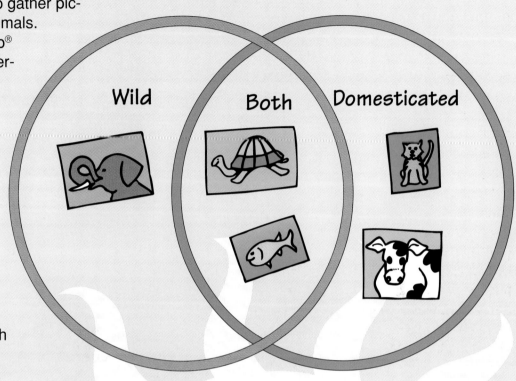

Hungry As A Lion!

Celebrate the end of your wild and woolly unit by making lion and lamb cookies. Roll out refrigerated cookie dough, cut into 3 1/2-inch circles, and bake as directed on the package. Then invite your youngsters to add the following ingredients to make these springtime cookies:

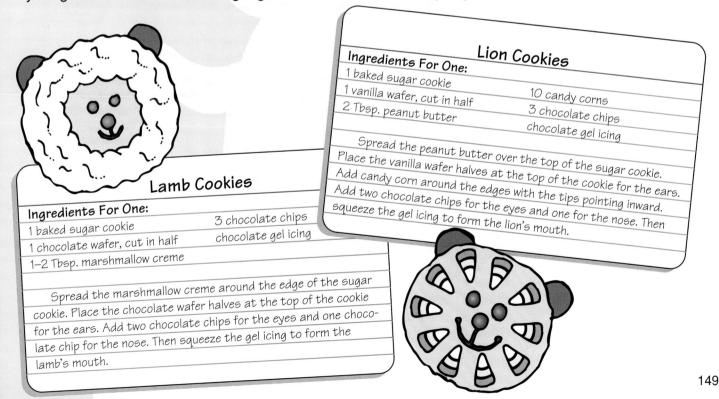

Lion Cookies

Ingredients For One:
1 baked sugar cookie
1 vanilla wafer, cut in half   10 candy corns
2 Tbsp. peanut butter   3 chocolate chips
                                    chocolate gel icing

Spread the peanut butter over the top of the sugar cookie. Place the vanilla wafer halves at the top of the cookie for the ears. Add candy corn around the edges with the tips pointing inward. Add two chocolate chips for the eyes and one for the nose. Then squeeze the gel icing to form the lion's mouth.

Lamb Cookies

Ingredients For One:
1 baked sugar cookie   3 chocolate chips
1 chocolate wafer, cut in half   chocolate gel icing
1–2 Tbsp. marshmallow creme

Spread the marshmallow creme around the edge of the sugar cookie. Place the chocolate wafer halves at the top of the cookie for the ears. Add two chocolate chips for the eyes and one chocolate chip for the nose. Then squeeze the gel icing to form the lamb's mouth.

Lion And Lamb Patterns

Use with "So It's Been Said" and "Lions And Lambs Math" on page 146.

Flannelboard Patterns

Use with "Lion And Lamb Lyrics" on page 148.

Pyramid Power

Celebrate National Nutrition Month® with a hearty helping of these activities that feed the mind and promote healthful eating habits!

ideas contributed by Linda Gordetsky and Angie Kutzer

Food Riddles

Introduce your children to the topic of nutrition by using the book *What Food Is This?* by Rosmarie Hausherr (Scholastic Inc.). Read aloud the riddle on each page before showing children the illustration. After sharing the book, invite each child to ask her own riddle about a favorite food. Follow this activity with a discussion about the importance of food. Explain that everyone needs a certain amount of food each day in order to grow and be active. Getting this amount of food is called *nutrition*. Inform your students that all food can be sorted into six groups. Name the groups, pausing after each one to see if students can identify any food items in that group. Then let the food follies begin!

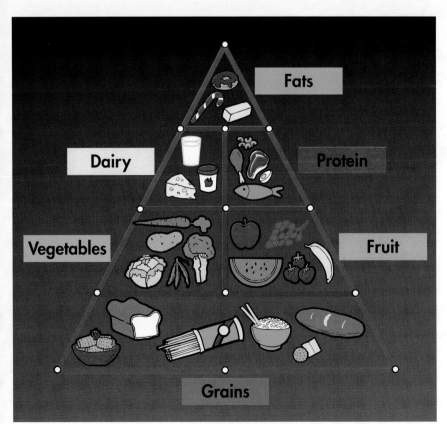

The Grub Groups

Guide your students' understanding of the basic food groups with this appetizing collage display. Prepare a large outline of the Food Guide Pyramid on a bulletin board by using pushpins and colorful yarn as shown. Write each food group's title on a different colored construction-paper strip and attach the strip beside its designated group's area on the display. Have each of your little ones search through magazines to find a picture of a food that he likes to eat. Instruct him to cut his choice from the magazine and return to the area in front of the display. Encourage each child to tell his classmates what he found and to name its correct group. Staple his food in its place on the display. If the display is not full of grub after everyone's turn, challenge your students to find more foods during their free time to add to the collage.

151

The Pyramid Poem

Reinforce the concept of the Food Guide Pyramid with this "munchy" masterpiece. During the first reading, point to each group on the pyramid as you spell out its specifics. Then serve more helpings of this poem and have youngsters do the pointing. (The numbers of servings noted in the poem reflect the minimum amounts needed daily.)

At the top of the pyramid
Sit lots of good treats.
But to be in good shape,
Eat just a few sweets.

The next group is dairy—
Milk, yogurt, and cheese.
For strong teeth and bones,
Eat two helpings of these.

Next to dairy are proteins—
Fish, eggs, nuts, and meat.
Two servings for energy;
These foods can't be beat.

Below is the fruit group
Full of vitamin C.
Two servings are needed
To keep you healthy.

Beside are the vegetables.
They're plants that we crunch.
To get lots of fiber,
Three servings we munch.

And, finally, the grain group—
Breads, pasta, and rice.
Eat six or more servings
Of these to feel nice!

Nutrition All Around

Provide lots of hands-on experiences for your little ones by including the following food props in your learning centers during this unit:

Building Area: Stuff empty food boxes and containers with paper, and encourage the construction of pyramid shapes!

Sand Table: Fill the table with sand, potting soil, or rice. Bury a variety of plastic veggies and invite children to dig them up with hand tools used for gardening.

Dramatic Play Area: Create a restaurant atmosphere with chef hats, order pads, aprons, menus, and play food.

Math Area: Wash and dry empty milk cartons, and label each one with a numeral. Provide a box of straws for counting practice and matching numerals to sets.

Art Area: Encourage the making of sweet treats! Fill this center with colored play dough, cookie cutters, rolling pins, and cupcake liners.

Reading Area: Roll over a play shopping cart full of good literature on the subject of food!

The Sensational Six!

Knowing the six food groups is important for obtaining good nutrition and balancing meals. Use these activities to focus on each food group.

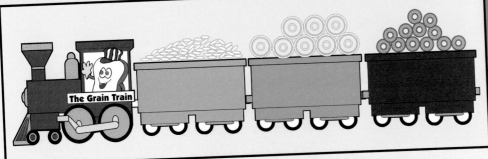

Pam Crane

Grains Are Great!

To prepare, enlarge and duplicate the train patterns on page 158 so that each child has one engine and three cars. Mix together a box of pasta, a box of rice, and a box of cereal. Put this mixture into bowls for your children to share. Cut a construction-paper strip that measures 6" x 18" for each child. Bring in a bowl of flour.

To begin this activity, have each child rub some flour between his thumb and fingers in order to feel its texture. Explain that this flour is actually a type of grass seed that has been ground into a powdery mixture. Refer back to the Food Guide Pyramid and have children name things that are made from grain. Then instruct your students to color and cut the train engine and cars from the paper. Have students assemble and glue their trains onto their construction-paper strips. Then encourage your little ones to sort and glue the rice, pasta, and cereal onto the separate cars. All aboard The Grain Train!

Dairy Delights

Emphasize the milk content in dairy products by making these "moo-velous" milk books. To prepare, obtain a classroom supply of small milk cartons. Open their tops and wash them out. When they are dry, cut the front and back panels from the cartons. To make the booklet pages, trace around the front panel of a carton four times on a sheet of paper. Program three of the pages with "Milk in my _____." Program the fourth page with "Milk is good for you!" Duplicate this master copy for each child.

To set the "moo-ood" for milk, read *No Moon, No Milk!* by Chris Babcock (Scholastic Inc.). After the story, direct your youngsters' attention back to the Food Guide Pyramid collage. Explain that all dairy products contain milk and that milk helps to make teeth and bones strong. Have your little ones name some dairy products. Distribute the photocopied sheet and the panels from one carton to each of your children. Instruct her to cut the pages apart and illustrate a different dairy product on each of the first three pages. On the last page, have her draw herself drinking a big glass of milk. When each child is finished, write her dictation on each page, arrange the pages between the panels, and staple the booklet at the top. Encourage your little ones to take their booklets home to share with their families.

153

Please Pass The Proteins!

Have your children imagine that they are cars. Ask them what they need to make them run. Accept all reasonable answers and stop when the answer is "Gas." Then ask what happens to them when they're all out of gas. Explain that the body needs food just like a car needs gas. *Protein* is one of the substances in food that provides gas, or energy, for the body. Refer to the Food Guide Pyramid display and name some foods that are rich in protein.

Teach your little ones the following rhyme. Invite each child to say the two-line stanza alone, filling in the blank with his favorite protein. Repeat the first verse together after each child's turn.

Eggs, nuts, meat, and fish.
Eggs, nuts, meat, and fish.
Put some protein on your dish.
Pick eggs, nuts, meat, or fish!

I like [protein food]; yes I do.
I eat proteins; how 'bout you?

Palatable Plants

The fruit and vegetable groups are similar in that they both contain foods that are plant parts. The horticultural difference is that *vegetables* may be the roots, leaves, stems, bulbs, or seeds of plants that have to be replanted annually; and *fruits* are the fleshy tissue containing the seeds of plants that live for more than two years without being replanted (perennials). Simplify this definition for children's understanding by saying that both fruits and vegetables are foods from plants; and fruits usually taste sweet.

For this fruit and veggie activity, enlarge and duplicate the mouse pattern on page 158 for each child. Discuss with your children the importance of eating fruits and vegetables because of all the vitamins and minerals that they contain. Share the book *Lunch* by Denise Fleming (Scholastic Inc.) with your children. Stop after each item the mouse eats, and ask your little ones if the item is a fruit or vegetable. Show the picture of the messy mouse on the last page and review what it ate. Encourage your children to name other fruits and vegetables that are the same colors. Hand each child a mouse pattern, and instruct him to color the mouse according to what fruits and vegetables he wants it to eat for dinner. Label each child's picture with his own menu to resemble the picture from the book. Display these pictures on a board with a paper-plate border and add the title "Dinnertime!"

Fat In The Hat

Show your little ones where the fats, oils, and sweets are located on the pyramid. Explain that they occupy the smallest part of the pyramid, to remind us to eat only a few. Bring in a hat full of items from this group—such as a candy bar, a snack-size bag of chips, an empty butter container, a soft-drink can, and a small bag of candy—and explain why each item belongs in this group. Play the following game with these items to improve problem-solving and visual-memory skills: Display the items and the hat on a tabletop. Ask a child to close his eyes while you hide one item under the hat. Invite the child to open his eyes and try to name the fat that's under the hat. Depending on the age group, you can add more items to increase the difficulty. Play until everyone has had a turn.

Not Again!

Use this game to help your children learn that variety is important in their diets. To prepare the game, make two identical sets of the food cards on page 157. Cut them apart and laminate them for durability. Place each set of the cards in a separate lunch bag.

To play, have two children sit across from one another, each holding a bag. To start, the children say, "Let's eat!" Each child reaches into his bag and pulls out one card. If the cards match, the children say, "Not again!", and the cards go back into the bags. If the cards do not match, the children say, "Mmmmm, something different!", and the cards stay on the table. Play continues in the same manner until all cards are on the table. Variety is the spice of life!

Skip To My Food!

This circle game will burn a few calories as your children skip around to improve their matching skills. Make multiple copies of a few of the food cards on page 157 so that each child has one. Cut out and then color each card, making sure the same foods look identical. Have your little ones stand in a circle. Distribute a card to each child and ask him to hold it so that the picture faces the outside of the circle. Choose one child to skip around the circle while singing the following song, inserting her food card's name where appropriate:

(sung to the tune of "Skip To My Lou")
I eat [food name]; so do you.
I eat [food name]; so do you.
I eat [food name]; so do you.
Tasty [food name]—good for you!

As she skips and sings, instruct the child to look at the other cards and find a child holding a match to her card. Have her tap him. He joins her in skipping and singing the verse again, looking for anyone else with a matching card. When all the matches have been found, collect their cards and choose a child holding a different card to skip. Play until the students run out of cards or energy—whichever comes first!

155

At The Most

Your little ones will practice matching, counting, and sorting in this nutrition activity. To prepare, duplicate the cards on page 157 so that there are two picture cards for fats, three cards for proteins, four cards for dairy, three cards for fruits, five cards for vegetables, and eleven cards for grains. Place these cards in a mixing bowl. On each of six index cards, write one of the following numbers: 2, 3, 3, 4, 5, and 11. Seat your children in front of a pocket chart. Put the number cards in a row at the bottom of the chart; then put one card from each food group into the chart (in its own row) to start the sorting. Invite each child to come forward, pick a card from the bowl, and place it in the correct row according to its food group. When all cards are sorted, have your children count each row and name the food group. Then direct one child to find the matching number and place it at the end of the row. Explain to your young eaters that these numbers and pictures show the *most* of a particular food group that should be eaten each day.

At The Least

To promote more healthful eating habits and balanced meals, make your children Keeping Track pockets. To make a pocket, cut a four-inch strip from the tab side of a letter-size file folder. Then cut the file folder in half as shown, making two folders. To make a pocket, open each folder, fold 1 1/2 inches from the bottom of the folder up, and staple the sides. Label the front of the mini folder "Keeping Track." Write "Eat It" on the left pocket and "Ate It" on the right pocket. Have children decorate the outsides of their folders by printing with vegetables, fruits, or pasta pieces dipped in paint.

Cut two-inch-square cards from colored construction paper that matches the colors of the titles on the Food Guide Pyramid display from "The Grub Groups" on page 151. Each child will need the following cards: one fat, two proteins, two dairy, two fruits, three vegetables, and six grains. These cards represent the *minimum* number of daily servings that a child needs from each of the food groups in order to maintain a balanced diet. When the paints on the folders have dried, place the servings cards in the "Eat It" pocket.

The next day, hand the folders to your children. Ask each child to tell what he ate for breakfast, and assist him in moving the corresponding cards over to the "Ate It" pocket. Do this again with your little ones after lunch and snacktime. Encourage your students to take their folders home and tell their parents about healthful eating. Challenge your little nutritionists to move the remaining servings cards to the "Ate It" pocket by eating the needed foods for dinner.

Food Cards

Use with "Skip To My Food!" and "Not Again!" on page 155 and "At The Most" on page 156.

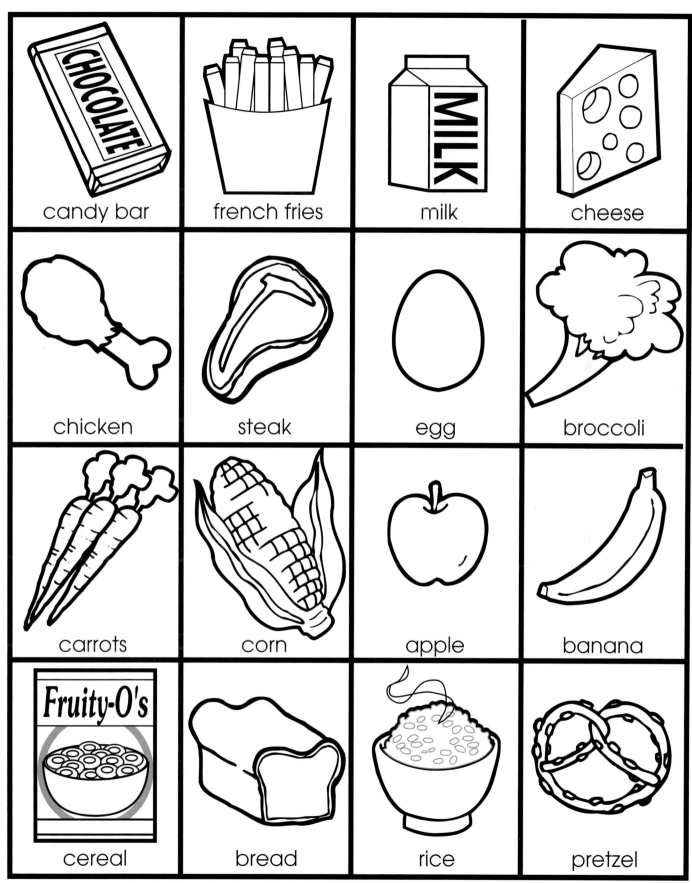

candy bar

french fries

milk

cheese

chicken

steak

egg

broccoli

carrots

corn

apple

banana

cereal

bread

rice

pretzel

Train Patterns
Use with "Grains Are Great!" on page 153.

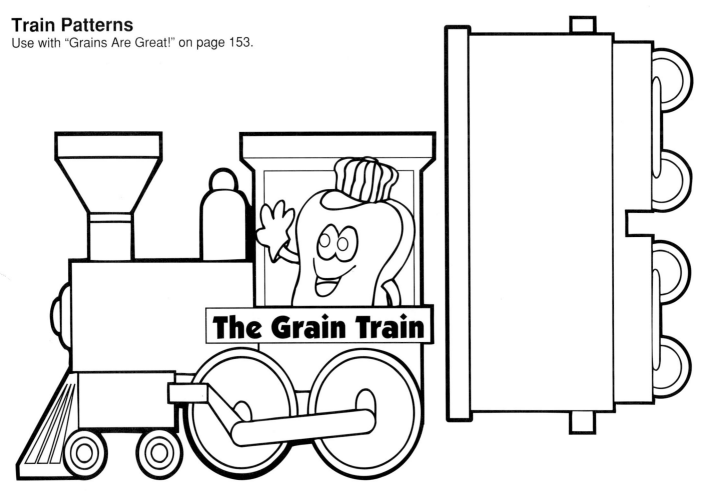

The Grain Train

Mouse Pattern
Use with "Palatable Plants" on page 154.

"Hares" To Bunnies!

Give a cheer because "every-bunny" loves bunnies! And what a perfect time to hop into a unit about rabbits with spring thriving and Easter arriving. So let Peter Cottontail guide you down the trail to lots of exciting bunny-related activities.

ideas contributed by Jan Brennan and Stacie Davis

This Little Bunny

Bound into your bunny unit with this rhyme and the cute bunny pattern on page 164. In advance enlarge the bunny pattern onto chart paper or poster board. Color it as desired; then use masking tape to attach the poster to your chalkboard. Next read the "This Little Bunny" poem below aloud to students. As you read the poem, point out the bunny's features on the poster. Afterward invite students to share what they know about rabbits. Write students' responses on the bunny poster; then hang it in a prominent classroom location.

Bunnies eat carrots.
Charles

They're soft.
Frankie

Bunnies are cute.
Dana

This Little Bunny

This little bunny has two big ears,
Long and tall to help him hear.
This little bunny has a nose so small,
It helps him smell—but that's not all.
This little bunny has strong legs to hop,
He runs and runs and doesn't like to stop.
This little bunny has short legs in front,
To help him balance when he's on a hunt.
And this little bunny has a fluffy round tail.
It's the last part we see when he hops
    down the trail.

—Jan Brennan

A Bonanza Of Bunny Facts

After students have had the opportunity to share their knowledge about bunnies, read aloud a nonfiction book such as *See How They Grow: Rabbit* photographed by Barrie Watts (Lodestar Books). Then share some more fascinating facts about rabbits with your little learners.

- Rabbits rely on their long, sensitive ears to help them hear sounds from all directions.
- Rabbits lose body heat through their ears. This helps keep them cool in hot weather.
- Rabbits have a very keen sense of smell that helps them sense when danger is near.
- Rabbits have very powerful back legs. If frightened, rabbits can leap ten or more feet to escape danger.
- Rabbits will run in a zigzag pattern to escape from enemies.
- Enemies of rabbits include coyotes, foxes, weasels, snakes, hawks, and owls.
- During the summer months, rabbits eat clover, weeds, and grass. During the winter months, rabbits eat twigs, fruit, and bark from bushes and trees.

Bunches Of Bunnies

Another interesting fact about bunnies—they have lots of babies! To emphasize this fact, share the story *Bunches And Bunches Of Bunnies* by Louise Mathews (Scholastic Inc.). After reading the story, explain that female rabbits reproduce several times a year. Each time rabbits give birth, they have approximately five babies.

Then try this activity to help students better understand this phenomenon. Use two stuffed rabbits to represent the mother and father bunnies and 25 cotton balls to represent baby rabbits. Then enlist students' help in selecting five different calendar dates. (For younger students, ask volunteers to point to five date squares on a yearlong calendar to determine the dates.) Designate those dates as the days on which baby rabbits will be "born." Next ask students to pretend that it is the first date they've selected and put five cotton balls next to the stuffed rabbits. If desired, sing "Happy Birthday To You" to the baby rabbits. Repeat this process four more times. Then enlist students' help in counting how many babies are born to one set of rabbits in a given year. My goodness—that's a lot of brothers and sisters!

Nibble, Nibble, Crunch!

Tell students that during the winter months—when grass and leaves are scarce or covered with snow—rabbits feed on twigs and bark. During the spring and summer months, rabbits feed on leafy green plants like clover, grass, and weeds. Rabbits also like to nibble on bean sprouts, peas, lettuce, and other vegetables.

Does all this talk of food have your little ones ready for a snack? If so, try making Rabbit-Food Salad. To make the salad, put bite-size lettuce and spinach pieces into a large bowl. (Introduce your students to different varieties of lettuce by using romaine, endive, and/or escarole in the salad.) Mix peas, bean sprouts, and sliced carrots with the greens and you've got yourself a tasty treat that any rabbit would envy! Provide a variety of dressings and give each child a serving of the salad in a disposable bowl. As each child samples his salad, read aloud *The Tale Of Peter Rabbit* by Beatrix Potter (Scholastic Inc.)

Bunny Tag

After reading aloud *The Tale Of Peter Rabbit*, discuss how Peter's desire for food from Mr. McGregor's garden led to all sorts of problems. Peter had to use speed to escape from the angry Mr. McGregor. Remind students that real rabbits use not only speed but also a zigzag running pattern to escape from their enemies.

With that fact in mind, head outdoors or to the gym to play a game of Bunny Tag. First select one volunteer to be Mr. McGregor. Have the remainder of the students pretend to be rabbits. Designate one area to serve as the rabbits' burrow. Tell each rabbit to find a spot away from the burrow and stand there quietly. Then, on a signal, have Mr. McGregor run toward the rabbits. If a rabbit feels that Mr. McGregor is too close, encourage him to jump forward, then zigzag back and forth as he runs toward safety in the designated burrow. If Mr. McGregor is able to tag a rabbit, the rabbit may be Mr. McGregor for the next round of play. Continue until your little bunnies are ready to flop!

Bunny Headbands

Get your little ones hopping with these bunny headbands. Provide each child with the following materials: one 2" x 24" strip of white construction paper, one 1" x 4 1/2" strip of white construction paper, two rabbit-ear shapes cut from white construction paper, one rabbit-nose shape cut from pink construction paper, a pink crayon, and glue. To make a headband, first fit each child's 2" x 24" paper strip to his head and staple the ends together. Have him use a pink crayon to color the ears as shown, then glue the ears to his headband. Next direct each student to glue his 1" x 4 1/2" paper strip to the headband as shown. Complete the project by having each child glue the construction-paper nose to the end of the construction-paper strip.

Bunny Melodies

Teach your students these tunes. Encourage students to wear their headbands while singing and acting out these songs.

I'm A Little Bunny
(sung to the tune of "I'm A Little Teapot")

I'm a little bunny, soft and sweet.
Here are my ears and here are my feet.
When I'm in the garden, I look for treats,
And nibble on all I like to eat.

My Bunny Hops
All Through The Garden
(sung to the tune of "My Bonnie Lies Over The Ocean")

My bunny hops all through the garden.
My bunny hops all through the yard.
I like to play tag with my bunny,
But trying to catch him is hard.

Come back, come back,
Oh, come back, my bunny, to me, to me.
Come back, come back,
Oh, come back, my bunny, to me.

My bunny is so soft and spunky.
My bunny is a friend to me.
My bunny is such fun to play with.
Come join us and you, too, will see.

Come back, come back,
Oh, come back, my bunny, to me, to me.
Come back, come back,
Oh, come back, my bunny, to me.

More Bunny Books To Nibble On

Here are some more good books about bunnies, just right for the Easter season—or anytime!

The April Rabbits by David Cleveland (Scholastic Inc.)
Bunny Trouble by Hans Wilhelm (Scholastic Inc.)
The Little Rabbit Who Wanted Red Wings by Carolyn Sherwin Bailey (Platt & Munk, Publishers)
Seven Little Rabbits by John Becker (Scholastic Inc.)

Come back, come back. Come back my bunny to me, to me.

Bunny Pattern
Use with "This Little Bunny" on page 160.

Here, Chicky, Chicky!

Youngsters delight in the sight of a soft, yellow chick. Encourage investigation and discovery with this coop full of chick activities.

ideas contributed by Lori Kent and Angie Kutzer

An Extraordinary Introduction

Storytime is the perfect time to introduce this chick unit. Put a stuffed toy chick in a paper bag; then read aloud *An Extraordinary Egg* by Leo Lionni (Scholastic Inc.) You probably won't finish the story without hearing cries of, "That's not a chicken!" After the reading, put on your acting face and with a puzzled look, ask your little ones why they didn't think the baby alligator was a chick. Pretending not to know what a chick looks like, ask them to describe one for you. With an understanding grin, pull the toy chick out of the bag and inform your group that chicks will be the next unit of study. Peep! Peep!

Plump Peepers

Your little ones will chirp with delight during this weighing activity. To prepare, fill several plastic eggs with different amounts of rice. Close each egg and tape around its seam to prevent the egg from separating. If desired, use paint pens to paint eyes and a beak on each egg. Have a student volunteer use a platform scale or a balance scale in order to weigh each egg. As each egg is weighed and compared, have a student sequence the eggs from heaviest to lightest. Leave the scale and eggs out for more weighing discoveries to be made during free time.

165

All Cracked Up

Hand and shoe prints hatch some excitement in this art project! Give each pair of students two sheets of white and one sheet of yellow construction paper. Help them trace each other's hands onto the white paper. Then have each student trace the bottom of her partner's shoe onto the yellow paper. Instruct each child to cut out her own hand and shoe prints. Direct her to turn the shoe print upside down so that the heel is at the top; then have her draw eyes (or glue on wiggle eyes) and a beak on the heel part of the cutout. To make the egg, glue the handprint cutouts—palms touching and fingers out at the sides—to the bottom of the chick. Display these newly hatched chicks on a bulletin board titled "All Cracked Up!"

An "Egg-cellent" Story

A chick's development inside an egg is a fascinating, yet hard-to-explain wonder for little ones. *Egg Story* by Anca Hariton (Dutton Children's Books) provides an excellent explanation for you to share with your children. After the story, let your little cheepers dramatize hatching as you teach them the following song:

The Chick In The Egg
(sung to the tune of "The Wheels On The Bus")

The hen on the farm lays a smooth white egg,
Smooth white egg, smooth white egg.
The hen on the farm lays a smooth white egg,
Cluck, cluck, cluck, cluck, cluck!

Inside the egg grows a little chick,
Little chick, little chick.
Inside the egg grows a little chick,
In twenty-one days.

The chick has a beak to crack the egg,
Crack the egg, crack the egg.
The chick has a beak to crack the egg,
Tap, tap, tap, tap, tap!

He hatches from the egg and flaps his wings,
Flaps his wings, flaps his wings.
He hatches from the egg and flaps his wings,
Flap, flap, flap, flap, flap!

The hen keeps her chick warm in the nest,
In the nest, in the nest.
The hen keeps her chick warm in the nest,
Peep, peep, peep, peep, peep!

Cheeper Sleeper

Encourage each of your youngsters to share his chick knowledge with his family by sending the stuffed toy chick from "An Extraordinary Introduction" on page 165 home for a sleep over. Put the chick in a straw-filled basket along with a journal, a favorite bedtime story, and some granola "chick feed" to share with its hosts. Attach a parent note to explain the activity and request that a page in the journal be written about the night's festivities. When the child and chick return the next day, read his journal entry to the class and invite him to share any other details about his sleep over. Your students will each be eager to be the next one who entertains!

The Reading Nest

Invite your children to relax in the reading nest while enjoying a chick story from the list below. To create a nest, fill an inexpensive baby pool with raffia and a few white pillow "eggs." Complete the environment by sprinkling a few colored craft feathers around the nest. This nest will entice every youngster in the room over to check out some chicks in print.

Books To Chirp About

Birthday Chickens
Written by Shirley Kurtz
Published by Good Books®

Minerva Louise At School
Written by Janet Morgan Stoeke
Published by Dutton Children's Books

Here Comes Henny
Written by Charlotte Pomerantz
Published by Greenwillow Books

Chick Chow

Your little chicks will love scratching and pecking for worms with this outside game. Make the worms ahead of time by bending brown pipe cleaners into curvy worm shapes. Then scatter the pipe-cleaner worms in a grassy area. Get a paper plate; then lead your class outside and divide them into small groups. Designate a certain number of worms for the groups to find. As a child finds a worm, have her run back to you and place it on the plate. On your signal, send one group at a time to "peck" for worms while the other groups count the worms that are placed on the plate. Be sure to have a bag of Gummy Worms® ready for the chicks who peck their way into a feeding frenzy!

The Sky Is Falling!

Your chick unit won't be complete until you introduce your youngsters to that infamous chick, Chicken Licken. Add a hip-hop twist to this traditional tale by using the rap version "Chickey Lickey" found on the Once Upon A Rhyme collection by CJ & Friends. (This tape can be ordered through National Educational Network at 1-800-537-6647.) Toes will be tappin' and wings will be flappin' to this funky beat. After several playings of the song, have student volunteers pantomime along with the music. Duplicate the characters on page 169 onto construction paper for each child. Have your little ones color and cut out the animal pictures, then tape the pictures to craft sticks for their own puppet show—to the beat, of course!

Chickie's Walk

This class-made big book will definitely be a group favorite! Read aloud the story *Rosie's Walk* by Pat Hutchins (Aladdin Books); then ask your students to recall some of the places Rosie visited. Emphasize any positional words that your children use to describe where Rosie walked. Inform your students that each of them will be illustrating a different place for Rosie's baby, Chickie, to visit. Give each child a piece of paper; then write her dictation as she tells you where the chick is walking. Remind her to use a positional word in her phrase. Staple the pages inside a simple, barn-shaped cover made from construction paper. Share the complete story of "Chickie's Walk" with your class.

A "Cheep" Snack

Gather the following ingredients together in your cooking center and assist your little ones in making these chick treats. Purchase (or ask parents to donate) a package of Nutter-Butter® cookies, plastic knives or craft sticks, vanilla frosting (tinted yellow), candy corn, and chocolate chips. To make a chick, spread frosting over a cookie; then add two chocolate-chip eyes and a candy-corn beak. These goodies will end your chick unit with lots of peeps, cheeps, and mmmmmms!

Taking Care Of Our Earth

The environmental concerns that launched the first Earth Day on April 22, 1970, continue to be today's concerns as we work to nurture our Earth back to health. Use these multidisciplinary activities to awaken your youngsters' awareness of ecological issues and to motivate them to take action in helping to restore our planet.

ideas contributed by Carrie Lacher and Mackie Rhodes

Sharing Nature

Capitalize on each child's curiosity and fascination with nature by making it a part of his daily environment—and promote an appreciation and respect for the earth in the process! In advance prepare a nature center with some magnifying glasses, measuring devices, a scale, paper, writing utensils, and a display area. For each child, duplicate the parent request letter on page 174; then laminate each letter for durability. Put the letter in a large, resealable storage bag labeled with the child's name. Each week send the bag home with the child. When he returns his nature item to school, invite him to place it in the nature center. If desired, write his dictated description or name of his item on a notecard and place the card with his item. Each time the child brings a new nature item to school, have him replace the item he brought previously. Encourage youngsters to make regular visits to the nature center to investigate the items on display. Engage them in discussions about the items and invite them to illustrate some of their discoveries. It's a natural fact—youngsters are fascinated by nature!

The Earth And I Are Friends

Introduce youngsters to a dear friend—Earth! To begin show students a globe. Explain that the globe represents Earth and its many different geographical features—such as land, oceans, mountains, and deserts. Invite a volunteer to help you locate your school's approximate location on the globe. If desired, mark that spot with a smiley-face sticker. Then read aloud *The Earth And I* by Frank Asch (published by Harcourt Brace & Company). Afterward ask youngsters to describe some ways in which they are friends with Earth. Can they name some things that make Earth sad? Happy? Write each student's response about an Earth-friendly activity on a small sheet of note paper. Then use a smiley-face sticker to attach each note to a large bulletin-board-paper cutout decorated to resemble Earth. Display the cutout with the title "Friends With The Earth."

Helping Out—The Three Rs

Summarize how each of us can help make Earth a cleaner place to live with these three words—reduce, recycle, and reuse. Explain each of these terms to students, giving a few examples of each. Then teach youngsters the hand motion shown for each term. Invite them to sing this song, performing the hand motions each time the three Rs are mentioned.

Reduce, Recycle, Reuse
(sung to the tune of "Three Blind Mice")

Reduce, recycle, reuse.
Reduce, recycle, reuse.

Now's the time to choose.
There must be no excuse.

It's up to each one of us to do
Our part to make the Earth clean, it's true.
So let's work together—yes, me and you!

Reduce, recycle, reuse.

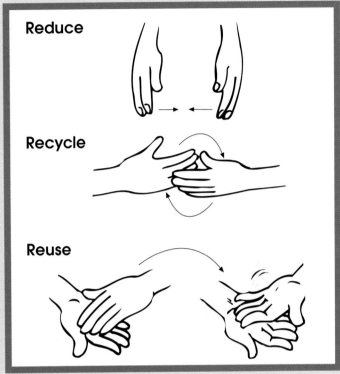

Earth-Friendly Families

Attract and hold the attention of your students and their families with these child-made magnetic reminders to participate in Earth-friendly activities. In advance duplicate the Earth pattern on page 173 on tagboard for each student. Also duplicate the song pattern on page 174 and the family letter on page 175 for each child. To make a magnet, have each child cut out his Earth and song patterns. Have him sponge-paint the Earth cutout with blue and green tempera paint. After the paint dries, instruct the child to glue the song onto his Earth cutout. Attach a strip of magnetic tape to the back of each child's cutout. Read a copy of the family letter to students; then have each child take home a copy of the letter with his magnet. Encourage youngsters to teach their families the song and to remind them to do their part in making our Earth clean.

Banding Together

Youngsters will identify with one another in their environmental efforts when they wear special armbands during Earth-friendly class projects. For each child, duplicate the armband pattern on page 176 on a sheet of tagboard. Have the child cut out her pattern; then invite her to embellish her cutout with her choice of boldly colored markers or glitter crayons. To make the armband, punch a hole near each corner of the cutout. Thread a separate length of narrow elastic through each hole on one side of the armband; then thread each piece of elastic through the hole on the opposite end of the band. Fit the armband to the child's arm and securely tie the elastic. Encourage each youngster to wear her armband during projects such as those described in "Pick A Project."

Pick A Project

Keep little ones continuously aware of the need to take care of our Earth by planning regular Earth-friendly projects. After obtaining permission from your school administrators, guide your class in selecting an area to "adopt" for scheduled cleanups. Or have students participate in seasonal projects such as planting in the spring, collecting paper trash from other classrooms after holiday celebrations, or making bird feeders from reusable items in the winter. Each time the children participate in an Earth-friendly project, invite them to wear their armbands made in "Banding Together."

Earth-Friendly Reading

This Is Our Earth
Written by Laura Lee Benson
Published by Charlesbridge Publishing

For The Love Of Our Earth
Written by P. K. Hallinan
Published by Ideals Children's Books

The Lorax
Written by Dr. Seuss
Published by Random Books For
  Young Readers

The Great Trash Bash
Written by Loreen Leedy
Published by Holiday House, Inc.

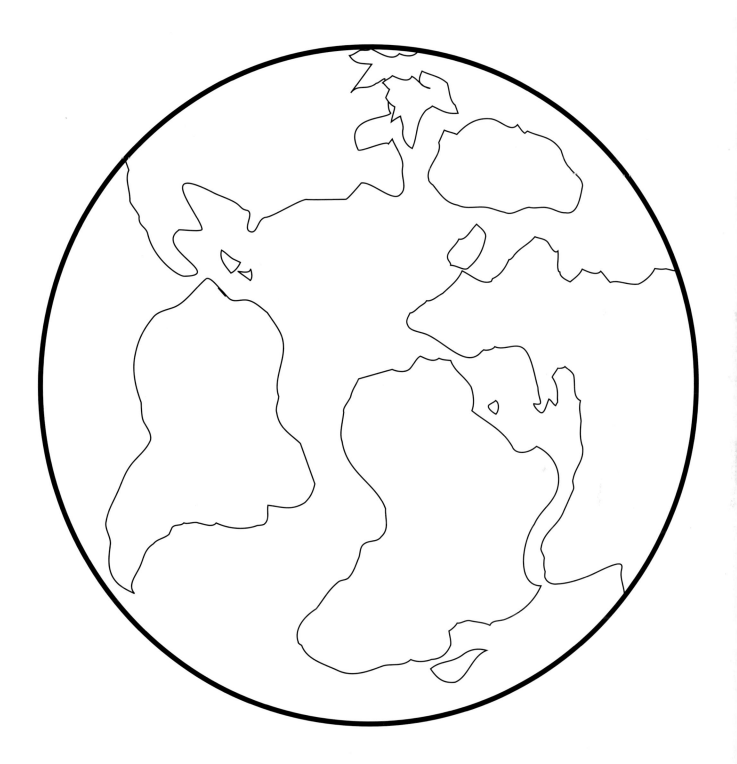

Parent Request Letter
Use with "Sharing Nature" on page 170.

Dear Parent,

Exploring and investigating things of nature is one way to help our children develop respect and appreciation for our Earth. As part of our study on Earth Day, it is requested that your child bring in an object of nature to include in our nature collection. Each week please take a little time to explore the outdoors with your child in search of an item to send to school—a pinecone, leaf, feather, unusual rock, or some other item. During your explorations, please be careful not to disturb the creatures and growing things in nature! Enclose the item in the bag provided and return the bag to school. Your child will have the opportunity to tell about the item and to add it to our collection.

Your cooperation and support in your child's education is always appreciated!

_____
(teacher)

Song Pattern
Use with "Earth-Friendly Families" on page 171.

Reduce, Recycle, Reuse
(sung to the tune of "Three Blind Mice")

Reduce, recycle, reuse.
Reduce, recycle, reuse.

Now's the time to choose.
There must be no excuse.

It's up to each one of us to do
Our part to make the Earth clean, it's true.
So let's work together—yes, me and you!

Reduce, recycle, reuse.

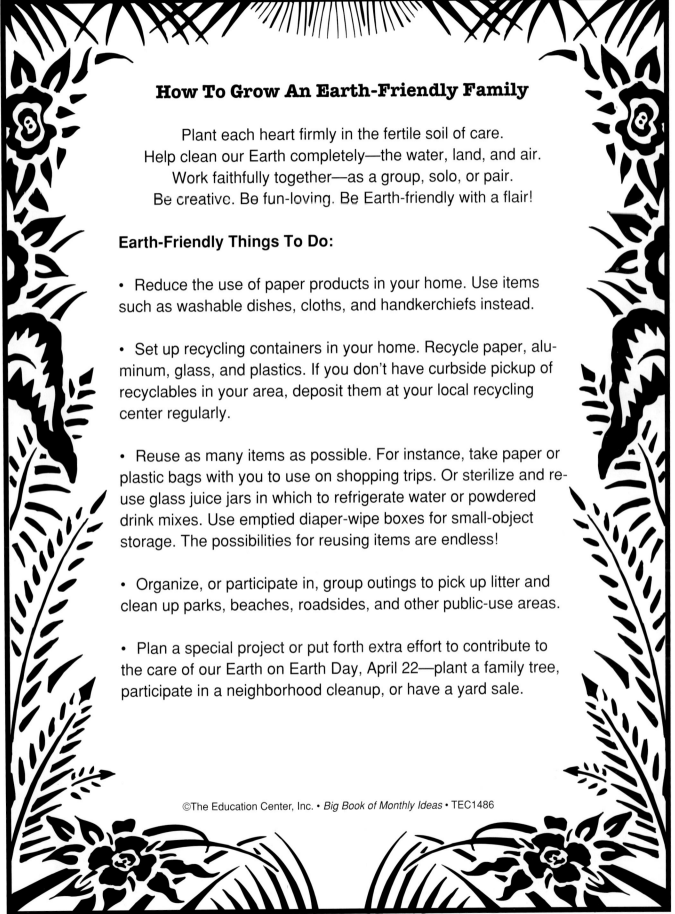

How To Grow An Earth-Friendly Family

Plant each heart firmly in the fertile soil of care.
Help clean our Earth completely—the water, land, and air.
Work faithfully together—as a group, solo, or pair.
Be creative. Be fun-loving. Be Earth-friendly with a flair!

Earth-Friendly Things To Do:

• Reduce the use of paper products in your home. Use items such as washable dishes, cloths, and handkerchiefs instead.

• Set up recycling containers in your home. Recycle paper, aluminum, glass, and plastics. If you don't have curbside pickup of recyclables in your area, deposit them at your local recycling center regularly.

• Reuse as many items as possible. For instance, take paper or plastic bags with you to use on shopping trips. Or sterilize and re-use glass juice jars in which to refrigerate water or powdered drink mixes. Use emptied diaper-wipe boxes for small-object storage. The possibilities for reusing items are endless!

• Organize, or participate in, group outings to pick up litter and clean up parks, beaches, roadsides, and other public-use areas.

• Plan a special project or put forth extra effort to contribute to the care of our Earth on Earth Day, April 22—plant a family tree, participate in a neighborhood cleanup, or have a yard sale.

Armband Pattern

Use with "Banding Together" on page 172.

FLOWER POWER

A BOUQUET OF BLOOMING IDEAS

Plant a garden of delights in your classroom with this flower-filled unit. Excite budding minds with this bouquet of springtime-fresh ideas; then watch bright eyes and happy smiles blossom on your little ones!

ideas contributed by Carrie Lacher and Sharon Murphy

FLOWER FACTS

Dig right into your flower study by bringing in a bouquet of fresh, inexpensive flowers. Include several different varieties. Invite youngsters to examine the flowers up close, using their senses of sight, touch, and smell. Encourage students to comment on the similarities and differences among the flowers.

After the flower exploration, ask students to contribute their knowledge to a chart titled "Flower Facts." Besides their hands-on experience, youngsters may want to tell about people they know who like flowers, or where flowers are found. After everyone has had a chance to contribute, have your students draw flowers in the margins of the chart paper. Display the chart on a classroom wall throughout your study.

Flower Facts

My mom likes flowers.
Jeffrey

We have yellow flowers in our yard.
Miguel

Some flowers are on trees.
Elizabeth

PAINT A RAINBOW

Flowers come in a variety of beautiful colors. Introduce your little ones to some of the many colors of flowers with the book *Planting A Rainbow* by Lois Ehlert (Harcourt Brace Jovanovich). In this story a mother and child plant flowers in a garden. They watch as bulbs, seeds, and plants grow into a rainbow of colorful blooms.

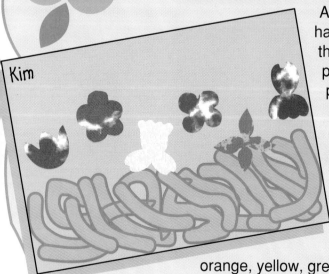

Kim

After sharing the text and vivid illustrations of the book, have each student create a rainbow—by painting, rather than planting! In advance add dish detergent to shallow pans of green, red, orange, yellow, purple, and blue tempera paint. Cut sponges into several different flower shapes. Provide each child with a 12" x 18" sheet of light blue construction paper. Have each child use the green paint to finger-paint the bottom of his sheet of paper to make grass. Next have students take turns dipping the flower-shaped sponges into the pans of paint and pressing them onto their paper. Ask more advanced students to sponge-paint the flowers in the order of the colors in a rainbow—red, orange, yellow, green, blue, and purple. After the paint dries, mount the rainbows on a bulletin board titled "Painting A Rainbow."

FLOWERPOT GIFTS

Even a child knows that flowers make wonderful gifts! Read the book *Flower Garden* by Eve Bunting (Harcourt Brace & Company) for a story of a garden gift; then invite each of your students to plant a flower as a gift for a school helper. If there are more helpers in your school than students in your class, be sure to plant extra flowers.

Provide each child with a miniature clay flowerpot and a variety of art supplies— such as paint pens and stickers—for decorating her flowerpot. After she finishes decorating, spray the pot with clear acrylic and allow it to dry. Then have each child fill her pot with potting soil and add a few fast-growing seeds, such as marigolds. Place the flowerpots in a sunny spot in your classroom. Assist students in nurturing their plants with the appropriate amount of water. Encourage your youngsters to examine their flowerpots daily to check for signs of growth.

Once the marigolds have bloomed, complete the project by making a gift tag as shown; then duplicate one for each student. Help each youngster write the name of a school helper on her gift tag; then have her sign her own name. Next have each child color and cut out her gift tag. Use tape to attach each student's gift tag to her flowerpot. Set the pots aside for students to distribute in "A Parade Of Petals" on page 181.

To: Mr. Amos
From: Beth
I planted this flower as a gift for you, To thank you for all the special things you do!

PETAL PAGES

Ben's Flower Book

Encourage youngsters to explore their creativity with their own unique flower books. For each child, duplicate the flower pattern on page 182 and trim the labels off the bottom. Glue the flower pattern to the front of a folded sheet of 18" x 24" construction paper. Add four sheets of white paper to the inside of the book; then staple along the fold. Print "[child's name]'s Flower Book" on the front cover.

Have each child use crayons or markers to decorate the front cover of her book. Next have students search for pictures of flowers in garden magazines and catalogs. Ask each child to cut out four pictures and glue one picture to each page in her book. Below each picture write the child's dictation describing the flower. Have the children share their finished books with classmates.

FLOWER ARRANGEMENTS

Sorting skills will be blossoming with this activity! To prepare, purchase silk roses, daisies, and tulips from a local craft store. Remove the blossoms from their stems. Place the blossoms in a basket or flowerpot. Next cut a picture of each of the three flowers from a garden magazine or catalog. Label each picture and attach it to a smaller flowerpot or basket.

Show your children photos of roses, daisies, and tulips. Place the labeled containers and the basket of blooms in the middle of your group. Help your students sort the flowers into the correct containers. To keep their classification skills growing, have your students sort the blooms by color, too.

Rose   Daisy   Tulip

179

FLANNELBOARD FLOWERS

Have some flannelboard fun with this rhyme that teaches the three basic parts of a flower: *stem, petals,* and *leaves.* Duplicate and color the flower and bee patterns on page 182. Laminate the designs before cutting out each one. Attach the hook side of a piece of self-adhesive Velcro® to the back of each cutout.

My flower grows up toward the sky,
Leaves and stem and petals high.

Place the flower on the flannelboard.

See the green leaves near the ground—
On the stem is where they're found.

Point to the leaves.
Point to the stem.

See the petals, count with me.
How many petals do you see?
1, 2, 3, 4, 5, 6, 7, 8, 9, 10

Point to each petal and count;

See the honeybee come callin',
Buzzin' 'round in search of pollen.

Place the honeybee on the flannelboard.

My flower smiles and says, "Hello."
The bee says, "Thanks!" before he goes.

Remove the honeybee from the flannelboard.

Tommy

petals

stem

leaves

THE PARTS OF THE FLOWER

Provide youngsters the opportunity to demonstrate their understanding of the three main parts of a flower by having them label their own flower pictures. Duplicate the patterns on page 182 for each student. Have each child color his flower and then cut out the flower-part labels at the bottom of the sheet. Provide help as each child glues a label to each flower part on his paper. Display the completed flower models for a garden of colorful knowledge sure to brighten your classroom!

A FLAVORFUL FLOWER

After making and eating these edible flowers, youngsters will have an even better knowledge of a flower's parts.

Ingredients For One:
2 vanilla wafers
1 spoonful peanut butter
8 miniature chocolate chips

10 pieces candy corn
1/2 celery stalk
vanilla icing, tinted with green
food coloring

Use a plastic knife to spread peanut butter on one vanilla wafer. Put a few miniature chocolate chips atop the peanut butter. Place the tips of the candy-corn pieces around the edge of the wafer to resemble petals. Place the celery stalk at the bottom of the flower to represent the flower's stem. Cut the other vanilla wafer in half. Spread the green icing on each half of the wafer. Place the wafer halves on opposite sides at the bottom of the stalk to represent leaves.

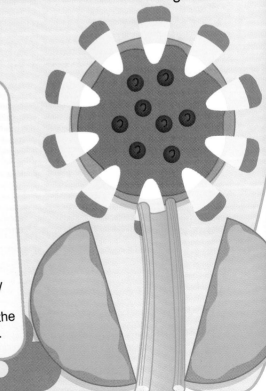

LAVENDER-FLOWER PLAY DOUGH

Fill your classroom with the wonderful aroma of lavender with this new variety of play dough.

Ingredients:
3 cups flour
2 cups water
3/4 cup salt
3 tablespoons oil

3 tablespoons cream of tartar
1/8 cup violet powdered tempera paint
10–20 drops lavender-flower essential oil
purple glitter

In a large pot, mix together the first five ingredients until smooth. Place the pot over medium heat, stirring constantly until the mixture forms into a large ball. While the mixture is still warm, place it on a floured cutting board and knead in additional flour until the dough has a silky texture. Add powdered paint and lavender essential oil and knead thoroughly. Sprinkle with purple glitter and knead again. Store in an airtight container.

Once the play dough is ready, give each child a small amount on a sheet of waxed paper. Invite him to mold the play dough or to flatten it and use small, flower-shaped cookie cutters to cut "scent-sational" flower shapes from it!

COUNTING ON FLOWERS

For counting practice with a flower theme, read the book *Counting Wildflowers* by Bruce McMillan (William Morrow & Company, Inc.). After sharing this colorful counting book with your students, have them use flower shapes and a flower wand to practice counting numerals. In advance, die-cut ten flower shapes from different colors of construction paper (or cut them by hand). Label each flower with a different numeral from "one" to "ten". Obtain a length of 1/4-inch dowel and hot-glue one or two fabric blossoms to one end of it. Next cut two lengths of 1/4-inch green fabric ribbon and hot-glue the ribbon lengths to the flower end of the wand. Invite each child, in turn, to use the flower wand to point to the numbered flowers as she counts them.

A PARADE OF PETALS

Conclude your flower theme with a springtime flower parade. In advance, purchase several pieces of fabric with flowery patterns. Create capes or skirts by cutting the pieces of fabric into large squares and rectangles. For each piece of fabric, attach the hook side of a piece of self-adhesive Velcro® to one corner and the loop side to the other corner as shown. To create flower hats, hot-glue fabric blossoms to several dress-up hats.

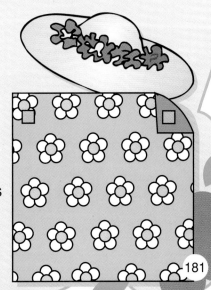

On the day of this activity, invite each child to put on either a decorated hat, cape, or skirt. Provide each child with his flowerpot gift for his chosen school helper. (See "Flowerpot Gifts" on page 179.) Now grab your flower wand and lead your parade of little ones around the school. Delight fin the surprised looks of school helpers as your parade stops to deliver flowerpots of thanks!

Patterns

Use the flower and bee patterns with "Petal Pages" on page 179
and "Flannelboard Flowers" on page 180.
Use all the patterns with "The Parts Of The Flower" on page 180.

Petals | Stem | Leaves

The Mamas And The Papas

Encourage your little ones to show their appreciation and say, "Thank you," to their moms and dads—or to whomever their primary caregivers are—with these fun-filled activities. Plan a special unit on parents or—if your school calendar allows—use these activities separately on Mother's Day and Father's Day.

ideas contributed by Diane Gilliam, Marie Iannetti, and Linda Ludlow

Mommies And Daddies Are Special

Begin your unit by reading aloud the books *Mommies* and *Daddies* by Dian Curtis Regan (Scholastic Inc.). Both books depict the special relationships between parent and child and the special things they do together. After reading these stories, have each child share with his classmates one special thing he does with his mom and one special thing he does with his dad.

Mommy And Daddy Songs

Start your morning routine or circle time with these songs about moms and dads!

(both sung to the tune of "B-I-N-G-O")

I love her and she loves me,
And Mommy is her name-o.
M-O-M-M-Y
M-O-M-M-Y
M-O-M-M-Y
And Mommy is her name-o.

I love him and he loves me,
And Daddy is his name-o.
D-A-D-D-Y
D-A-D-D-Y
D-A-D-D-Y
And Daddy is his name-o.

(both sung to the tune of "Twinkle, Twinkle, Little Star")

Mommy, Mommy, let me say,
"I love you in every way.
I love you for all you do.
I love you for being you."
Mommy, Mommy, let me say,
"Have a Happy Mother's Day!"

Daddy, Daddy, let me say,
"I love you in every way.
I love you for all you do.
I love you for being you."
Daddy, Daddy, let me say,
"Have a Happy Father's Day!"

Marvelous Moms

Honor moms with these cute cards, gorgeous gifts, crafty corsages, and a special celebration!

"Thumb-thing" Special

Creative fingerprint art is the focal point of these special Mother's Day greeting cards. In advance, prepare two shallow pans of tempera paint: one green and the other any bright color of your choice. Add a few drops of dishwashing liquid to each pan. To make a card, fold a 12" x 18" sheet of construction paper in half. Then cut out a 6" x 9" rectangle of white drawing paper and glue it to the front of the card.

Draw a small circle near the top of the paper. Have a child dip her thumb into the pan of bright-colored tempera paint. Then have her repeatedly press her thumb onto the paper around the circle to create the petals of a flower. Have her glue a length of green yarn under the flower to create a stem as shown. Ask her to dip her other thumb into the pan of green tempera paint, then press some thumbprint leaves next to the yarn stem. Have her glue a yellow or orange pom-pom atop the circle in the center of the petals. To complete her card, glue a copy of the poem on page 188 below the flower; then help each child personalize the inside of her card with a message and her signature.

Teatime Invitation

Host a special tea party to honor the special mothers (or caregivers) of your students. In advance program one copy of the tea-party invitation on page 190 with the date and time of your celebration. Then duplicate a class supply of the programmed invitation and the patterns on page 188. Have each child color and cut out the patterns and invitation. Instruct him to squeeze glue on the sides and bottom of the back of his teacup cutout only (leaving the top free from glue); then mount the cutout in the center of a sheet of 9" x 12" construction paper. Have him glue the title cloud above the teacup. Show each child how to fold his copy of the invitation in half three times—so that it is approximately the size of a tea bag. Help each youngster glue the tea-bag tags back-to-back, then tape the ends of a length of thin string to the tag and to the folded invitation, so that it resembles a tea bag. Once the glue on his teacup has dried, have each student slip his folded invitation inside it. Encourage your little ones to take their invitations home to their moms. Tea, anyone?

A Treasured Keepsake

Showcase students' masterpieces in this unique classroom art gallery that highlights mothers. In advance, collect or purchase an inexpensive picture frame for each child. Have each child draw or paint a portrait of his mother on paper sized to fit the frame. Assist him in writing or copying "My Mom" at the top of his picture; then have him write his name at the bottom. Insert each picture in its frame; then display the framed works of art in your classroom. Leave the pictures in your classroom as a decorative display for the "Teatime Party Fun!" activity (page 185), or send the pictures home as special mementos for Mother's Day.

A Corsage For Mom

Have your little ones present these special corsages to their moms on the day of your tea party (see "Teatime Party Fun!"). Help each youngster make a corsage by completing the following steps: Use colorful markers to embellish each of five paper coffee filters. Stack these filters; then pinch the stack together at the center. Bend a five-inch length of green pipe cleaner in half. Then slip the pinched portion of the filters between the open ends of the pipe cleaner. Tightly wrap a length of masking tape around the pinched filters, securing the pipe cleaner in place. Carefully pull the coffee filters apart to open the flower. Attach a large safety pin to the back of each child's completed flower, and the corsages are ready to wear!

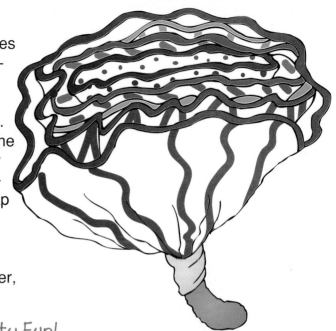

Teatime Party Fun!

It's party time—actually tea-party time! Prepare for your tea party by having little ones help you bake a batch of sugar cookies. Use heart-shaped cookie cutters and candy decorations to make the cookies extra special. Borrow a large, electric coffeepot from your school's cafeteria and fill it with water. Encourage your students to help you set up a serving table with a festive tablecloth, platters for the cookies, a sugar bowl, a pitcher of milk, and, if desired, some fresh flowers in a vase.

When the mothers have arrived, have your students sing "Welcome To Our Teatime" and present the corsages to their moms (see "A Corsage For Mom"). Have each child give her mom a tea bag to place in her special cup or mug; then let the moms fill their cups with hot water. Ask each mother to pour some of her tea (or some juice) into a thoroughly washed, play teacup for her child. Invite the mothers to prepare their tea to their liking and partake of the cookies. After the refreshments, encourage each child to present her mom with her framed portrait (see "A Treasured Keepsake" on page 184) and her Mother's Day card (see " 'Thumb-thing' Special" on page 184). What a wonderful day for some very special ladies!

Welcome To Our Teatime
(sung to the tune of
"I'm A Little Teapot")

Welcome to our teatime.
We're glad you're here,
Because you are so very dear.
We hope you like the things
we've made for you...
To show how much we do love you!

185

Super-Duper Dads

Make dads feel special with great greetings, terrific T-shirts, splendid stories, and a sweet treat just for them!

A Handful Of Love For Dad

Invite youngsters to hand over lovely Father's Day messages with these cards. For each card, duplicate the large heart pattern on page 189 on red construction paper and the smaller heart pattern and poem boxes on white paper. Have each child trace around his own hand twice on a sheet of red construction paper; then assist him in cutting out these hand shapes, the hearts, and the poem boxes. Instruct each child to draw a self-portrait on his white heart cutout; then have him glue this white heart atop the red heart. Have each youngster cut apart the poem boxes and glue the poem on his hand cutouts as shown. Staple the hand cutouts to the top of the heart as shown; then intertwine the fingers to close the card. What a heartwarming surprise for Dad!

A Sweet Day For Dad

Plan a Doughnuts-For-Dads celebration as a sweet way for children to show their appreciation to their fathers. In advance, duplicate and program one copy of the invitation on page 190 with the date and time of your celebration; then make a copy of the invitation for each child. Have each child glue her copy of the invitation to the inside of a folded sheet of construction paper. Then help her cut out a simple doughnut shape from manila paper. Provide tempera paints, brushes, glue, and candy sprinkles.

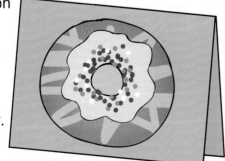

Have each child use the materials provided to decorate her doughnut cutout. When the glue and paints have dried, have her glue her doughnut to the front of the invitation. Encourage your little ones to take their invitations home and hand deliver them to their dads.

Terrific T-Shirts

Won't Dad be proud to sport this "hand-some" T-shirt? In advance ask each family to send in one adult-size, white T-shirt from home. Pour several colors of fabric paint into separate shallow containers.

Working with one or two students at a time, place a piece of cardboard or folded newspaper inside each shirt and smooth the shirt flat. Pin or tape a sheet of construction paper over the center front of each shirt. Then invite each child to press one hand into a color of paint and make handprints randomly on the front of her shirt—around the piece of paper. Have disposable wipes handy for cleanup, and encourage children to repeat this process a few times with other colors of paint.

When the paints have dried, remove the construction paper from each shirt and use a squeeze bottle of fabric paint to write the message "The Best Dad—Hands Down!" in the open space. Allow the paint to dry for a day or two. Then assist each child in wrapping her shirt in colored tissue paper. Have her present this gift to her dad during the Doughnuts-For-Dads celebration (see page 187), or send it home as a special gift.

Father's Day Book

Help your little ones make a meaningful Father's Day gift. To prepare a set of book covers for each child, fold and cut a sheet of 12" x 18" construction paper as shown. Help each child fold the top flaps over to make a collar for the shirt. Then have him glue the collar down securely. Invite each youngster to use crayons to draw a necktie, bow tie, pocket, or shirt design. Next staple a few 7" x 9" sheets of copy paper between the covers of each student's book. On the first page of his book, have each child write (or write for him) "I love my dad because..." and draw a picture of himself with his dad. On each of the following pages, have him illustrate special things about his dad or cut out and glue magazine pictures that depict activities he enjoys doing with his dad. Set the books aside for youngsters to share with their dads during your Doughnuts-For-Dads party.

Doughnuts, Anyone?

Prior to your Doughnuts-For-Dads party, teach youngsters to recite the poem below. On the day of your celebration, borrow a large coffeepot from your school cafeteria and prepare coffee. Have little ones help you set up tables with festive table coverings and trays of assorted doughnuts and doughnut holes. In one corner of your classroom, set up a table with a manual juicer, a glass pitcher, small paper cups, and a bowl of orange halves.

As each dad arrives, have him join his child at the "juice bar" to make some freshly squeezed orange juice. Then have each child invite his dad to partake of a few doughnuts and coffee. After the refreshments, encourage each child to sit with his dad and share the book made in the "Father's Day Book" activity. Then have youngsters recite the poem they learned. At the end of the poem, have each child give his dad a big hug! Then complete this special day by having each child present the card (see "A Handful Of Love For Dad" on page 186) and T-shirt (see "Terrific T-Shirts" on page 186) that he made to his dad. A perfect end to a perfect day!

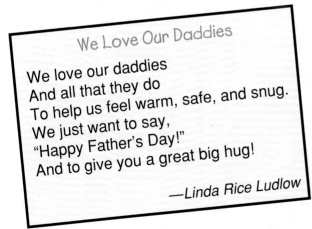

We Love Our Daddies

We love our daddies
And all that they do
To help us feel warm, safe, and snug.
We just want to say,
"Happy Father's Day!"
And to give you a great big hug!

—Linda Rice Ludlow

Tea-Party Invitation Patterns
Use with "Teatime Invitation" on page 184.

A Cup Of Tea
For Mommy And Me!

Tea-Bag Tags

I Love You

I Love You

Mother's Day Card Poem Use with " 'Thumb-thing' Special" on page 184.

This little flower is special, you see,
Because it was made from a part of me.
My painted thumb made each flower part
To show I love you with all my heart!

Happy Mother's Day!

Look inside
so you can see

Who loves you best.
Of course, it is ...

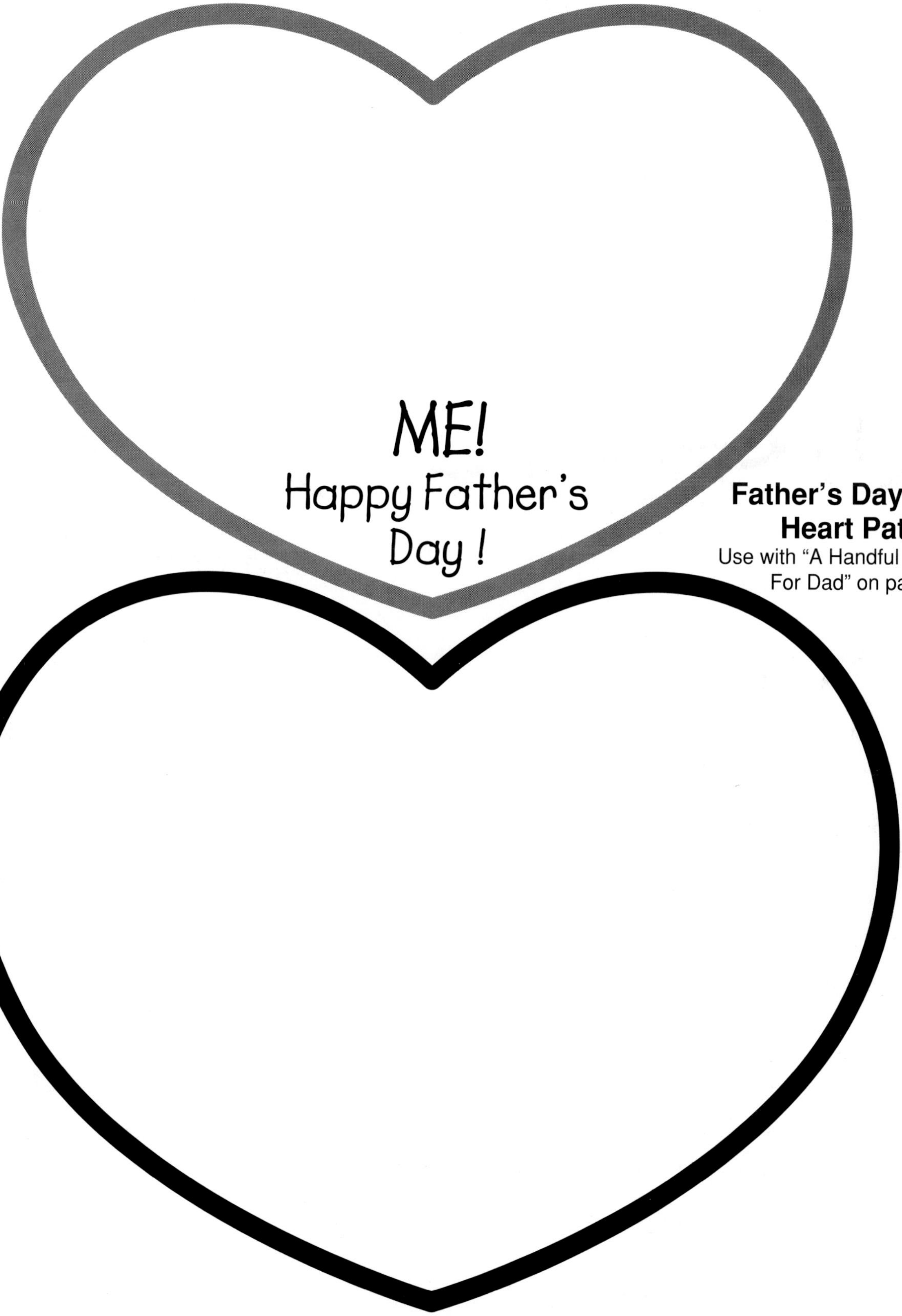

ME!
Happy Father's
Day !

**Father's Day Card
Heart Patterns**
Use with "A Handful Of Love
For Dad" on page 186.

Tea-Party Invitation
Use with "Teatime Invitation" on page 184.

You are invited to our Mother's Day Tea Party.
We hope you can come.
Please bring your favorite teacup or mug with you.

The party is on _____ at _____.

               (date)   (time)

Doughnuts-For-Dads Invitation
Use with "A Sweet Day For Dad" on page 186.

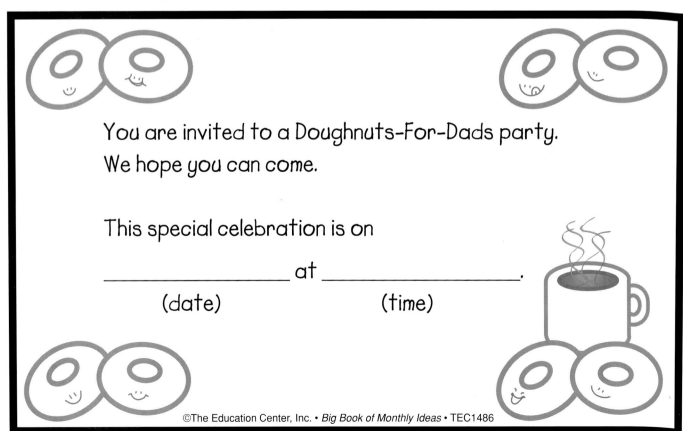

You are invited to a Doughnuts-For-Dads party.
We hope you can come.

This special celebration is on

_____ at _____.

     (date)   (time)

A Day At The Beach

Generate a wave of learning excitement when you and
your youngsters use this cross-curricular beach unit!

ideas contributed by Barbara Backer and Mackie Rhodes

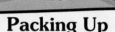

Sand, Surf, And Sun

Dive into your beach study by reading aloud
At The Beach by Anne and Harlow Rockwell
(Macmillan Publishing Company). Afterward find
out if any students have ever been to the beach.
Ask them to tell about their experiences—the
things they did or saw at the beach. Encourage
those students who have not been to the beach
to tell about an imaginary beach experience.
Randomly write their responses on a length of
light brown butcher paper edged along the bottom with a blue paper-strip wave. If desired,
place a sticky note labeled with each child's
name beside her response. Invite several children at a time to find their responses, then illustrate and autograph them. Remove all the sticky
notes from the completed beach scene; then
display the scene with the title "At The Beach."

In The Shade

The beach forecast calls for bright sunshine—but the sun's glare will
be no problem for youngsters when they make these sun visors to wear!
To prepare, duplicate the sun-visor pattern on page 195 on tagboard for
each child. Have the child cut out the pattern, then decorate it with sea-
creature sponge prints. To make a visor band, cut out the center of a
paper plate. Keep the center cutout for use in "Cool Breezes" on page
192. Cut through the resulting outer ring; then round the ends to resemble
a sun visor. Have each child glue his visor cutout along the edge of the
band. Then place the visors aside for youngsters to wear during the
imaginary beach trip in "The Beach At Last!" on page 192.

Packing Up

A trip to the beach means planning ahead and
packing necessary items to make it a fun day in
the sun. Engage youngsters in some critical de-
cision-making and organizational skills by having
them pack a bag for a beach adventure. To prepare, gather a large beach bag and an assortment of items that may be used at the beach—
such as sunglasses, sunscreen, a beach towel,
a swimsuit, a pail, and a shovel. Add some other
unrelated objects to the collection, also—such as
blocks, a flashlight, and a coat. Invite each student in turn to select an appropriate item from
the collection to take to the beach. Ask him to
explain why he made his choice; then have him
put the item in the bag. After the bag is packed
and ready to go, put it aside to use with "The
Beach At Last!" on page 192.

Cool Breezes

Just in case there's not a beach breeze to please, encourage youngsters to create their own breezes with personalized beach fans. If your students made the visors in "In The Shade" on page 191, have them use the center cutouts from the paper plates to make their fans. Or provide tagboard circle cutouts for the fans. To make a fan, cut across the circle to create a straight edge; then encourage each child to use markers or crayons to decorate his fan cutout as desired. Have the child glue the fan to a wide craft stick. Set the fans aside to be used in "The Beach At Last!"

A Beach Song

Anticipation over their beach trip will peak when youngsters sing this bouncy song. On a sheet of chart paper, write a student-generated list of things seen at the beach—such as a sand castle, an umbrella, or a seagull. Then invite each student in turn to replace the underlined word in the song with a word from the list. Repeat the song as often as student interest dictates.

I'm Going To The Beach
(sung to the tune of "The Farmer In The Dell")

I'm going to the beach.
I'm going to the beach.
I think I'll see a [lifeguard] there.
I'm going to the beach!

The Beach At Last!

After all that preparation, it's finally time to go to the beach! So grab your camera and head out for a picture-perfect beach day. In advance select an open or sandy outdoor area to represent the beach; then prepare the area by scattering seashells around it. Have students gather their visors made in "In The Shade" on page 191 and fans made in "Cool Breezes." Ask a volunteer to carry the bag prepared in "Packing Up" on page 191. Lead the class to the pretend beach. Then have each child, in turn, remove several articles from the bag to use as he role-plays a beach activity. (If he selects clothing, you might attach those items over his own clothes with clothespins). Take an instant photo of each child at the imaginary beach—swimming, surfing, building a sand castle, or engaging in another "beachy" activity; then have him return the items to the bag. After returning to the classroom, mount each child's picture on a sheet of construction paper. Write his dictation about his adventure at the bottom of the page. Bind the pages between two construction-paper covers; then write the title "Fun At The Beach!" on the front cover. Put the book in the reading center for students to enjoy.

If The Shell Fits...

Move into it! Fascinate little ones with facts about the hermit crab's transient lifestyle; then invite them to explore size relationships in this discovery center. To prepare, collect several hard blocks—wooden or plastic—of different sizes and shapes. Cut a sponge to match the size and dimension of each hard block. Then gather an assortment of boxes in various sizes and shapes. Tell youngsters that a hermit crab lives inside a shell in order to protect its soft body. To get inside the shell, the crab twists and curls its body. When it grows too big for its shell, the crab moves into a larger one.

Invite each child in turn to compare the sizes, shapes, and textures of the blocks in the center. Then ask her to pretend that each sponge block is a soft-bodied hermit crab searching for a new shell home—a box. Instruct her to fit each make-believe crab into a shell. Have her place the corresponding hard block beside each box containing a sponge crab. Prompt her to compare each block to the box. Will the hard block fit inside the box? Why or why not? Why did the corresponding sponge block fit in the box? If the hard block were a crab, would it need a shell? Why or why not? Then encourage the child to engage in some dramatic beach play using the blocks and boxes as well as other props to represent beach life.

House Hunting

Teach youngsters this rhyme and the corresponding hand gestures about a house-hunting hermit crab.

Hermit crab has a special house.	*Form roof with hands.*
He lives in a borrowed shell.	*Cup one hand over other fist.*
But when he grows much bigger,	*Spread open hands apart.*
The shell doesn't fit so well.	*Shake head from side to side.*
Up and down the beach he goes,	*Point finger back and forth.*
Scanning left and right.	*Point finger left and right.*
Searching for a brand-new house—	*Shade eyes with hand.*
A shell that fits just right.	*Cup one hand over other fist.*
When he finds that perfect shell,	*Point finger at pretend shell.*
You see him almost grin.	*Point to mouth and smile.*
"Hello, new house!" he seems to say,	*Wave at pretend shell.*
"I think I'll move right in!"	*Slide fist into cupped hand.*

193

I Went To The Beach

Youngsters will enjoy learning new hand signs as they recite this verse about a visit to the beach. If desired, encourage students to create additional verses and hand signs to add to these.

I went to the beach
And what did I see?
A *bird* on the sand
Looking at me!

I went to the beach
And what did I see?
A *fish* in the water
Splashing at me!

I went to the beach
And what did I see?
A *shell* in the sand
Sparkling at me!

I went to the beach
And what did I see?
A *crab* in its shell
Waving at me!

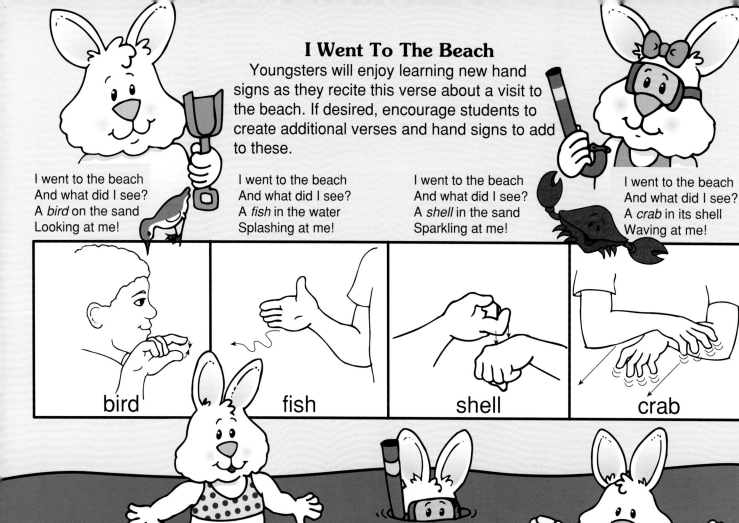

bird   fish   shell   crab

Beach Booklets

Students will be delighted to share the rhyme in "I Went To The Beach" with their families using these individual booklets. For each child, duplicate the booklet pages on page 196 on white construction paper; then make a same-size front cover for the booklet. Have the child cut apart the booklet pages and then stack the pages and cover. Staple the booklet along the left edge and write the title "I Went To The Beach" on the front cover. Instruct youngsters to complete each page following the suggestions provided; then invite them to take their booklets home to read with their families.

- Page 1: Trace the bird footprints with glue; then sprinkle sand over the glue.
- Page 2: Sponge-print a fish on the page. After the paint dries, glue a wiggle eye onto the fish.
- Page 3: Color the shell with glitter crayons.
- Page 4: Use watercolors and a cotton swab to paint the crab.

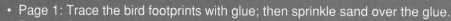

Beach Reading

A Beach Day
Written by Douglas Florian
Published by Greenwillow Books

A House For Hermit Crab
Written by Eric Carle
Published by Picture Book Studio

Sea Squares
Written by Joy N. Hulme
Published by Hyperion Books For Children

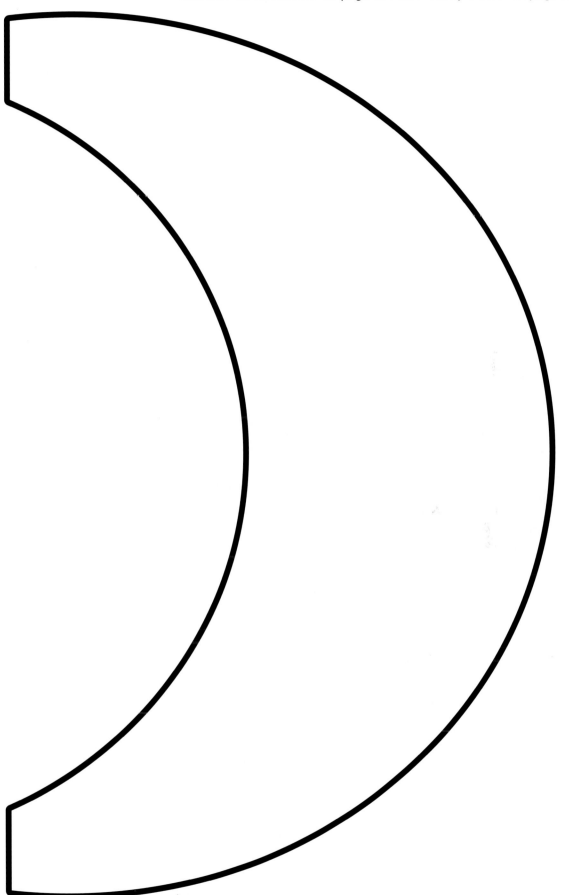

Booklet Pages

Use with "Beach Booklets" on page 194.

I went to the beach
And what did I see?

A *bird* on the sand
Looking at me!

1

I went to the beach
And what did I see?

A *fish* in the water
Splashing at me!

2

I went to the beach
And what did I see?

A *shell* in the sand
Sparkling at me!

3

I went to the beach
And what did I see?

A *crab* in its shell
Waving at me!

4

JUNE

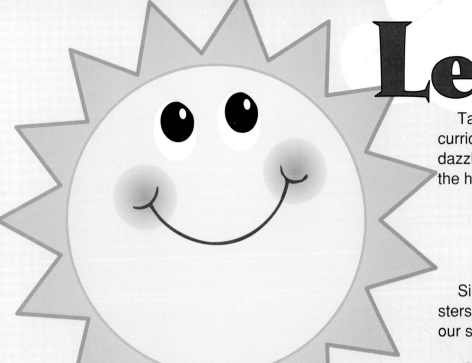

Let The

Take a walk on the sunny side of the curriculum with this hot collection of dazzling activities that are sure to warm the hearts of your little sunseekers!

by Lori Kent

Sing A Song Of Sunshine

Sing this sunny tune to help youngsters understand the many benefits of our spectacular star.

(sung to the tune of "When Johnny Comes Marching Home")

The sun is shining in the sky—a star—so bright.
It shines down on the earth and gives us
  warmth and light.
The sun helps plants and flowers grow.
It gives us clouds and bright rainbows.
Oh, the sun is shining high, in the sky.
What a beautiful sight!

Warm-Up

Now that students are shining with anticipation, introduce your sunshine unit with a brainstorming session. In advance, cut a large circle from yellow bulletin-board paper; then cut several strips from orange bulletin-board paper. Read aloud *Sun Up, Sun Down* by Gail Gibbons (Harcourt Brace Jovanovich, Publishers). Afterward have your little ones recall some facts about the sun; then print each fact on an orange strip. Display the strips around the yellow circle on a wall in your classroom for reference during the remainder of your unit.

A Time To Shine

Spread some sunshine throughout your classroom in preparation for this dazzling unit. Hang yellow and orange crepe-paper streamers and lengths of metallic ribbon from the ceiling of your room to give the feel of sparkling sunshine. Next use yellow tape to make a sun shape on your floor, making as many sun rays as there are children in your classroom. Sprinkle a path of gold plastic confetti (available at party-supply stores) from the door of your classroom to the sun on the floor. On the first morning of your unit, play some lively tropical music in the background; then greet your little ones at your classroom door wearing a wide-brimmed hat and sunglasses. Invite each child to follow the confetti path, then sit on a sun ray. What a sunny way to start the unit!

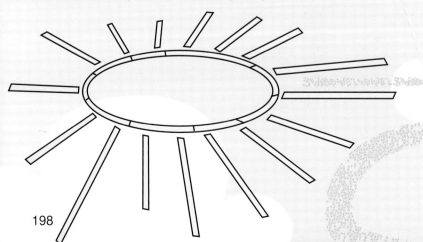

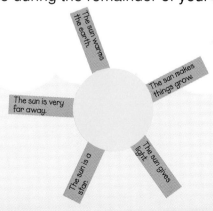

Sun Shine!

Warm Up And Melt Down

Your youngsters will be powered up on solar science after participating in this experiment that demonstrates the sun's warmth. Provide each child with a few spoonfuls of chocolate chips inside a resealable plastic bag. Instruct each child to place his bag near a sunny window or outside in a sunny spot. Have students check the bags every ten minutes. Ask volunteers to guess why the chips melted. Write their comments on a sheet of chart paper. Lead students to the conclusion that the heat from the sun melted the chocolate chips. Save the bags of melted chips to make Peanut Butter Power Bars as a tasty follow-up to this activity.

Peanut Butter Power Bars

Put the information your little ones have learned about the sun's heat to yummy use with this solar-powered snack. To make one power bar, have a child spread a thin layer of peanut butter onto a graham cracker; then cut a corner from the bottom of a bag of melted chips (see "Warm Up And Melt Down"). Instruct her to gently squeeze the bag of melted chips, drizzling the chocolate over the peanut butter. Serve the Peanut Butter Power Bar with a cup of milk. Yum-yum-yummy!

Sunshiny Faces

Create a sparkling display of sunshiny faces with this bright idea. Duplicate a class supply of the sun pattern (page 204) onto yellow construction paper; then cut out all the suns. Have each youngster paint a cutout using a mixture of thinned yellow-colored glue to which clear glitter has been added. Have her cover the outside edges of the sun cutout with orange-colored glue, then sprinkle on clear glitter. When the glue has thoroughly dried, cut out the center of each sun as indicated. Tape a photo of each child to the underside of her sun, so that her picture is framed within the circle. Display your little sunshines on a bulletin board with the title "Spectacular Stars!"

Colorful Light

After participating in these outdoor centers, your little ones will discover that a little ray of sunshine contains all the colors of the rainbow.

Prism Center

Spread a white sheet on the ground; then challenge students to use prisms to see the sun's rainbow of light reflected onto the sheet.

Bubble Center

Mix up a batch of bubble solution by combining 1 3/4 cups of dishwashing liquid and 14 cups of water in a large tub or bucket. Add a collection of bubble blowers. Then, as a child blows a bubble, encourage him to notice the rainbow of colors on each bubble as the sun shines through the bubble solution.

Water Zone

Invite students to pour water from watering cans, or spray water with a garden hose. Remind them to look for the rainbows caused by the sun's light shining through the water droplets.

Shine On Me!

Provide youngsters with a firsthand opportunity to see the sun in action. On a sunny day, plan to take your students for an outdoor walk around your school. During the walk, encourage your little sunseekers to notice things that the sun shines on; then return to your classroom to make these individual booklets. Duplicate a supply of the booklet pages from page 205; then cut them apart. Invite each student to illustrate as many pages as she wishes, showing things that the sun shines on. Then write her completion to the sentence "Sunshine on _____," on each page. Encourage her to illustrate a final page showing the sun shining on herself. Complete its sentence to read "Sunshine on [Child's name]." Staple the pages together between construction-paper covers.

Sun Prints

Your little ones will delight in this project that uses the sun's light to create interesting prints. In advance, gather some small items, such as keys, feathers, leaves, necklaces, doilies, combs, forks, and seeds. To make a print, lay a sheet of blue construction paper outside in bright sunlight. Place a variety of objects on the paper. Leave the paper in the sun for several hours; then remove the objects. Your youngsters will be amazed to see images of the objects that the sunlight could not shine through.

Sunny Centers

Let the sun shine into your center activities with these ideas.

Art Center

Watch your students' interests soar when you enhance your art center with some of the supplies listed below.

- yellow and orange paint to which gold glitter has been added
- yellow, orange, and red crepe and tissue paper
- yellow, orange, and red colored glue
- yellow, orange, and red construction paper
- gold, silver, and clear glitter
- strips of Mylar® or metallic ribbon
- paper plates

Block Center

Place a floor lamp or clamp a utility lamp to a shelf in your block area so that children can experiment with making shadows. Before opening the center, discuss safety precautions with your youngsters regarding the use of the lamp. (As always, supervision is the best precaution.)

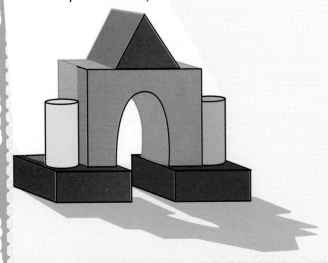

Music Center

Add a little razzle-dazzle to your music center with these terrific tambourines. To make one, paint the bottom of a paper plate yellow and allow it to dry. Fold the plate in half; then glue lengths of yellow and orange crepe paper to the inside rim of half the plate. Add several spoonfuls of dried beans to the inside of the folded plate; then staple the edges together. Invite youngsters to shake their tambourines while listening to a few of the sunny songs listed below.

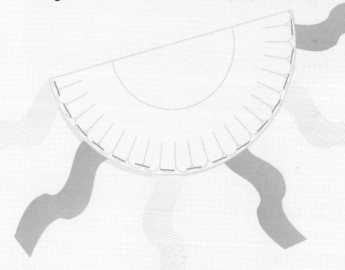

"Sunshine Medley"
Sung by Greg and Steve
Rockin' Down The Road; Youngheart Music, Inc.

"Get Up & Get Going/This Land Is Your Land"
Sung by Anna Moo
Making Moosic; Music For Little People

"May There Always Be Sunshine"
Sung by Charlotte Diamond
10 Carrot Diamond; Hug Bug Records

Play-Dough Center

Add a little solar shine to your play-dough center with this sparkling recipe.

Sparkling Play Dough

1 cup all-purpose flour
1/2 cup salt
1 cup water
1 Tbsp. cream of tartar

1 Tbsp. vegetable oil
yellow food coloring
lemon extract
clear glitter

Mix the flour, salt, water, cream of tartar, and vegetable oil with the desired amount of food coloring and lemon extract in a pan. Place the pan over low heat and stir until the mixture forms a ball that pulls away from the sides of the pan. Remove the pan from the heat, and place the dough on a flat surface. Knead in as much glitter as desired. Continue kneading until the dough is smooth and pliable. Store in an airtight container.

Math Center

Your little ones will be catching more than rays at this math center that focuses on patterning and number skills. On the floor or on a tabletop in your math area, use masking tape to make a sun design. Vary the length of each ray. Challenge each student to use a set of math counters to create a pattern along a sun ray. Extend this activity by asking each child to count the number of manipulatives she placed along each ray. What a sunny center!

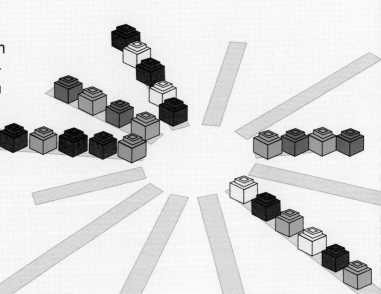

Reading Center

Heat up your reading center with these sizzling stories.

When The Sun Rose
Written by Barbara Helen Berger
Published by Philomel Books

Sun Song
Written by Jean Marzollo
Published by HarperCollins Publishers, Inc.

Sunshine Celebration

Your little ones will be ablaze with sunny attire after making these suits and souvenirs to culminate your sunshine unit!

Sunbeam T's

Top off your sunshine unit by making these cool sunbeam shirts. Send home copies of the parent letter on page 206 requesting that each child bring a clean, white T-shirt to school. Assist each child in pulling up sections of his T-shirt, then twisting a rubber band around each section. Dye each shirt yellow according to the package directions on a box of Rit® Dye. When each shirt is thoroughly dry, remove the rubber bands to reveal bright, yellow sunbursts. Groovy!

Sunny Visors

Your youngsters will be ready for lots of fun in the sun when they team up these nifty visors with sunbeam shirts (see "Sunbeam T's"). For each child, trace a sun visor pattern (page 195) onto tagboard; then cut it out. Invite a student to decorate his visor using his choice of art materials. Punch a hole in each end of the visor. Thread a length of string elastic through each hole and tie them in place. Tie the lengths of elastic together to provide a snug fit. Your little ones will be proud to wear their sunny suits for all to see.

Sunshine Souvenir

Mark the end of your sunshine unit by providing each student with a sunshine souvenir. Duplicate a class supply of the award on page 206 onto yellow construction paper. Take a photo of each child wearing his sunbeam T-shirt and sun visor. Program an award for each child; then attach his picture. Present him with his award on the last day of your unit. What a sunny delight!

Souvenir Of A Sunny Unit

Name Mark Kidney
Date June 18, 2001

Sun Pattern
Use with "Sunshiny Faces" on page 199.

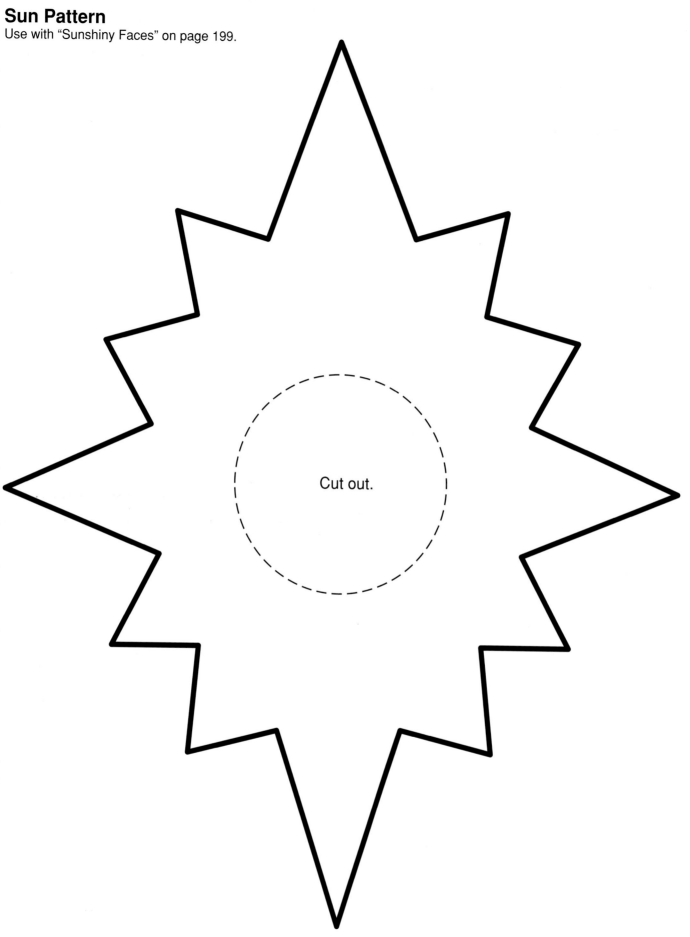

Cut out.

Sunshine on _____ .

Sunshine on _____ .

Parent Letter
Use with "Sunbeam T's" on page 203.

Dear Family,

To commemorate our sunshine unit, we will be making sunburst T-shirts. You can help us by sending a clean, white T-shirt to school. Please label the inside of the shirt with your little sunseeker's name. At school each child will have an opportunity to tie-dye his/her shirt yellow. Don't be surprised if your child comes home beaming with pride over a "sun-sational" shirt!

Please send a T-shirt to school by _____.

(date)

Thanks so much for your help!

Sunshine Award
Use with "Sunshine Souvenir" on page 203.

Souvenir Of A Sunny Unit

Place photo here.

Name _____

Date _____

Footloose And Fancy-Free

Kick off your shoes and jump feetfirst into this unit filled with curriculum-related activities about barefootin'.

by Mackie Rhodes

Barefootin'

What better way to begin a barefootin' unit than to invite youngsters to bare their soles—the soles of their feet, that is! In advance, send each child home with a copy of the parent letter on page 211. After students bring in the requested items, have each child remove his shoes and socks. Instruct him to wet his washcloth, then wring the excess water from it. Squirt a small amount of liquid soap onto his cloth. Have the child wash, then towel-dry, his feet thoroughly. As youngsters wash their feet, encourage them to say this "sole-ful" chant, whispering the word *barefootin'* each time it is recited.

Take your soap and water, and scrub your feet clean.
Barefootin'. *(pause)* Barefootin'.
A-rub 'em and a-scrub 'em. You're a foot-cleaning machine!
Barefootin'. *(pause)* Barefootin'.
Grab a towel. Dry 'em quick. The cleanest feet you've ever seen.
Barefootin'. *(pause)* Barefootin'.
Two fancy-free feet with a sparkle and a sheen!
Barefootin'. *(pause)* Barefootin'.

Fancy Footwork

Challenge youngsters to put their best feet forward in this no-hands activity. To begin, divide your class into student pairs. Tell youngsters that you have some really hard jobs for them to do; then assign each pair a simple task to complete, such as assembling a puzzle, building a block tower, looking at a book, or drawing a picture. When the partners comment on how easy their assignments seem, "suddenly remember" to tell them that they cannot use their hands to do the tasks. They must use only their feet! After each student pair succeeds at its task (or decides that it cannot be accomplished using only feet), assign a different task to the partners, rotating the assignments so that each pair has an opportunity to try several different tasks. Afterward discuss the ease or difficulty with which students performed the tasks with their feet. Look, Ma! No hands!

Reflections Of The Sole

Encourage youngsters' story recall skills with this idea that truly mirrors their soles. Ask each student or student pair to select a rhyme or story, such as "Two Little Blackbirds" or *The Three Little Pigs.* Using washable markers, help each child decorate the sole of each of her feet to represent a different character from the rhyme or story. Then have the student(s) sit in front of a floor mirror so that she (they) can see the reflected soles of her (their) feet—or foot puppets. Encourage the child(ren) to practice performing the rhyme/ story with the foot puppet reflections in the mirror. If desired, invite students to perform their rhymes/stories with their puppets facing the class.

PIGGY PAINTING

What else can little piggies do other than going to the market or eating roast beef? Why, paint a passel of pretty colors, of course! To introduce youngsters to the primary colors and color combinations, read *Mouse Paint* by Ellen Stoll Walsh (Harcourt Brace & Company). Remind students that the mice in the story mixed the paint colors with their feet; then invite students to use their feet to do a little piggy painting of their own. To prepare, spread out a length of bulletin-board paper on the floor. Put a small amount of each color of fingerpaint—red, blue, and yellow—on the paper; then have a child step barefoot into two different paint colors. Encourage him to mix the colors with his feet to create a new color. What color did his little piggies make? After the child finishes mixing colors, ask him to remove the excess paint from his feet with a disposable wipe, then wash and dry his feet thoroughly. Or, if desired, extend this activity with "Dogs Come In All Sizes."

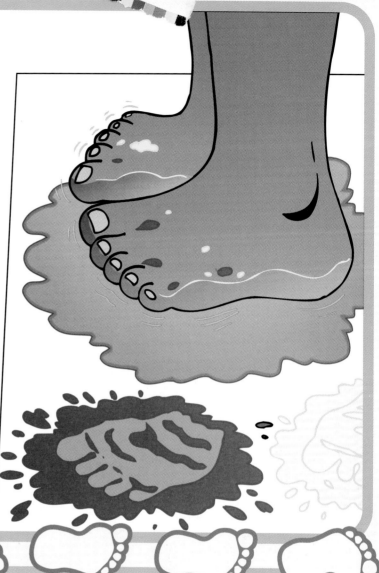

DOGS COME IN ALL SIZES

If youngsters participated in "Piggy Painting," you might have them extend that activity with this foot-printing idea. Before each child washes the paint from his feet, ask him to make a footprint on a sheet of construction paper. After his footprint dries, have him carefully cut around the outline of the print, then label the back of his cutout with his name. Collect all the cutouts in a large shoe; then place the shoe in a math center. To use the center, tell students that a commonly used word for feet is *dogs*. Then, as student pairs visit this center, encourage them to sequence the footprints—or dogs—by size. It's true: dogs come in all different sizes!

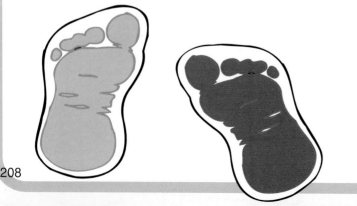

TOE JAMMIN'

A toe-tappin' good time awaits your little ones with this idea. To warm youngsters up for this activity, invite them to imitate simple rhythmic patterns that you create by stomping or tapping your bare feet. Then increase the difficulty by foot-clapping rhythms for students to repeat. Afterward challenge students to imitate the patterns using rhythm instruments—such as bells, rhythm sticks, or cymbals—held between their toes. Conclude your toe-jammin' session with an invitation for youngsters to make the barefootin' music of their choice to accompany some lively recordings.

DO THE WALK!

Can you do the walk? Challenge youngsters to perform creative walk patterns with this activity. To begin, show students the *heel, ball, sides,* and *toes* of your bare feet; then have the children point to these parts on their own feet. After youngsters are familiar with the foot vocabulary, ask them to watch you walk on just your heels or your toes, or one of the other named parts. Then invite youngsters to imitate your walk. After they practice walking on the different parts of their feet, have students gather into small groups. Ask a leader to guide her group through an obstacle course as they walk on an assigned foot part. Let's do the walk!

TEXTURE TALK

Build youngsters' descriptive vocabulary when you introduce them, feetfirst, to a variety of textures. In advance, duplicate and cut from tagboard one copy of the foot pattern on page 211 for each texture to be represented, such as sand, rice, play dough, fingerpaint, plastic grass, or wood chips. Create a sample of each texture on a separate foot cutout; then attach two wiggle eyes and a pipe-cleaner mouth near the toe end of each cutout. Mount each textured cutout onto a separate large sheet of construction paper labeled with the texture's name. Then partially fill a separate large box lid (or tray) with each of the different textured substances. Invite each student, in turn, to step barefoot into each box lid. Ask him to describe the feeling of the substance's texture. Record his responses in speech bubbles on the sheet representing the corresponding textured cutout. Afterward display the finished miniposters on a bulletin board with the title "Texture Talk: 'Feet-uring' [teacher's name]'s Class." If desired, add to this display with photos you snapped during your little ones' texture exploration.

Play Dough

soft

squishy

cold

209

Frolicking Feet

Enhance youngsters' observation skills while creating in them a new appreciation for the many movements of their feet. To begin, have youngsters sit on the floor and lift their feet into the air. Ask them to examine the different ways their feet move. Then help youngsters identify the parts of their feet—the *toes, balls, arches, heels, sides, soles,* and *ankles.* Ask a volunteer to stand up and move around the room in a suggested fashion, such as walking, jumping, or skating. Have the rest of the class watch his feet closely as he moves. What individual foot actions make it possible for that child to move in that way? After each discussion, invite the entire class to perform the same action, in follow-the-leader fashion, paying particular attention to the different foot movements involved. Wow! These fine-tuned actions make for fun, frolicking feet.

Hot Potato, Tootsy-Style

Here's a ticklish circle game designed to promote group cooperation, quick problem solving, and lots of laughter. Have youngsters sit in a circle of chairs facing one another. Explain that they will play a game of Hot Potato, but instead of passing the potato with their hands, they will pass it with their feet. Create a small potato from a crumpled piece of paper; then have students pass the potato feet-to-feet around the circle. Chorally count the number of passes made before the potato is dropped. If desired, invite each child who successfully completes the pass to give himself a round of foot-applause. Ready, set, pass! And no tootsy-tickling allowed!

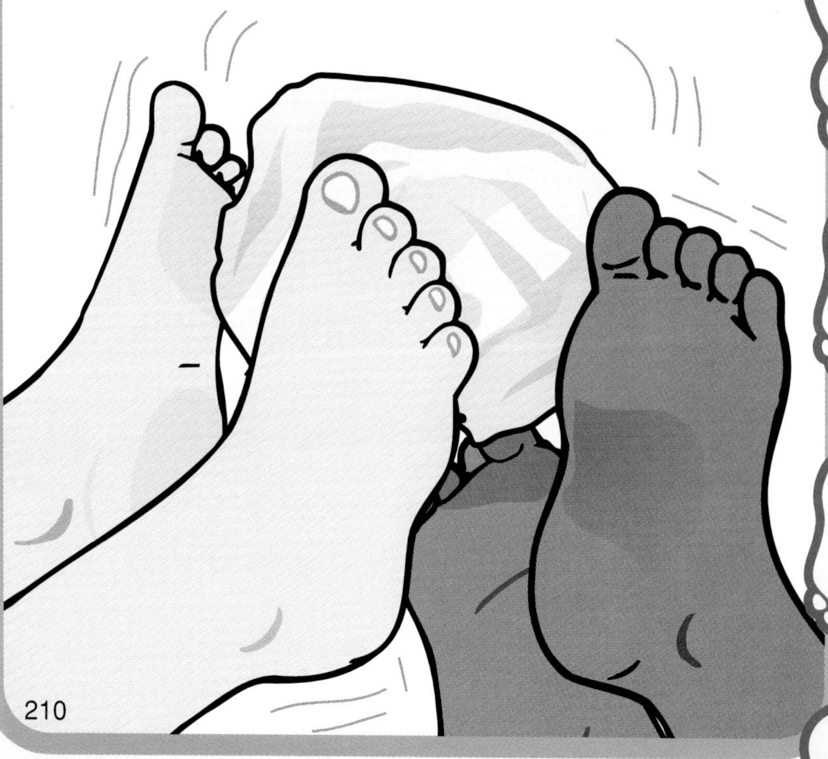

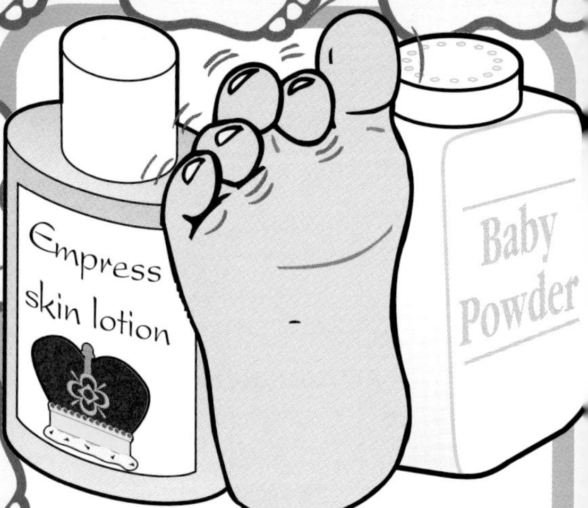
Empress skin lotion
Baby Powder

Pampered "Peds"

Expand the vocabulary of your little ones just a little further as they indulge in a bit of foot-pampering. Just prior to rest time, tell your class that when *ped* is heard in a word, it is usually in reference to the foot or feet. For example, a *pedestrian* is someone who travels by foot. Or a bike or car *pedal* is operated by a foot. Then, if desired, have youngsters wash their feet again, as in "Barefootin' " on page 207. Invite students to gently rub lotion and/or powder on all the different parts of their feet, informing them that when they take care of their feet in this way, they are giving themselves a type of *pedicure.* Ahhh! Feels good. Now put those "peds" to bed.

Parent Letter

Use with "Barefootin' " on page 207.

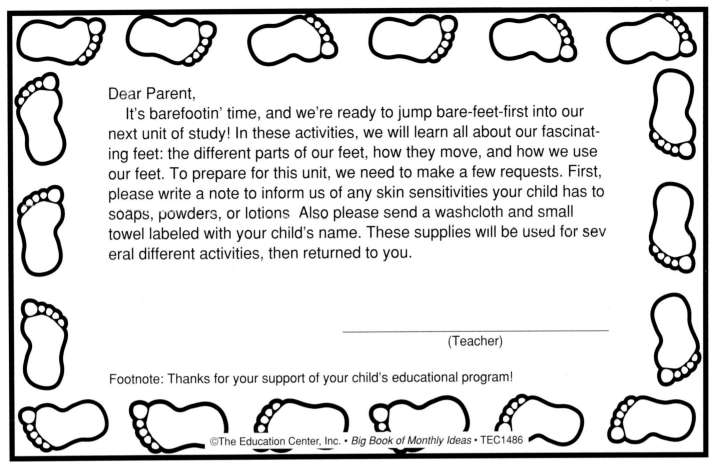

Dear Parent,

It's barefootin' time, and we're ready to jump bare-feet-first into our next unit of study! In these activities, we will learn all about our fascinating feet: the different parts of our feet, how they move, and how we use our feet. To prepare for this unit, we need to make a few requests. First, please write a note to inform us of any skin sensitivities your child has to soaps, powders, or lotions Also please send a washcloth and small towel labeled with your child's name. These supplies will be used for several different activities, then returned to you.

_____
(Teacher)

Footnote: Thanks for your support of your child's educational program!

©The Education Center, Inc. • *Big Book of Monthly Ideas* • TEC1486

Foot Pattern

Use with "Texture Talk" on page 209.

©The Education Center, Inc. • *Big Book of Monthly Ideas* • TEC1486

Ladybug Pattern

Use with "A Ladybug Hunt" on page 213.

Life-Cycle Patterns

Use with "Life Cycle Of A Ladybug" on page 215.

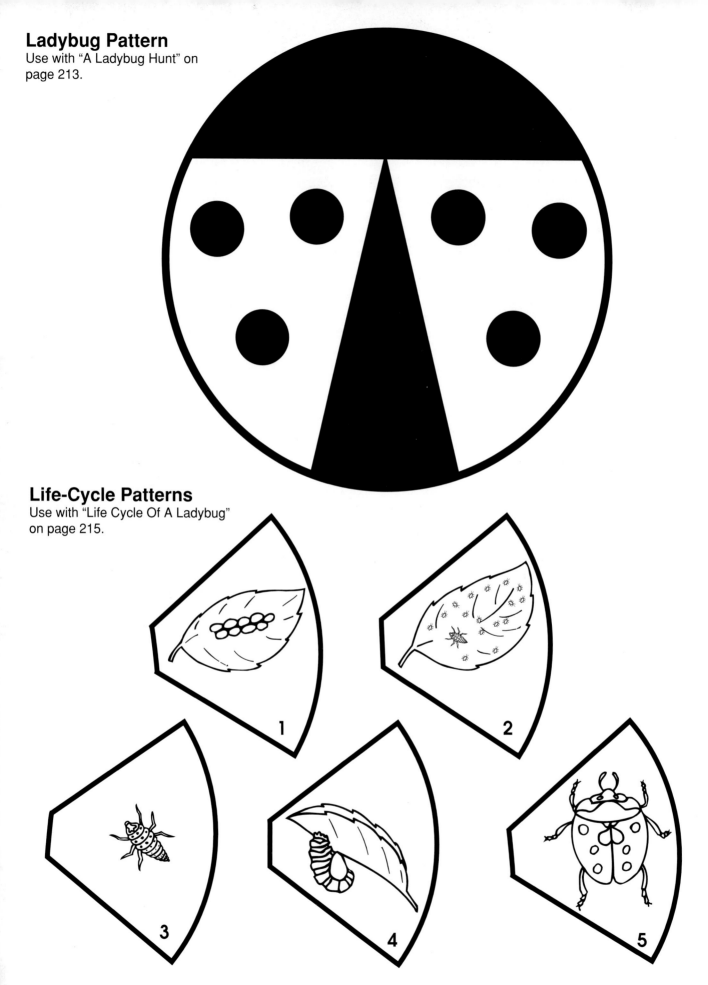

1
2
3
4
5

Look—Ladybugs!

Youngsters will go buggy over this unit on those pretty polka-dotted inhabitants of the garden—ladybugs! So ask them to flit on over and explore these ever-so-interesting insects.

ideas contributed by Diane Gilliam

A Ladybug Hunt

Prepare an indoor ladybug hunt to introduce your students to some facts about ladybugs. First duplicate ten copies of the ladybug pattern on page 212 onto red construction paper. Cut out the patterns; then staple an equal-sized, white paper circle behind each cutout. Then fold each ladybug cutout up, as shown, and write a ladybug fact from "Buggy—But True" on the white circle below it. Hide the completed ladybugs around your classroom—or around your school or center—where little ones can spot them.

When you are ready to begin your ladybug unit, inform youngsters that they will be going on a ladybug hunt. Show them a large, clear jar and explain that you'll be collecting the ladybugs they find in this jar for further study. Then lead the way, perhaps spotting the first paper ladybug yourself to get things started. After your students have collected all the ladybugs you've hidden, return to your circle area and ask volunteers to pull the ladybugs from the jar, one at a time, as you share the fact printed on each one. If desired, share drawings or photos from a good nonfiction book to further your discussion. Have youngsters tell about their own experiences with and observations of ladybugs. Then, if desired, engage little ones in painting a flower-garden mural. Post the mural on a bulletin board, and add the ladybug cutouts and a title that reads "Ladybug Lingo."

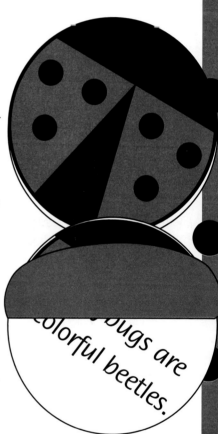

Ladybugs are colorful beetles.

Buggy—But True

- Ladybugs are colorful beetles.
- Ladybugs have three body parts, two antennae, and six legs.
- A ladybug's transparent wings are hidden beneath hard wing cases.
- Ladybugs can be red, orange, yellow, or black.
- Ladybugs can have anywhere from 0 to 22 spots.
- A ladybug's favorite food is aphids.
- A ladybug can eat 100 aphids a day.
- Some ladybugs protect themselves from birds by playing dead.
- One ladybug can lay hundreds of eggs.
- Many ladybugs hibernate during the winter.

Paper-Plate Puppets

Reinforce the appearance of a ladybug and strengthen fine-motor skills with this paper-plate project. Provide each youngster with a thin white paper plate, crayons, some black construction-paper scraps, scissors, glue, eight black pipe-cleaner halves, and a 1" x 6" strip of black construction paper. Show the children how to draw black lines on each plate to resemble a ladybug's head and two wing cases. (You may want to do this in advance for younger children.) Instruct each child to color her plate as shown. Then invite her to cut any number of small circles from the black paper before gluing them in place on the wing cases. Assist each child in punching three holes on each side of her ladybug and two on the head. Then have her thread a pipe-cleaner half through each hole and twist its ends together to create six legs and two antennae. Finally staple each child's 1" x 6" strip to the back of her plate to create a handle for her ladybug puppet.

Encourage little ones to manipulate their puppets as they sing "I'm A Ladybug" (to the tune of "Found A Peanut"). Are your little beetles ready for Broadway?

I'm a ladybug.
I'm a ladybug.
I eat aphids off a leaf.
I have six legs and two feelers.
And my wings are underneath.

Bake Up A Batch Of Bugs

Your little ladybug lovers will be scurrying to taste these scrumptious cupcakes! Either in advance or with your students' help, prepare a batch of strawberry cupcakes from your favorite cake mix. Then have each child frost a cupcake with vanilla frosting. Have him carefully roll the top of his cupcake in a container of red sugar crystals. Then provide each youngster with a six-inch length of licorice lace and a few chocolate chips. Demonstrate how to use pieces of licorice to form the ladybug's head and wing cases. The chocolate chips will serve as spots. If desired, provide Runt® candies, and have each child use these to form eyes and a mouth on his ladybug. Then invite youngsters to enjoy their cupcake creations while you read aloud *The Grouchy Ladybug* by Eric Carle (HarperCollins Children's Books).

Life Cycle Of A Ladybug

Have your youngsters studied the metamorphosis of a butterfly? Then they'll be fascinated to learn that ladybugs, too, have a larval life cycle. In advance, prepare the materials to help each student create a growth wheel that illustrates this life cycle. For each child, stack two six-inch paper plates together. Use sharp scissors to poke a hole through the centers of the two plates; then attach them with a brad. Cut a pie-shaped wedge from the top plate as shown, being careful to avoid the center. Print the words "The Ladybug Life Cycle" on each of the top plates. Then, if desired, duplicate the illustrations on page 212 for each child.

Share *The Ladybug And Other Insects* (A First Discovery Book) by Gallimard Jeunesse and Pascale de Bourgoing (Scholastic Inc.) for a clear and concise description of the ladybug's life cycle. On a sheet of chart paper, sketch the five stages in a circular flowchart (or use enlarged copies of the reproducible illustrations on page 212). Model how to retell the life cycle of the ladybug, using the pictures as cues. Invite some student volunteers to retell the life cycle using your chart.

Then have each youngster make his own growth wheel. Distribute the prepared plates. In the open space below the cutout wedge, have each child either draw or glue the duplicated illustration for the first stage. Then have him rotate the top plate until that picture can no longer be seen. He is then ready to draw or glue his second illustration. Have students continue until they've illustrated (or colored, cut, and glued) all five stages and numbered them accordingly. Then assess their understanding by having them use the growth wheels to describe the ladybug's life cycle.

Stage 1: A ladybug lays *eggs* on the bottom of a leaf.

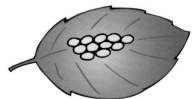

Stage 2: Larvae hatch out of the eggs and begin to eat aphids.

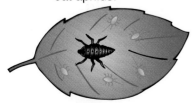

Stage 3: Each larva grows bigger and sheds its skin.

Stage 4: A larva attaches itself under a leaf and sheds its skin once more. It is now called a pupa.

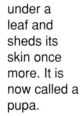

Stage 5: A few days later, a ladybug emerges from the pupa.

Ladybugs To The Rescue!

You've told little ones that ladybugs like to eat aphids. Now explain why that ladybug diet is so beneficial to humans. Read *What About Ladybugs?* by Celia Godkin (Sierra Club Books For Children) or simply explain that aphids are pesky little bugs that enjoy sucking the juices out of plants and flowers. Aphids can destroy a vegetable or flower garden if left to their own devices, and gardeners often bring in ladybugs to control the aphid population.

Invite youngsters to create a garden scene with some beany buggy art to remind them of the ladybug's importance. In advance, spread a bag of dried lima beans on sheets of newspaper and spray-paint one side of the beans red. When the paint is dry, provide each child in a small group with some painted beans, a sheet of light blue construction paper, an assortment of construction-paper scraps, scissors, glue, and a black permanent marker. Invite the children to make garden scenes by cutting and tearing construction-paper shapes, and gluing them onto the light blue backgrounds. Then show children how to use the black marker to decorate a red-painted bean so that it resembles a ladybug. Have them glue a few ladybugs to their garden scenes. Have each child finish her project by writing or dictating a sentence about ladybugs in the open space at the top of her paper.

Ladybugs are good because they eat aphids.

Nathaniel

La-La-La-Ladybug

Teach youngsters this song and its accompanying motions. Then encourage them to sing the song for their families and share all they've learned about ladybugs.

I'm A Bug
(sung to the tune of "I'm A Nut")

I eat aphids; don't you know?	*Point to chest with thumbs.*
I eat aphids so I'll grow.	*Make muscles with both arms.*
I eat aphids; they're the best!	*Rub tummy.*
They're for me; don't want the rest.	*Shake head "no" and hold palm out to indicate "stop."*
I'm a bug.	*Clap, clap.*
I'm a bug.	*Clap, clap.*
Ladybug, ladybug, ladybug.	*Clap, clap.*

Getting Wet!

The heat is on! And there's no better way to cool down on a hot summer day than to get wet—whether from a light misting or from a soaked-to-the-bone drenching. Here's a deluge of ideas to choose from for a water-day celebration or just for a few beat-the-heat activities. Prior to your wet activities, send each child home with a copy of the letter on page 224 so that parents can plan and prepare ahead, too. Got your swimsuit and towel? Ready…set…let's get wet!

ideas contributed by Mackie Rhodes and dayle timmons

Bath-Time Blitz

Splish, splash! Let's all take a bath! Try this activity for some good, clean fun. Partially fill several wading pools (or large plastic tubs) with water; then add scented children's bubble bath to each pool. Finish filling the pools with a spray of water to create lots of foamy bubbles. Position the water hose or a sprinkler near the pools. Put several washcloths and a few water and bath toys in each pool; then add one or two seated children to each bubbly pool. Invite students to splash around, playing with the toys and taking an imaginary bath. If desired, inspire youngsters' bath-time "scrubbies" with a recording of Hap Palmer's "Take A Bath" from *Learning Basic Skills Through Music: Health And Safety* (Educational Activities, Inc.). After each child finishes his bath, encourage him to rinse off in a spray of water or under the sprinkler.

I'm singin' in the rain

Shower Savvy

Do some of your youngsters prefer a shower to a bath? To accommodate these students, secure a hose with a sprayer attachment over a low-hanging tree branch or a piece of playground equipment. Supply the shower area with a washcloth, back scrubber, and shower cap; then turn on the water and lock the sprayer attachment so that a steady spray of water flows from it. Invite students to step into the shower, in turn, for a thoroughly delightful scrubbing. Don't be surprised to hear your shower-savvy students bellow a few operatic refrains above the pitter-patter of the water!

Bathe The Babies

Students will immerse themselves in the roles of parenthood when they engage in this dramatic water-play activity. To begin, partially fill several plastic tubs with water to represent bathtubs. Add bubble bath, washcloths, sponges, and water-filled shampoo bottles to each of the tubs. Have towels, empty containers of baby powder, and powder puffs nearby. Invite each child, in turn, to bathe a plastic, immersible doll—her imaginary baby—in a tub. Encourage her to pamper her baby during bath time and afterwards with a gentle towel drying and powdering. If desired, prompt youngsters to sing a bath-time version of "This Is The Way" (sung to the tune of "Mulberry Bush").

Laundry Time

While youngsters are assuming the roles of parents, invite them to add their own flair to a redundant parental task—the laundry. To prepare, partially fill a water table or several plastic dishpans with water. Add a small portion of mild laundry detergent or a scented liquid soap to the water. To the side, set up a clothesline and a container of spring-type clothespins. Then have small groups of students take turns washing doll and baby clothes in the soapy water. Show them how to wring the water out of the washed items, then hang the clothes on the line to dry. With youthful enthusiasm and creativity, students will discover that grown-up chores can be fun!

A Wet Letter Day

Have a Wet Letter Day—and accomplish a bit of classroom cleaning in the process! To begin, explain to your class that things in the classroom—like things in their homes—need to be cleaned periodically. Then select a letter of the alphabet, such as *T*, or any letter currently being studied. Have youngsters gather a collection of classroom items beginning with that letter that can be put in the water. For example, they might choose a towel, a T-shirt, a corresponding sponge letter, or plastic toys, such as a truck, a tiger, or a sand mold of the numeral 2. Ask each child to place her choice in a partially filled water table; then invite students to rotate turns playing at the water table. As youngsters engage in their wet letter play, encourage them to sound out the names of the items in the water, paying particular attention to the beginning sound of each. It's a Wet Letter Day!

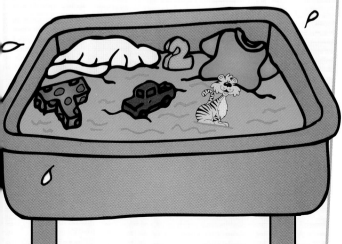

Wet And Wonderful
Sensory Experiences

Try these sensory-stimulating activities to give youngsters still more reasons to get wet!

Piggies In The Puddle

A sensory treat awaits your little ones with this muddy listening game. To prepare a mud puddle, cover the bottom of a wading pool with purchased potting soil or topsoil; then mix water with the soil until it reaches a thick, soupy consistency. To play, ask a small group of students to role-play little pigs. Explain that when pigs get hot, they cool off by wallowing in mud. Then have the pigs circle around the mud puddle as you recite the rhyme below. Fill in the blank at the end of the rhyme, prompting youngsters to respond appropriately. Continue the game, providing a different response at the end of the rhyme each time so that every student has the opportunity to get in the mud. After the game, have students hose themselves clean. Aaahh, cool mud.

Hot little piggies circle round and round.
Into the mud you go if your name starts with this sound:
[sound/letter].

arm

charm

Slime Time, Rhyme Time

Help youngsters slime into some "ooey-gooey" rhyming practice with this activity. To begin, divide your class into pairs of students. Instruct each student pair to create slime by mixing one cup of water, two cups of cornstarch, and a small amount of green washable paint in a plastic container. If necessary, add small amounts of water to the slime until a thick, soupy consistency is achieved. Then ask a child in each pair to name a body part. Challenge her partner to say or create a corresponding rhyming word; then invite each child to rub a bit of slime on the named part of her body. Repeat the procedure, having the partners switch roles so that they take turns naming a body part, then a rhyming word. After each pair has become all slimed out or rhymed out, hose the slime off each student with a spray of water.

Sticking Together

If the names of their body parts just won't stick in students' memories, here's a cooperative game that might help. To begin, spray a large quantity of shaving cream into several large tubs to represent glue; then randomly place the tubs in a spacious outdoor area. To play, repeat the name of a body part to create a rhythmic chant. Have youngsters move around the play area, chorally repeating the chant while tapping that body part on themselves. On the signal, "Stick!", each youngster will find a partner, then scoop out a dollop of glue from the nearest tub. Each partner will rub glue on herself at the named body part; then she will "stick" herself to her partner's glued body part. For example, each student pair might be stuck together elbow-to-elbow or ankle-to-ankle. To separate the stuck-together students, spray a shower of water over each pair to wash away the glue. Then repeat the game, chanting the name of another body part.

We're stuck!

Swamp Stomp

Conclude this sensory section with a good old-fashioned swamp stomp. To create a swamp, arrange an obstacle course to include the mud-filled pool from "Piggies In The Puddle" and a large tub of slime from "Slime Time, Rhyme Time" on page 220. Also position one or more large containers of the shaving-cream glue from "Sticking Together" in the obstacle course. Place a water sprinkler at the end of the swamp course. Tell youngsters that each sensory substance represents a swamp texture. For example, the mud might represent swamp mud (of course!) while the green slime might be swamp scum. The shaving-cream glue might be swamp foam and the spray from the water sprinkler swamp mist. Explain the path of the swamp stomp, including such actions as swimming through the swamp mud, splashing through the swamp scum, and wading through the swamp foam. Then invite each child, in turn, to negotiate his way through the murky, mushy swamp—completing the course with a grand-finale swamp stomp dance through the swamp mist. A swampy delight!

Cool 'Em Down

Is it just too hot for your little ones to enjoy the wet, sensory activities in this section? If so, cool 'em down with ice. Simply add ice to the mud puddle from "Piggies In The Puddle" and the slime mixture from "Slime Time, Rhyme Time" on page 220. If desired, also drop a few ice cubes into each tub of shaving-cream glue in "Sticking Together." Before long all your students will agree: It's cool to get wet.

Splish, Splash, Wet In A Flash

Are your students waterlogged yet? If you find them asking for more, try some of these splashy carnival-type games to keep them wet and learning.

Teatime

This "tea-totally" terrific activity will challenge youngsters' resourcefulness and problem-solving abilities. In advance tint a gallon of water with several tea bags. Fill a plastic teacup with the tea; then place the gallon of tea and the cup several feet away from an empty tea pitcher. Explain that each child will take the cup of tea and empty its contents into the pitcher—only she must accomplish this task without the use of her hands! Invite each child, in turn, to employ her problem-solving savvy to figure out how to maneuver the cup to the pitcher. Refill the cup as necessary. After every child has had a turn, invite the class to enjoy cups of real tea—using their hands, of course! Pinkies up.

Ready, Aim, Squirt!

It's target-practice time—got your spray bottles ready? To play this game, label each of several plastic cups with a different numeral, letter, or shape. Assign each cup to a different child; then have the assigned children sit side by side on the ground. Ask each student to balance his cup on his head with the labeled side aligned with his back. Then equip another student with a spray bottle and the title of Squirter. Have the Squirter stand a few feet behind the seated children. Ask him to name the label on one of the cups; then challenge him to squirt that cup off the head of the child on whom it is balanced. If necessary, adjust the nozzle of the spray bottle so that its water stream has enough pressure to move the cup, but isn't uncomfortable for a child in the stream's path. Give each child an opportunity to be the Squirter. Bull's-eye!

Gotta Regatta

No outdoor water play would be complete without boats! Use this boat-making idea to promote parent involvement and creativity. In advance, send home a copy of the request letter on page 224 with each child. After your students bring their family-designed boats to class, set up a wading pool filled with water. Offer each child a turn to show her boat to the class and to explain how she and her family made it; then ask her to demonstrate how it moves in the water. Afterward invite small groups of youngsters to use their boat creations in a small-scale regatta at the wading pool. You've gotta regatta!

Toe Fishing

After the last boat crosses the finish line, there's still more water fun to be had! Simply drop some marbles into the bottom of the wading pool; then stir in some bubble solution to make a foamy topping on the water. Invite several volunteers to sit in chairs placed around the pool's edge. Challenge them to use their toes to catch and remove as many marbles from the pool as possible. Ask each toe fisher to compare the number of marbles he caught to the number caught by his companions. Then return the marbles to the pool, foam up the bubble solution, and invite another group of students to do some toe fishing.

Watermelon Wrap-up

Now that youngsters have saturated their exteriors with all this wet play, offer them some red, juicy watermelon with which to wet their interiors. As the children pick out their watermelon seeds (either by mouth or by hand), invite them to toss or spit the seeds into the wading pool. Then have youngsters take one last hoopla through a sprinkler or spray of water to rinse off the sticky watermelon juice. All wet—inside and out!

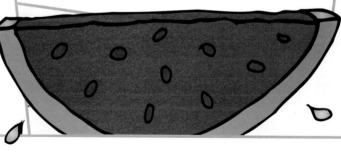

Wet Side Stories

Invite youngsters to dry out with one of these books about getting wet.

Better Not Get Wet, Jesse Bear
Written by Nancy White Carlstrom
Published by Simon & Schuster

No More Water In The Tub!
Written by Tedd Arnold
Published by Dial Books For Young Readers

Splash!
Written by Ann Jonas
Published by Greenwillow Books

Joe's Pool
Written by Claire Henley
Published by Hyperion Books for Children

Parent Letter
Use with "Getting Wet!" on page 218.

We're going out to get wet.
Buckets of fun, you bet!
Splish, splish, splash, splash.
Soaking wet in a flash!

Date: _____

Place: _____

We're planning some wet, wonderful fun! Please send the following items for your child on the date above. And why not plan to beat the heat yourself? Just slip into your swimsuit and come join us!

_____ swimsuit
_____ bath towel
_____ sunscreen
_____ sunglasses

_____ change of clothes
_____ flip-flops or water shoes (optional)
_____ large, resealable plastic bag (for wet clothes)

Parent Request Letter
Use with "Gotta Regatta" on page 223.

Dear Parent,

Our class needs your help with a regatta (that's a special word for boat races) planned for _____. Please take time
(date)
with your child to create a boat for our regatta. The boat could be made of something as simple as a plastic soda bottle or a foam meat tray with a paper sail. After you and your child complete the boat, test it in a tub of water or a wading pool to make sure it floats. Then send the boat to school with your child on or before the regatta date. Have fun!

Thanks for your support,

_____
(teacher)

On The Lookout For A Cookout!

Summertime is the perfect time for a cookout. So fire up students' appetites for learning with this tasty thematic unit.

ideas contributed by Vicki Mockaitis Pacchetti

Barbecue Brainstorm

Get your cookout unit off to a hot start by gathering your little ones together for a mouthwatering discussion about this tasty topic. In advance cut a hamburger patty from brown construction paper and two bun halves from tan construction paper. Glue the three pieces of paper together to resemble a hamburger as shown. Mount the cutout onto a flat surface such as your easel or a bulletin board. During group time, ask student volunteers what types of foods are cooked on grills. Write students' responses on the giant hamburger. Then have students share other words and phrases associated with cookouts and barbecues. Responses might include cookout tools, games, or paper products. After recording these responses, display the hamburger cutout on a classroom wall.

hot dogs   napkins
paper plates   smoke
potato chips   ketchup
picnic table   hamburgers
grill   potato salad

Singing Chefs

What's the next best thing to having a cookout? Singing about one! In advance bring in a toy grill. Or create a pretend grill by placing a wire baking rack atop a cardboard box. If desired, add rocks or spray-paint Styrofoam® balls black to resemble charcoal; then place them in the box. Gather students in a circle around the grill and teach them this summertime tune and its accompanying movements.

Let's All Have A Cookout Today
(sung to the tune of "Here We Go 'Round The Mulberry Bush")

Let's all have a cookout today, a cookout today,
   a cookout today.
Let's all have a cookout today, and fun in the summer sun.
                     Clap hands to each beat.

There's the grill that cooks the food, cooks the food,
   cooks the food.
There's the grill that cooks the food; that's how the food gets done.
                     Point to the grill.

Flip the burgers and the hot dogs, and the hot dogs,
   and the hot dogs.
Flip the burgers and the hot dogs—enough for
   everyone.
                     Pretend to flip a burger with a spatula.

Gather the chips, dips, and your friends, and your friends,
   and your friends.
Gather the chips, dips, and your friends, and let's all eat
   a ton...MUNCH!
                     Signal "come here" with your hands.

                     Pretend to take a huge bite.

Mustard

Pepper

Hamburger Patterns

Cook up some patterning practice with this appetizing activity. In advance duplicate several copies of the burger ingredients on page 229 for each student. Then cut a 4" x 18" strip of construction paper for each child. Distribute the burger patterns and a strip to each student. Have each student color and cut out her burger ingredients. Then challenge each child to use the cutouts to create a repetitive pattern, such as *lettuce, tomato, cheese, lettuce, tomato, cheese.* After checking each child's pattern, have her glue her cutouts to her construction-paper strip. Voila—patterns that look good enough to eat!

Build A Burger

Build basic-skills knowledge with this small-group activity. Duplicate, color, and cut out several sets of the burger ingredients on page 229. Mount each picture on a piece of tagboard; then laminate the pictures for durability. Label the pieces in each set with numerals, shapes, or letters; then place each set in a resealable plastic bag. (Each bag will have two buns, one patty, a piece of lettuce, a piece of cheese, and a tomato slice.)

To begin the game, distribute a bag to each student in the group and have him empty it in front of him. Then—depending on the skill you choose—announce a shape, letter, numeral, or beginning sound and have each child search for a match on his burger ingredients. If a child has a match, he places that piece to the side. Play continues in this same manner as each student uses his matches to build a stacked burger. The first student to have six matches (and a stacked burger), announces, "I built a burger!" Continue play until each child has built his burger. Change skills on the game pieces by wiping off the original programming with a spritz of hairspray.

One-Of-A-Kind Burgers

Encourage your young chefs to try their spatulas at creating their own burger recipes—the crazier, the better! Will it be a chocolate-pickle burger or a rose-petal burger? After each child has decided on the ingredients for her burger, give her a sheet of paper and have her illustrate her burger. Then write each child's dictation describing her burger on her individual page. Compile all the recipes into a class book titled "One-Of-A-Kind Burgers." Then share this class menu and listen to your hungry ones giggle for more!

We're Having A Cookout

Play this fun memory game with your little ones, and watch their excitement for cookouts grow! (This game also makes a great lead-in to the next activity, "All Decked Out For Dramatic Play.") To prepare for the game, bring in a large cooler and a variety of cookout items, such as plastic squeeze bottles for ketchup and mustard, a checkered vinyl tablecloth, tongs, a spatula, an apron, plastic or paper plates and cups, plastic utensils, and napkins. Place the cookout items in the cooler and have a small group of students form a circle around the cooler. Begin by having a student choose a cookout item from the cooler and say, "We're having a cookout, and I brought the [cookout item]." The student then returns with his cookout item to his spot in the circle. Then invite another student to choose an item from the cooler. Have him repeat the first child's sentence, and add the name of his own cookout item. Continue until each child has had a turn. Encourage students to look at the items in their classmates' hands to help them remember the previous items listed.

All Decked Out For Dramatic Play

Transform your dramatic-play area into a deck or patio to encourage role-playing throughout your cookout unit. Stock the area with the props and cooler used in "We're Having A Cookout," a pretend grill (see "Singing Chefs" on page 225), and some child-size lounge chairs, a petite picnic table, or a blanket or two spread on the floor. Also gather an assortment of plastic cookout-type food, or cut sponges or felt to resemble hot dogs and hamburgers. Encourage children playing in the area to use the cookout items and foods as they have their own cookout. Now, who wants burgers and hot dogs?

Hot Potato—Cookout Style

Play this cookout version of Hot Potato to sharpen students' gross-motor skills. In advance ask each child to bring an oven mitt to school. (Be sure to locate some extra mitts in case some students forget.) You will also need an uncooked potato and some aluminum foil. Gather students in a circle and place the pretend grill from "Singing Chefs" (page 225) in the middle of the circle. Explain to your youngsters that some people wrap food in foil before placing it on a grill. Then wrap the potato in foil and place it on the pretend grill. While the potato is "cooking," have students put on their oven mitts. Once the potato is "hot," play a selection of music and send the potato around the circle. Remind each student that since the potato is "hot," he can touch it only with his hand that's wearing the mitt. At random intervals, stop the music and send the student holding the potato to the middle of the circle until the next round. Briefly "reheat" the potato and begin play again.

Hamburger Cookies

Conclude your cookout unit with this delicious burger-making experience.

Ingredients For Patties (makes 25–30):

2 Tbs. cocoa
1/4 cup milk
1 cup sugar`
1/4 cup butter
1/4 cup peanut butter
1 cup uncooked oatmeal

Ingredients For One Cookie:

2 vanilla wafers
1 Tbs. patty mixture
vanilla ready-to-spread frosting
yellow and red food coloring
sesame seeds
water

In advance divide the frosting into three small jars. Use food coloring to color one-third red (ketchup) and one-third yellow (mustard). Leave one-third white (mayonnaise). Place a plastic knife beside each jar.

Prepare the patty mixture using a pot and a portable burner. Stir together the cocoa and the milk. Add the sugar and the butter, and boil about three minutes. Add the peanut butter and the uncooked oatmeal; then stir until the peanut butter has melted. Remove from heat and stir until mixture begins to thicken. Allow the mixture to cool slightly; then have students make their hamburger cookies while the patty mixture is still pliable.

To make a hamburger cookie, a student chooses and spreads the condiments she wants on the flat side of one vanilla wafer. Next she forms a tablespoon of the patty mixture into a patty, stacks the patty atop the condiments, and then tops the make-believe burger with the other vanilla wafer. Finally she dampens the top vanilla wafer with a wet paper towel and sprinkles a small spoonful of sesame seeds on it. Ready for a bite?

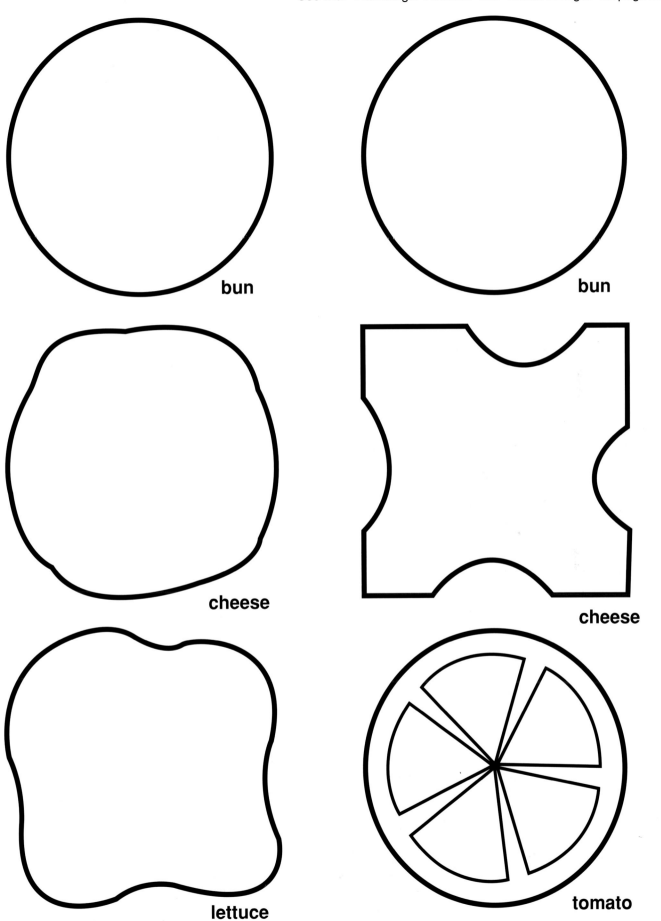

bun

bun

cheese

cheese

lettuce

tomato

Everybody's Yellin' For Watermelon!

This juicy assortment of watermelon activities will have youngsters' mouths watering. Have fun serving up this favorite slice of summer!

ideas contributed by Lucia Kemp Henry and Angie Kutzer

Guess What?

Begin the melon madness by having your little ones play the parts of supersleuths. Hide a watermelon in a box. On the outside of the box, write clues describing the watermelon. During circle time, show the box to your students and read the clues aloud. Invite volunteers to guess what's inside. After all guesses have been made, unveil the mighty melon. As an extension, challenge older students to list other descriptive words or phrases for a watermelon.

Oval shape, hard outside, soft inside, crunchy, has stripes

We are family...

Melon Mania

Watermelons aren't the only ones! The other members in their gourd family include muskmelons, pumpkins, squash, cucumbers, and zucchini. Haul an example of each of these gourds into the classroom for older students to compare, contrast, and examine. Or, for younger children, bring in the three most common melons—a watermelon, cantaloupe, and honeydew—for comparison. Call attention to the color(s), pattern, smell, and texture of the outside of each melon; then slice each one in half to investigate the inside. They're all melons and/or gourds, yet each has its own unique characteristics, just like us!

Juicy, Juicy, Juicy

Use the three cut melons from "Melon Mania" to give youngsters' taste buds a treat. Cover one half of each melon with plastic wrap and place it near a piece of paper labeled with its name. Then cut the other half of each melon into bite-sized cubes, saving the watermelon seeds for later. Put each melon's pieces into a separate bowl and place each bowl beside the corresponding covered melon half. Invite each child to sample the melons. Then have her vote for her favorite by placing a sticker on the paper that's labeled with her choice. Tally the votes with your students by counting the stickers aloud. Have a volunteer report the winning melon. For older youngsters, you may want to graph the data on a picture or bar graph. Before putting away the covered melon halves for another snacktime, take a photo of each child holding the watermelon to use in the booklet described on page 231 (see "A Slice Of Reading"). Conclude this juicy activity by reading *Anansi And The Talking Melon* retold by Eric A. Kimmel (Holiday House, Inc.).

Watermelon

That Wonderful Watermelon!

Help your youngsters learn this short fingerplay to introduce them to the parts of a watermelon.

A watermelon is round | *Make a circle with arms and hands.*
And as hard as your head. | *"Knock" lightly on head with fist.*
The *rind* is green, | *Clasp hands together to show melon.*
And the *flesh* is red. | *Open hands to show melon's inside.*

A watermelon tastes good | *Take a bite from a pretend melon slice.*
And is a juicy treat. | *Rub tummy.*
But the *seeds* inside, | *Point to the inside of cupped hand.*
You do not eat. | *Shake head "no."*

The seeds.
The flesh.
The rind.

Mighty fine!

A Slice Of Reading

Review the parts of a watermelon with this slice of summer reading. For each child, cut one green construction-paper semicircle at least eight inches long on the straight side. Then cut a slightly smaller semicircle from red construction paper and an even smaller semicircle from laminating scraps or transparency film. Then assemble a watermelon slice by stapling the semicircles together as shown. Working with one small group at a time, invite each child to use a permanent black marker to draw seeds on the clear layer of her watermelon slice. Then circulate and ask each child to name the parts of the melon as you point them out: *seeds, flesh,* and *rind.* Use a black permanent marker to label each layer of the watermelon as shown.

When a youngster has successfully named all the watermelon parts, flip her watermelon slice over and print the words "Mighty fine!" on the back. Then present the photo taken of her during "Juicy, Juicy, Juicy" on page 230 and have her glue it above the text. (Or have her illustrate a picture of herself eating watermelon in the available space.) Encourage little ones to take these simple-to-read slices home to show off their knowledge for their families. What a way to ripen beginning reading skills!

A Watermelon Tree?

Why not? Celebrate summer with a classroom tree loaded with these watermelon ornaments. Give each youngster half of a large Styrofoam® ball. Have him paint the rounded side green and the flat side red. If desired, spray the dried paint with a layer of clear gloss. After the gloss is dry, direct the child to glue on a few real watermelon seeds. Then insert a green pipe cleaner, as shown, and twist the end to make a hook for hanging. Let each child hang his summertime delight on a tree branch placed in a gravel-filled flowerpot. What a sight for summer eyes!

Works Of "W-art-ermelon"

Decorate your room with these wild and wacky works of art. Give each child a large sheet of white construction paper. Provide two shades of green paint and brushes for each child to paint a large rind on her paper. Then give choices for filling in the fleshy part of the melon—for example, red fingerpaint, crayon, colored chalk, sponge paint, tissue paper, or even lipstick! For even more fun, explain to your little ones that watermelon flesh can actually be white, yellow, orange, or pink, depending on the variety. Then give youngsters even more colorful options for completing their slices. When the materials used on the artwork are dry, have each child glue on real seeds or black construction-paper dots from a hole puncher. Hang these melons on the wall or in the hall, but be careful—they're awfully juicy!

Allison

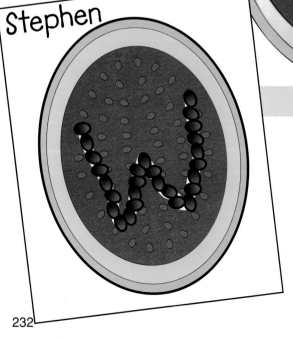

Stephen

Fine-Motor Melon

Put clean, leftover watermelon seeds to good use in this fine-motor activity. For each child, duplicate a watermelon slice on white construction paper from the pattern on page 234. Have him color his melon slice; then use a marker to write a large *W* in the center. Encourage him to trace the letter with glue, then add watermelon seeds to cover the glue lines. If desired, cut out each child's melon and use it as a front cover for a book of words that begin with *W*. Worms and whales and watches, oh my!

Watermelon Puzzlers

Duplicate an even number of watermelon slices from the pattern on page 234 onto white construction paper. Color the rinds green and the centers of the slices red. Cut out all the slices and mount half of them onto separate pieces of construction paper. Laminate the melon cards and the remaining slices for durability. Then cut the remaining slices so that each one fits together in a unique way. Vary the number of pieces according to the abilities in your group. Insert one melon card and one cut-up melon slice into a resealable plastic bag to make a puzzle kit. These puzzles serve up lots of fun, no matter how you slice 'em!

Just "Ripe" For Review

Gather your little ones around this watermelon patch for a rollicking review of basic skills. To prepare, duplicate a large supply of the watermelon slice pattern on page 234 onto green construction paper. Cut out the slices and—if desired—color the flesh red and use a black crayon to draw lines across the back of the pattern to resemble the outside of a watermelon. Then label each slice with a letter, a numeral, a sight word, a colored dot, a shape, or another skill you'd like reinforced. (For older students you may even want to mix skills together.) Spread the cutouts on the floor, facedown, along with strands of green curly-ribbon "vines" to make a big watermelon patch. Choose a few volunteers to walk around the patch while the rest of the group chants the following rhyme. When the rhyme ends, have each volunteer pick a melon and tell what is found on the "inside." If she is correct, reward her with a watermelon-flavored treat, such as jelly beans, and have her pick someone to take her place in the patch. If she is incorrect, have her stay in the patch until she finds a melon that's just "ripe"!

Watermelon, watermelon, watermelon rind.
Pick one up and tell us what you find!

Triangle.

A Behavior "In-seed-tive"

Keep your classroom juicy all summer long by using seedless watermelon-slice cutouts to encourage appropriate behavior. Personalize a cutout for each student. Allow her to either glue a real watermelon seed or add an inked fingerprint "seed" to her slice for each day of good behavior. When a designated number of seeds have been accumulated, reward her with a watermelon-flavored or watermelon-scented treat.

Rachel

Watermelon Slice Pattern
Use with "Fine-Motor Melon" on page 232 and "Watermelon Puzzlers" and "Just 'Ripe' For Review" on page 233.

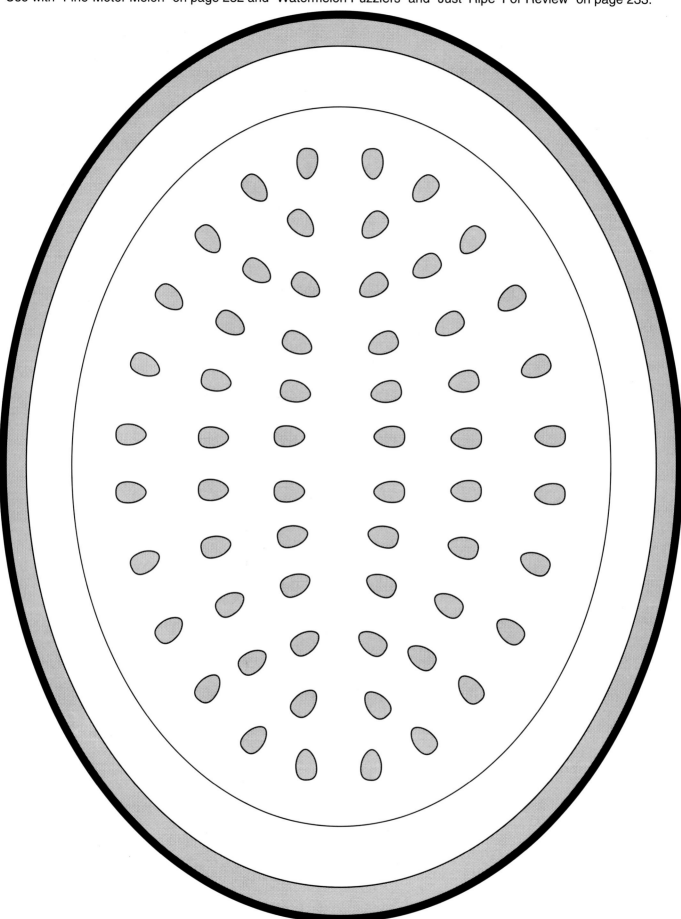

Index